Second Edition

THAT'S ASL

Visualization of American Sign Language

Kendall Hunt publishing company

Diane McDonagh

Photographs by David Penney

Cover and interior images by David Penney.

Kendall Hunt
publishing company

www.kendallhunt.com
Send all inquiries to:
4050 Westmark Drive
Dubuque, IA 52004-1840

Textbook Alone ISBN 978-1-5249-0258-2
Textbook and Website ISBN 978-1-5249-0257-5

Printed in the United States of America

Contents

Dear Students, Teachers, Parents and Friends:

Thank you for purchasing my book! I hope you will find it to your benefit. It's been an exciting process for me to get my book published, as it's always been a dream of mine.

This book is designed to help you find a certain category or topic within each chapter unlike a dictionary. I've created the structure to be less complicated. I guarantee that you will find the structure of this book to be most helpful. It is designed to help you easily retain and remember information.

I wanted to share some history about American Sign Language to give you a better understanding about the rich history of the language. Laurent Clerc was a deaf teacher , teaching the deaf students at a school for the deaf called Institut National de Jeunes Sourds de Paris, France. Thomas Gallaudet from Connecticut visited the school in France and was impressed by what he discovered. Thomas Gallaudet asked Laurent Clerc to join him in America to start a similar school. Thomas Gallaudet taught Laurent Clerc to write English while Laurent Clerc taught him French Sign Language. They traveled by ship for approximately 52 days from Paris to the United States and on that journey their friendship began while they each instructed the other in their perspective languages. On April 15, 1817, together the men established and founded the first school for the deaf called American School for the Deaf in Hartford, Connecticut. As time went by, some signs have changed and vary by state. For example: there are 24 different signs for the word " birthday" and most of them are made up of two signs for this one word. In different part of the United States people talk differently from people in other parts of the United States. Depending upon where a person lives and grows up will determine the accent he/she will have. People from the Southern part of the United states talk slightly different than people in the Northern part of the United States. People from the Midwest compared sound different and use different words than people from the East and West coast of the United States. The same is true for signs. Some signs are regional signs. A person's dialect cannot be changed and it is the same for Deaf and Hard of Hearing people. They respected each state's regional signs, using what was appropriate depending upon where I was.

You will notice the categories in the book show there is often more than one sign for one word. I'm hoping this will meet your needs based on the region you live in and will be to your satisfaction. If you see something missing that you feel should be added and will help others, please inform me and I will add your suggestion to the next edition of this book. The email address is visualizationofasl@gmail.com

Overall, I hope you enjoy my book, it has given me great pleasure to write it and share it with you.

Enjoy!!!!

Smiles,

Diane

Alphabet

A

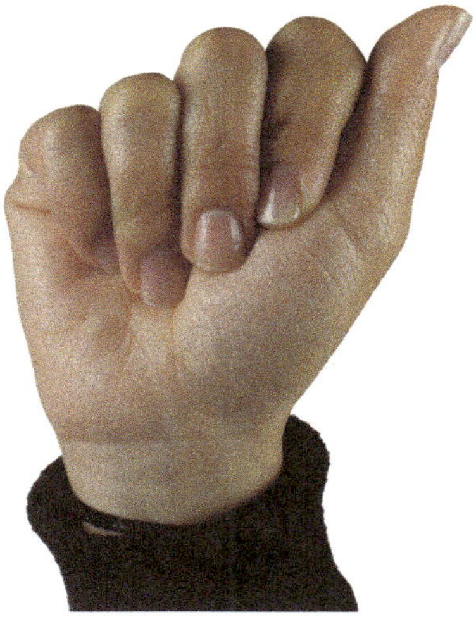

B

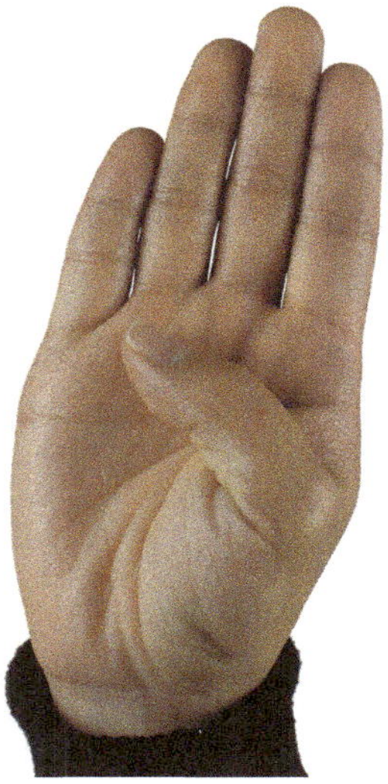

C

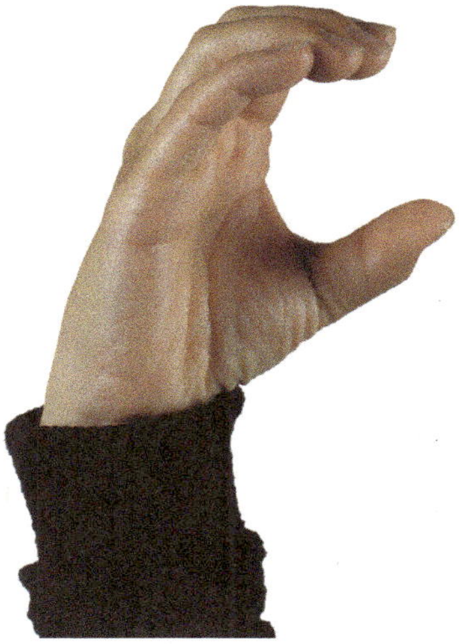

D

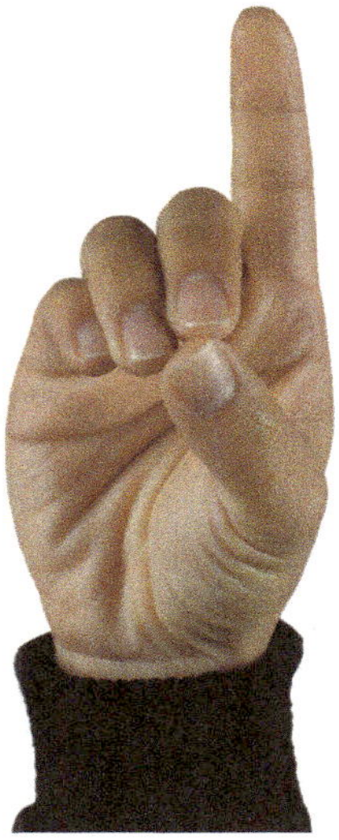

E

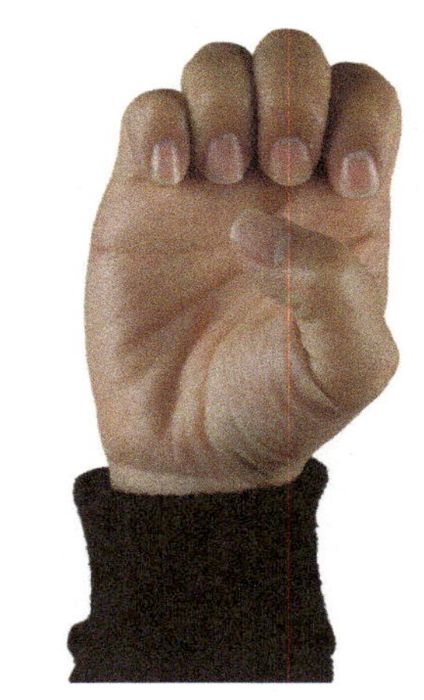

F

G

H

I

J

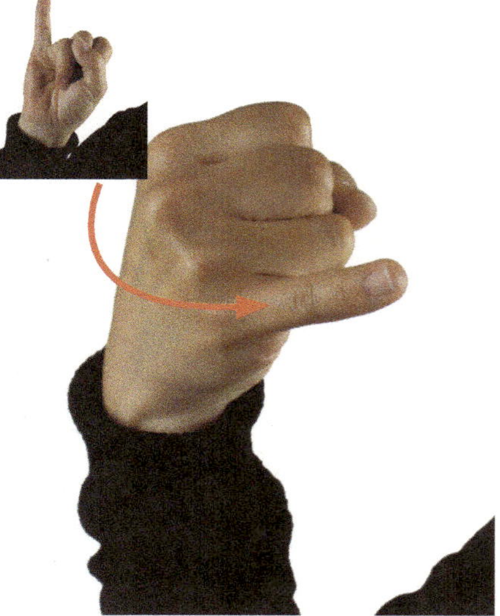

K

L

M

N

O

P

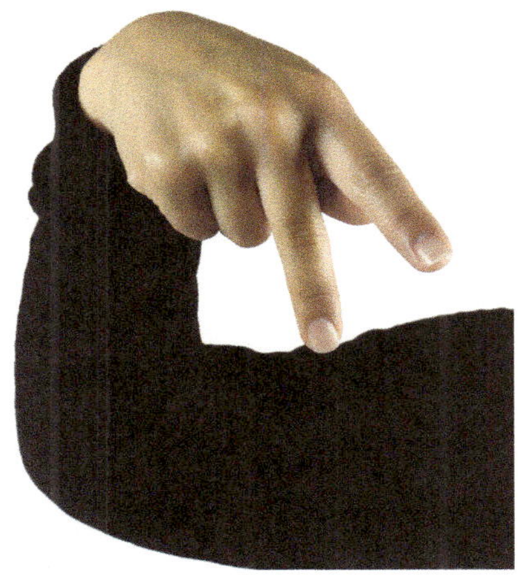

Q

R

S

T

U

V

W

X

Y

Z

Numbers

1

2

3

4

5

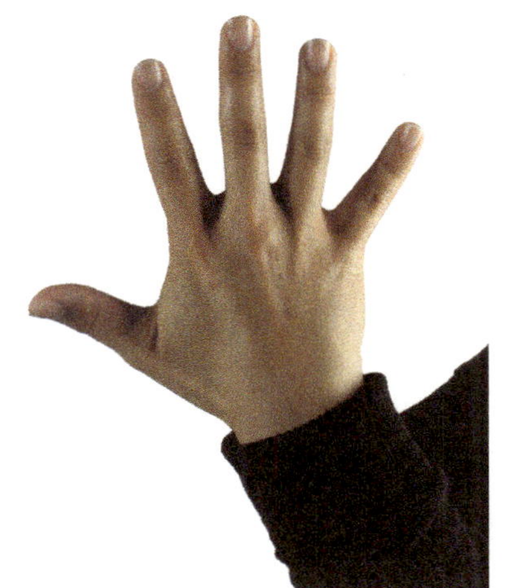

6

7

8

9

10

11

12

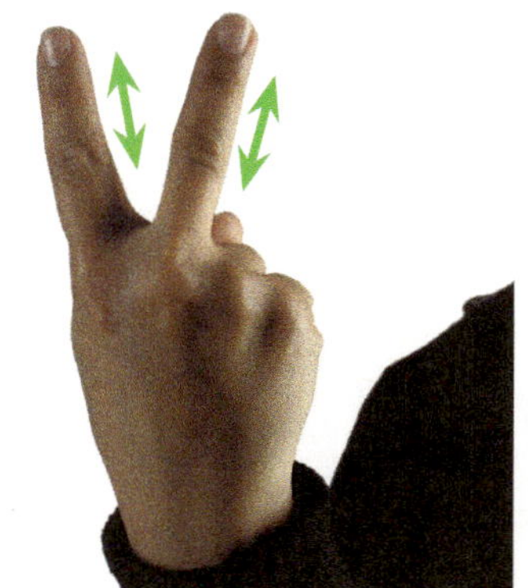

13

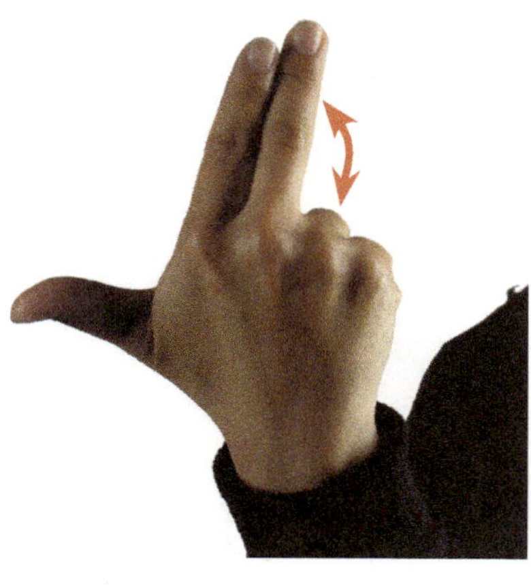

14

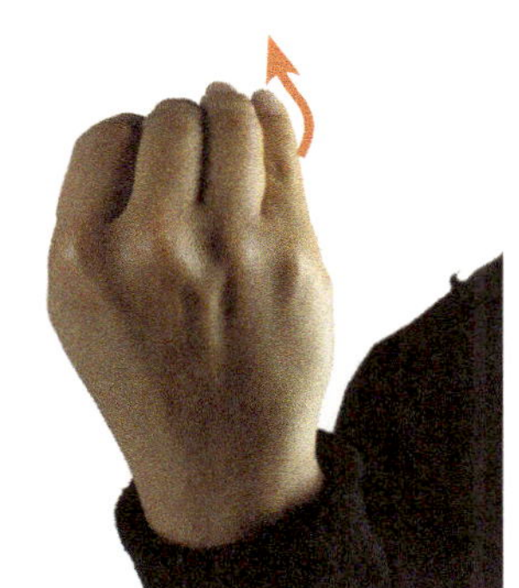

15

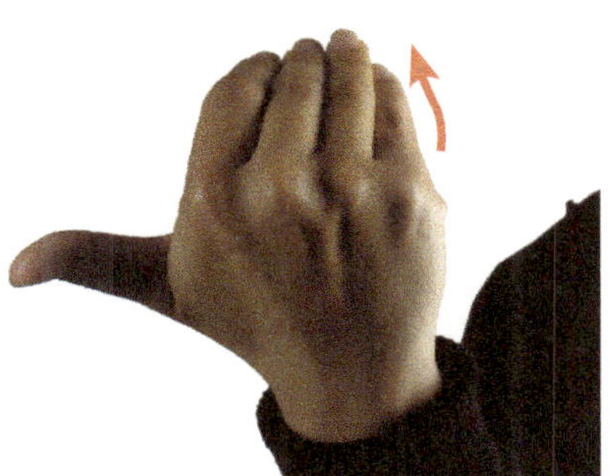

16

17

18

19

20

21

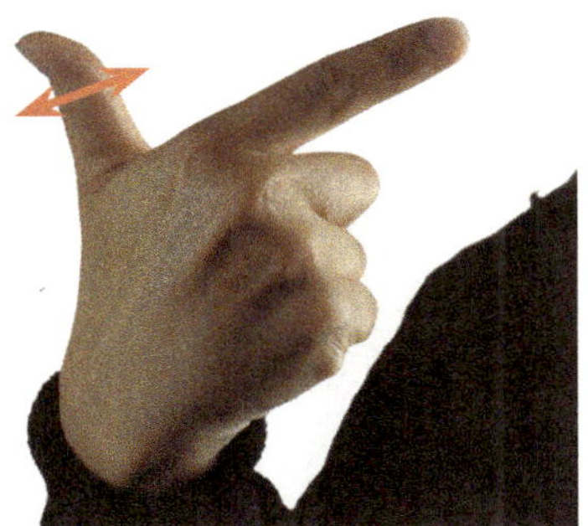

22

23

24

25

26

27

28

29

30

40

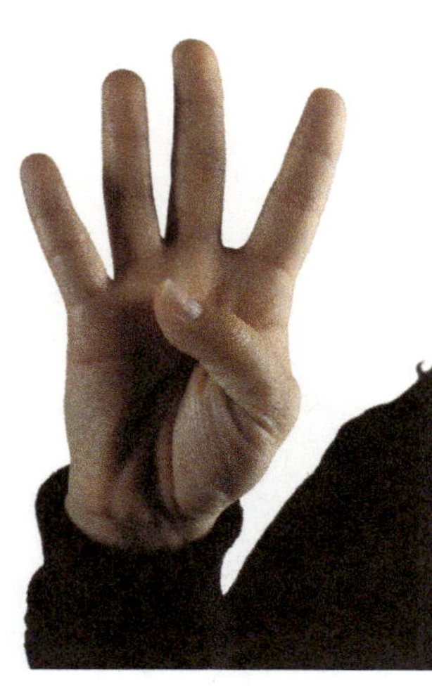

50

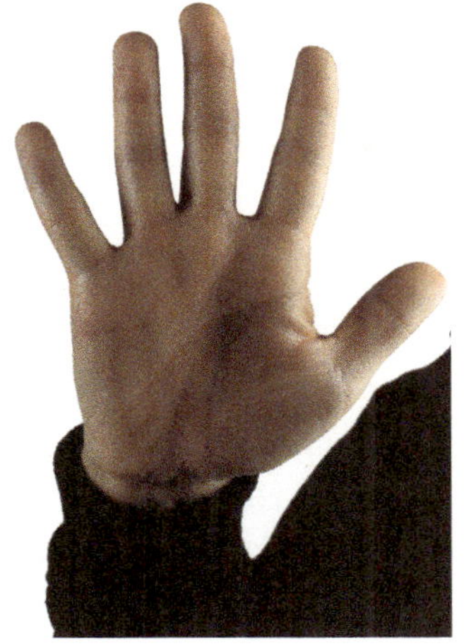

60

70

80

90

100

CHAPTER

1 Family, Relatives and Friends

1. MOTHER, MOM
   "5" open handshape facing sideways taps on your chin once.

2. FATHER, DAD
   "5" open handshape facing sideways taps on your forehead once.

3. **GRANDMOTHER, GRANDMA**
"5" open handshape facing sideways taps on your chin and moves forward twice.

4. **GRANDFATHER, GRANDPA**
"5" open handshape facing sideways taps on your forehead and moves forward twice.

5. **BROTHER**
1st "L" handshape facing sideways stays still while the 2nd "L" handshape facing sideways on your forehead moves downward touching each other once.

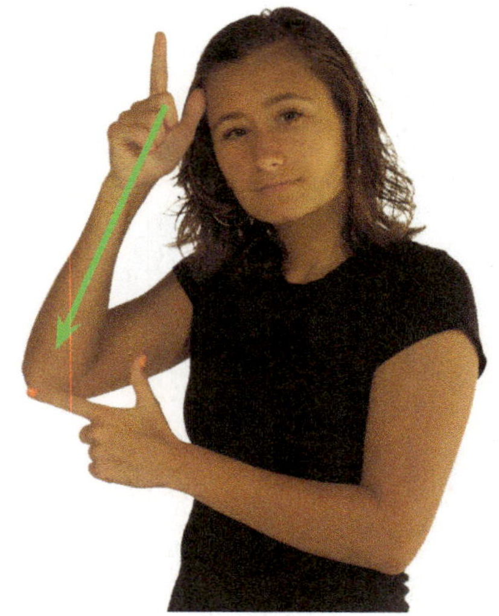

6. SISTER

1st "L" handshape facing sideways stays still while the 2nd "L" handshape facing sideways on your jaw moves downward touching each other once.

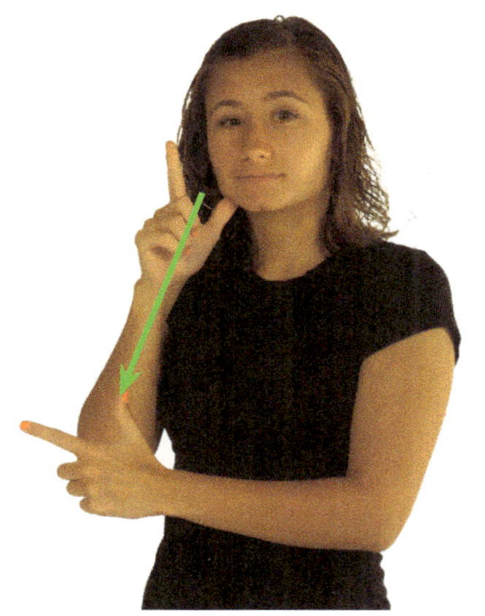

7. MOTHER-IN-LAW

Sign "mother" as above then 1st "5" closed handshape facing sideways stays still while the 2nd "5" handshape changes to "L" handshape facing sideways taps on the 1st "5" closed handshape's fingers and slides down slightly once.

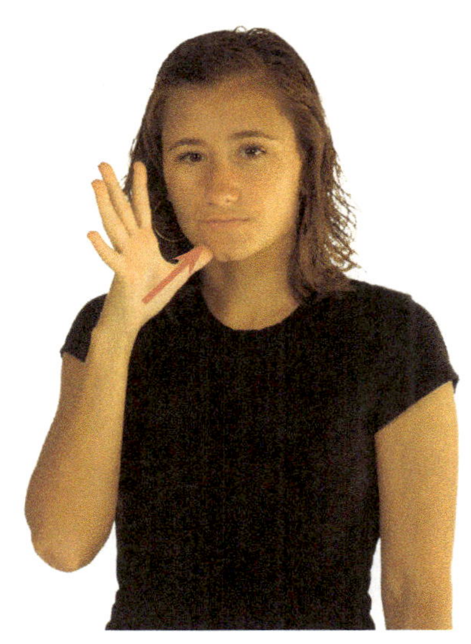

8. FATHER-IN-LAW

Sign "father" as above then changes to 1st "5" closed handshape facing sideways stays still while the 2nd "5" handshape changes to "L" handshape facing sideways taps on the 1st "5" closed handshape's fingers and slides down slightly once.

9. BROTHER-IN-LAW

Sign "brother" as above then changes to 1st "5" closed handshape facing sideways stays still while the 2nd "5" handshape changes to "L" handshape facing sideways taps on the 1st "5" closed handshape's fingers and slides down slightly once.

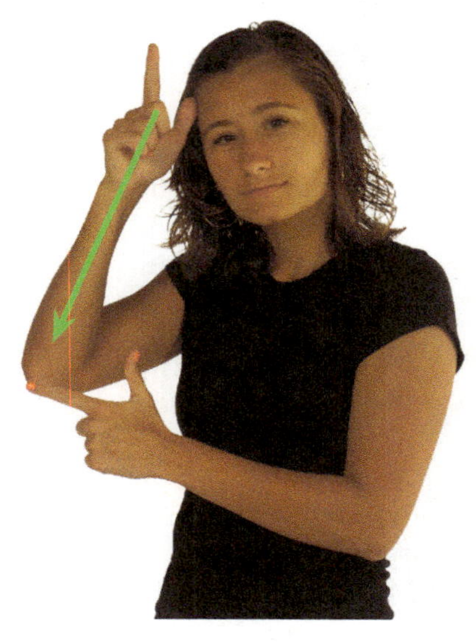

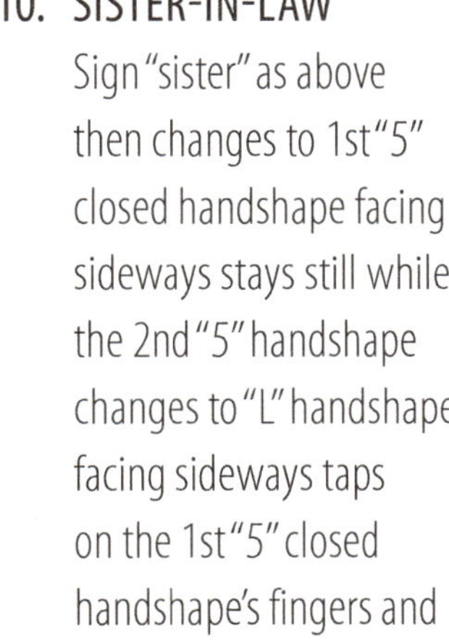

10. SISTER-IN-LAW

Sign "sister" as above then changes to 1st "5" closed handshape facing sideways stays still while the 2nd "5" handshape changes to "L" handshape facing sideways taps on the 1st "5" closed handshape's fingers and slides down slightly once.

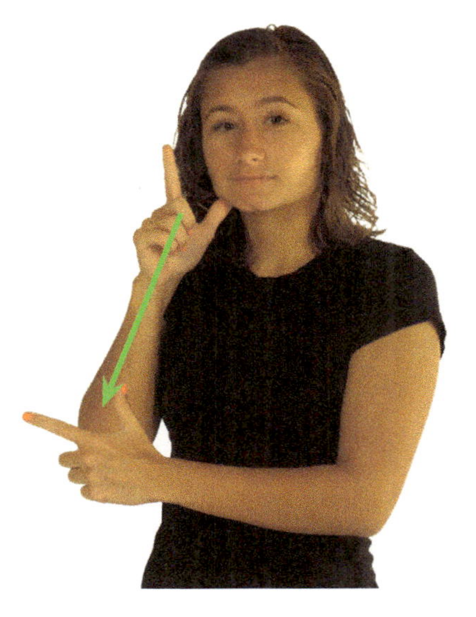

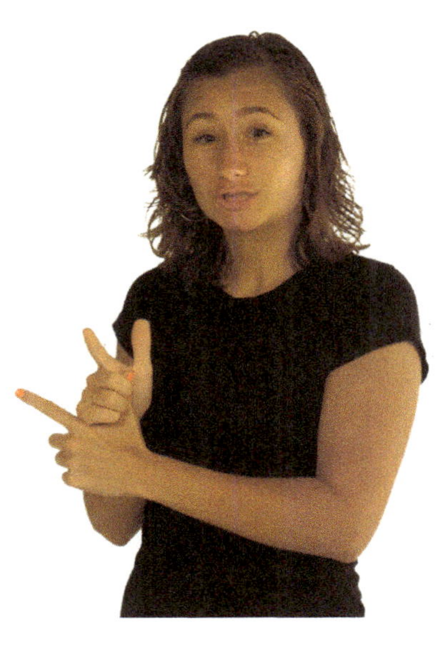

11. STEPMOTHER

1. "1" handshape facing sideways touches on your nose and moves downward slightly once and sign "mother" as above.

2. Variation of Stepmother: "L" handshape facing down away from your body flips over once then sign "mother" as above.

12. STEPFATHER

1. "1" handshape facing sideways touches on your nose and moves downward slightly once and sign "father" as above.

2. Variation of Stepfather: "L" handshape facing down away from your body flips over once then sign "father" as above.

13. STEPBROTHER

1. "1" handshape facing sideways touches on your nose and moves downward slightly once and sign "brother" as above.

2. Variation of Stepbrother: "L" handshape facing down away from your body flips over once then sign "brother" as above.

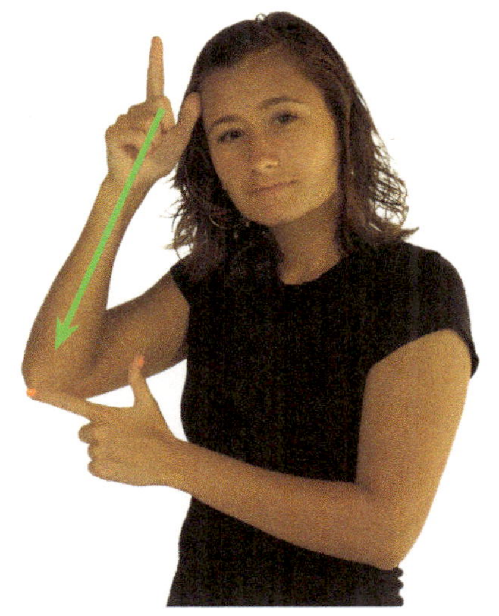

14. STEPSISTER

1. "1" handshape facing sideways touches on your nose and moves downward slightly once and sign "sister" as above.

2. Variation of Stepsister: "L" handshape facing down away from your body flips over once then sign "sister" as above.

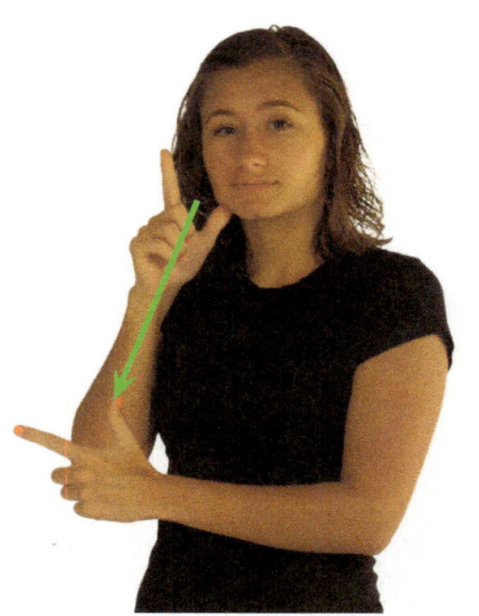

15. HALF BROTHER

"1" handshape moves down slightly and changes to "2" handshape quickly once then sign "brother" as above.

16. HALF SISTER

"1" handshape moves down slightly and changes to "2" handshape quickly once then sign "sister" as above.

17. UNCLE

"U" handshape facing outward near the side of your temple twists sideways repeatedly.

18. AUNT

"A" handshape facing outward near your cheek twists sideways repeatedly.

19. COUSIN

"C" handshape facing outward near your temple twists sideways repeatedly. If it's a male cousin, you sign "C" outward near your head and twist sideways repeatedly.

20. BOY
"5" closed handshape sideways bends bringing all fingers together at the thumb in front of your forehead moves up and down repeatedly or once.

21. GIRL
"10" handshape's thumb on the side of your cheek moves downward repeatedly or once.

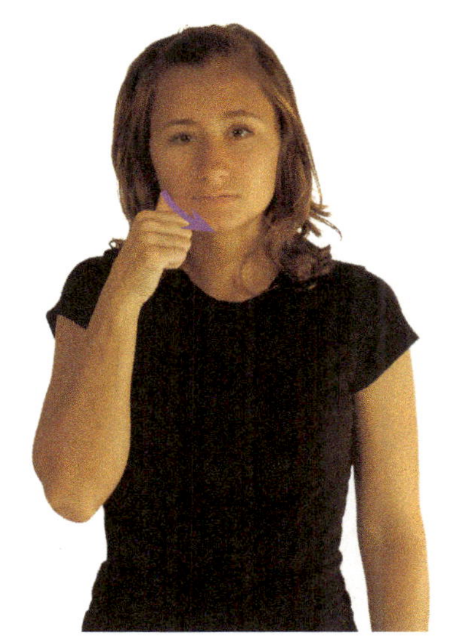

22. BOYFRIEND
Sign "boy" as above then 1st "X" handshape facing up while the 2nd "X" handshape facing down touch each other and turn over once.

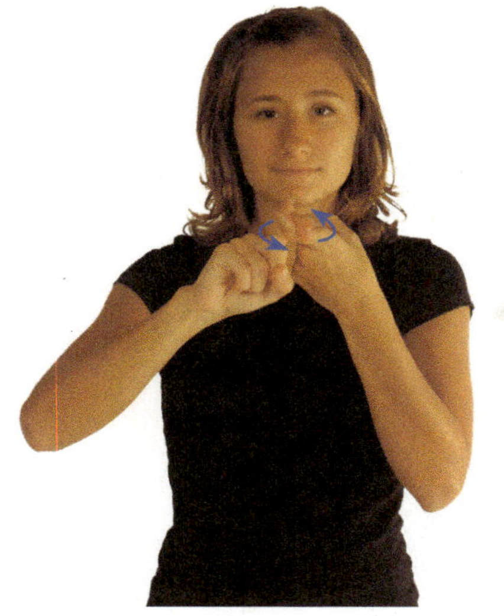

23. EX-BOYFRIEND

Fingerspell E-X then sign "boyfriend" as above.

24. GIRLFRIEND

"10" handshape's thumb on the side of your cheek moves downward repeatedly or once 1st "X" handshape facing up while the 2nd "X" handshape facing down touch each other and turn over once.

25. EX-GIRLFRIEND

Fingerspell E-X then sign "girlfriend" as above.

26. FAMILY

Both "F" handshapes facing outward touches each other and moves around as a cirlce finishes with both "F" handshape's little fingers touching each other once.

27. HUSBAND

Sign "boy" as above then changes to 1st "5" curved handshape facing up stays still while the 2nd "5" curved handshape facing down clasp together once.

28. WIFE

Sign "girl" as above then changes to 1st "5" curved handshape facing up stays still while the 2nd "5" curved handshape facing down clasp together once.

29. EX-HUSBAND

Fingerspell E-X then sign "husband" as above.

30. EX-WIFE

Fingerspell E-X then sign "wife" as abcve.

31. FRIEND

1st "X" handshape facing up while the 2nd "X" handshape facing down touch each other and turn over once.

32. GOOD FRIEND, BEST FRIEND

1. Both "X" handshapes like "friend" above and move upward tightly once or repeatedly.

2. "R" handshape facing yourself move back and forth once or repeatedly.

33. RELATIVE

Both "R" handshapes touch each other and move outward in a circle then touch again facing yourself once.

34. GENERATION, ANCESTRY

1. "5" closed handshape facing yourself in front of your upper shoulder while the 2nd "5" closed handshape facing yourself in the side of your body moves forward alternating repeatedly.

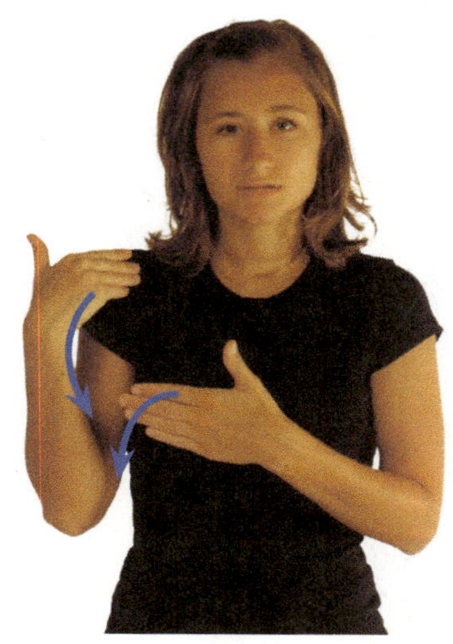

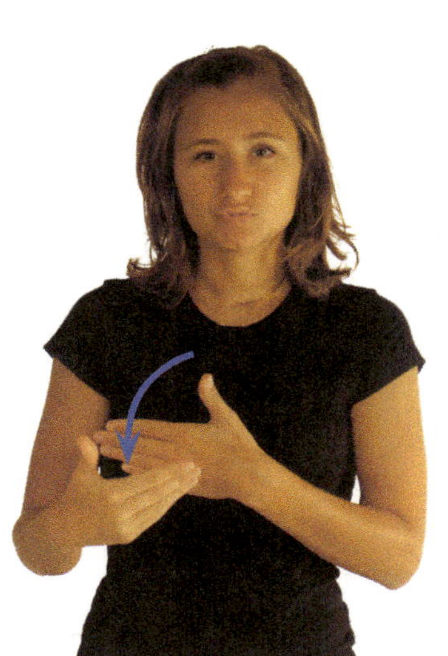

2. Variation of "Generation, Ancestry" "H" handshapes and sign the same "generation" as above.

35. PARTNER

1st"5" closed handshape facing yourself stays still while the 2nd "5" closed handshape puts in between the 1st "5" closed handshape's thumb and fingers brushes sideways and sign person: both "5" closed handshapes on both side of your ribs and move downward once.

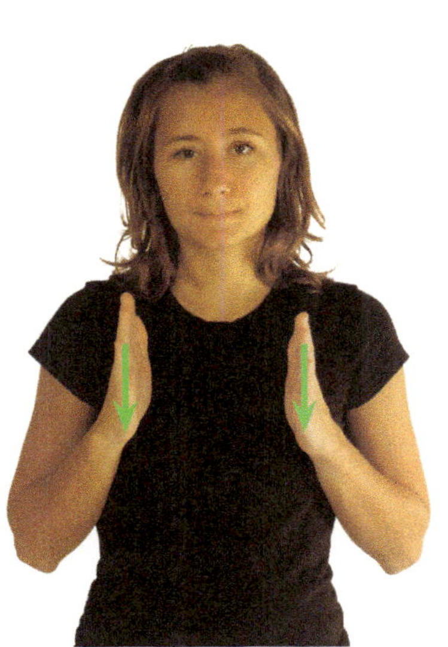

36. PARENTS

Sign "father" as above moves downward to your chin as " mother"once OR sign "mother" as above moves upward to your forehead as "father" once.

37. TWINS

"V" handshape facing sideways on the side of your chin slides down and moves to the other side of your chin and slides down once.

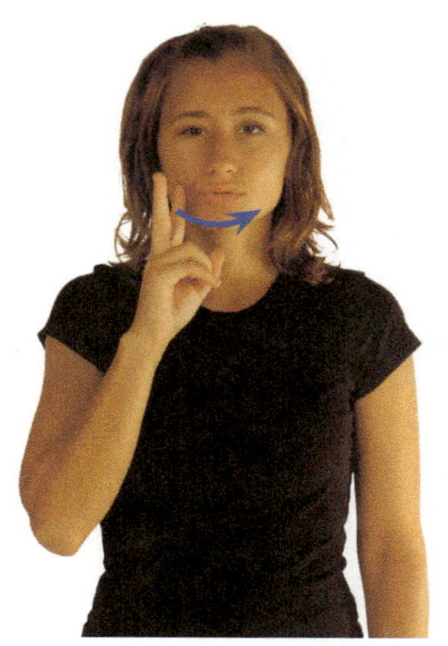

38. TRIPLET

"3" handshape. "1 finger" facing sideways touching on the side of your chin slides down and moves to the other side of your chin and slides down once.

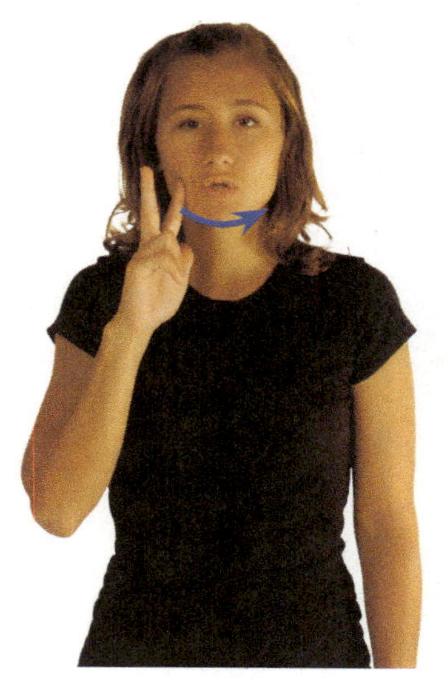

39. ADULTS

Both "5" closed and bended handshapes facing each other and move hands up alternating and repeatedly.

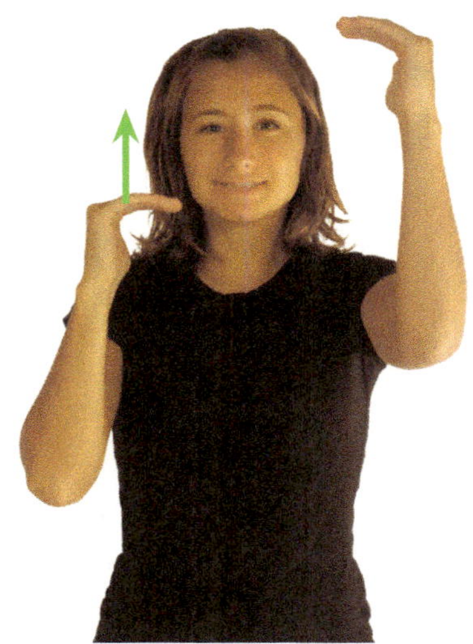

40. COUPLE

1. 1st "V" handshape facing sideways stays still while the 2nd "V" handshape's fingers touching the 1st "V" handshape's fingers move alternating and repeatedly.

2. "V" handshape facing yourself wiggle fingers back and forth repeatedly.

41. NIECE

1. "N" handshape near your cheek twists repeatedly.

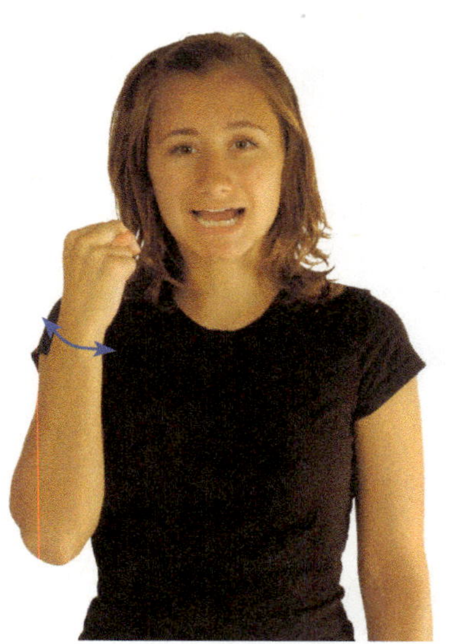

2. Variation of "Niece"

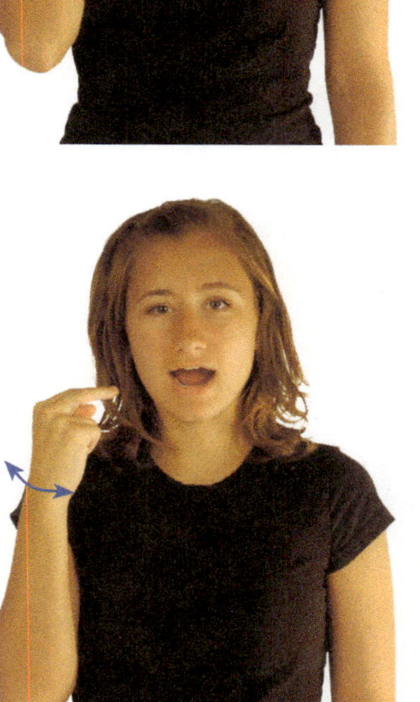

42. NEPHEW

1. "N" handshape near your temple twists repeatedly.

2. (no picture) Variation of "Nephew": Sign "Nephew" as above but with the alternative handshape for "N". (See Niece, above as reference)

43. CHILDREN

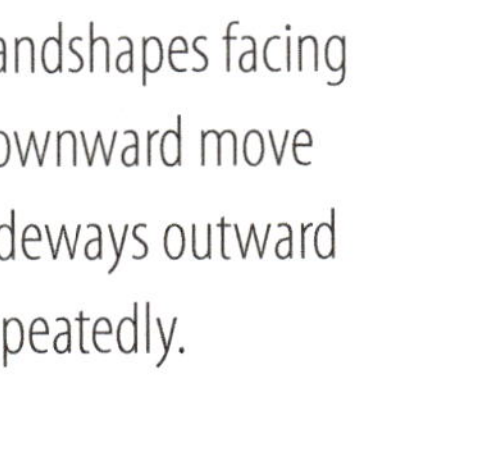

Both "5" closed handshapes facing downward move sideways outward repeatedly.

44. CHILD

"5" closed and bended handshape facing down near the side of your hip stays still like a height of a small child.

45. BABY

1st "5" bended handshape facing up near your stomach while the 2nd "5" bended handshape facing up touches on the top of the 1st "5" bended handshape move back and forth repeatedly.

46. KID

"1 finger & little finger" handshape. "1 finger" under your nose palm facing down move little finger up and down repeatedly.

47. WEDDING
Both "5" closed handshapes on both sides of your body move toward your stomach and hold hands together.

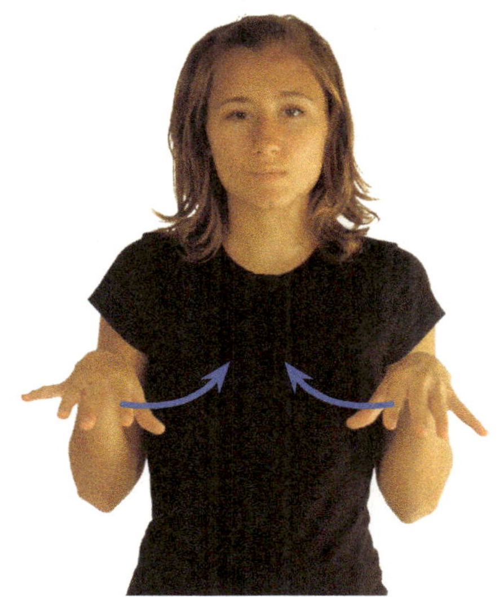

48. MARRY
1st "5" curved handshape facing up stays still while the 2nd "5" curved handshape facing down clasp together once.

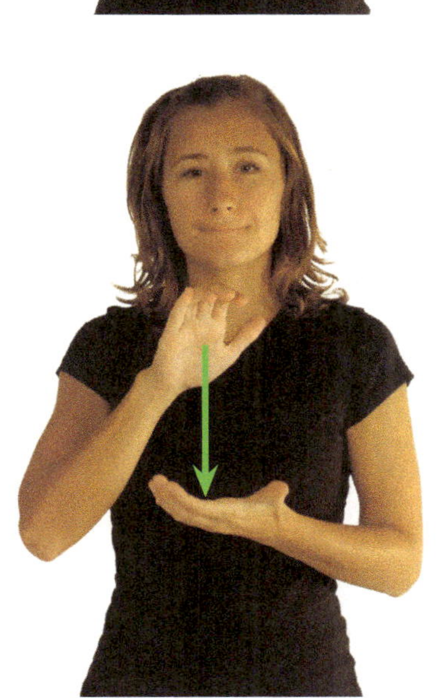

49. ENGAGE, ENAGEMENT

1. 1st "5" handshape facing down stays still while the 2nd "E" handshape touches on the top of the first "5" handshape's 3rd finger once.

2. 1st "5" handshape facing down stays still while the 2nd "F" handshape touches on the top of the first "5" handshape's 3rd finger once.

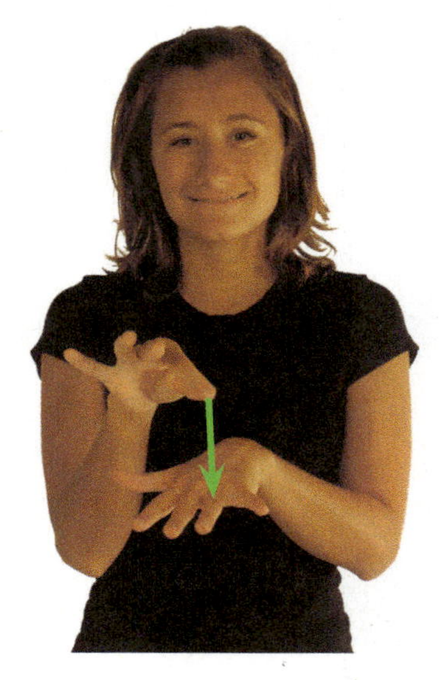

50. PREGNANT

"5" open handshape facing down near your stomach moves outward once.

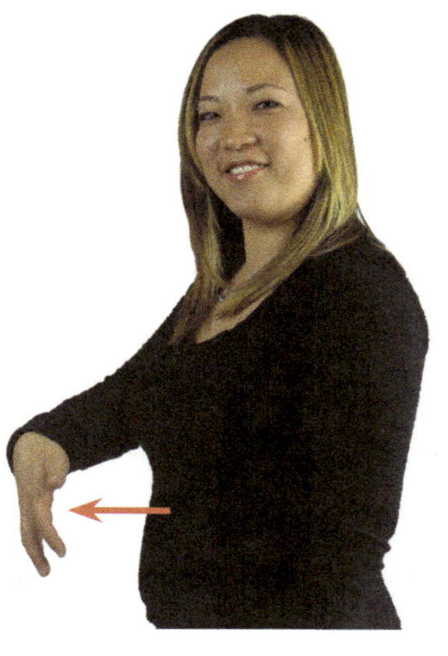

51. DIVORCE

1. Both "D" handshapes facing sideways touch each other and move forward and sideways at the same time.

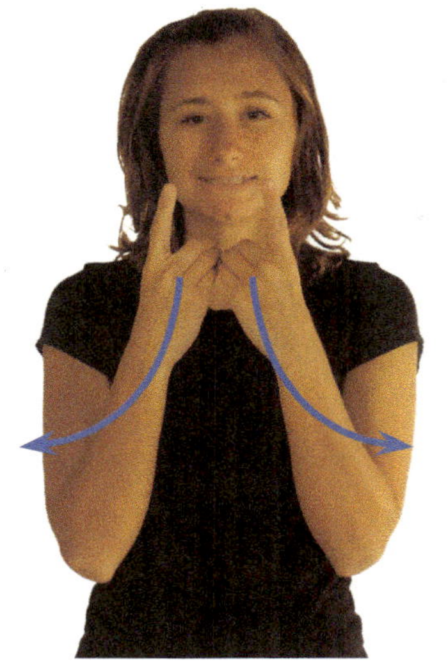

2. Sign "marry" as above and move out forward out sideways at the same time.

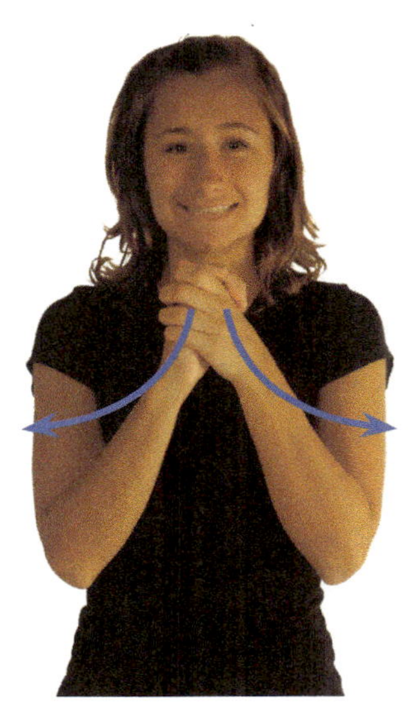

52. DAUGHTER

Sign "girl" as above then changes to "baby" once.

53. SON

Sign " boy" as above then changes to "baby" once.

CHAPTER 2

Pronouns, Nouns and Indefinite Pronouns

1. I, ME
   "1" handshape points toward your chest.

2. WE, US
   "1" handshape pointing down facing yourself touches on the side of shoulder moves forward to other shoulder.

3. YOU
"1" handshape points outward.

4. THEY
"1" handshape pointing outward moves from one side to other side

5. HE, SHE & IT
"1" handshape points away from your body.

6. MY
   "5" closed handshape on your chest once.

7. YOUR
   "5" closed handshape points outward once.

8. MYSELF
   "A" handshape facing yourself on your chest repeatedly.

9. YOURSELF
"A" handshape facing outward away from your body moves back and forth repeatedly.

10. THEMSELVES
"A" handshape facing outward away from your body moves from side to other side.

11. HER & HIS
"5" closed handshape points to a female/male.

12. OUR

"5" curved handshape on the side of your chest moves to other side of shoulder.

13. OURSELVES

"A" handshape on the side of your chest moves to other side of shoulder.

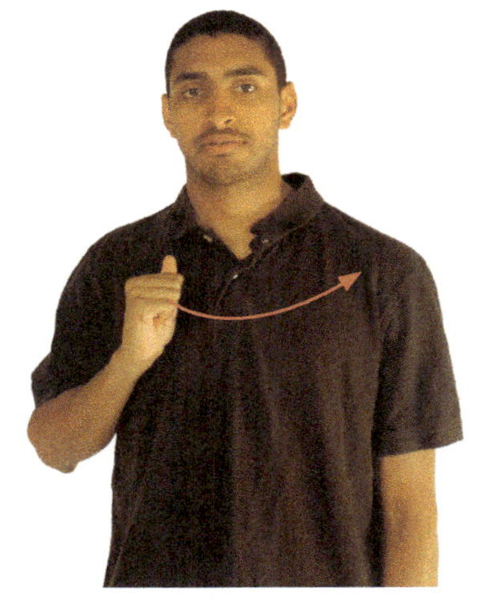

14. EACH

1st "A" handshape facing sideways stays still while the 2nd "A" handshape touches the knuckles to thumb on the 1st "A" handshape and moves downward repeatedly.

15. SOMEONE

"1" handshape moves in a circular motion continually.

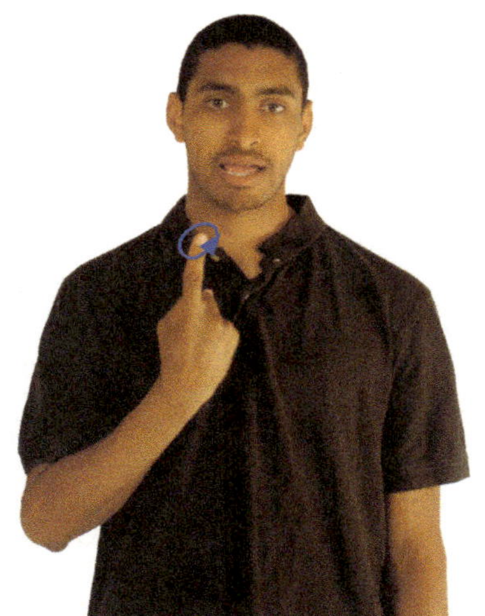

16. SOMETHING

same sign as "someone" (shows "curious" facial expression)

17. ANY

"A" handshape sideways sweeps movement away from your body once.

18. ANYONE

"A" handshape same as above and changes to "1" handshape.

19. ANYTHING

"A" handshape same as above then changes to "5" handshape facing up and moves outward once or twice.

20. EVERYONE

sign "each" as above then changes to "1" handshape.

21. OTHER

"A" handshape facing sideways moves outward once.

22. EACH OTHER

1st "10" handshape facing up 2nd while the "10" handshape facing down circles alternately around continually.

23. FELLOWSHIP
    1st "5" open handshape wiggling facing up while the 2nd "5" open handshape wiggling facing down alternate continually.

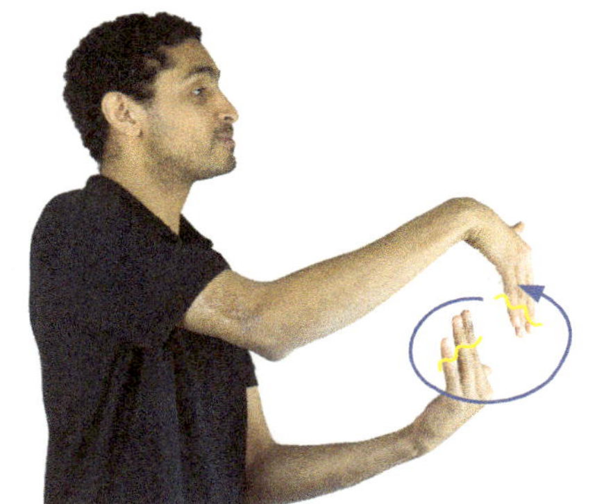
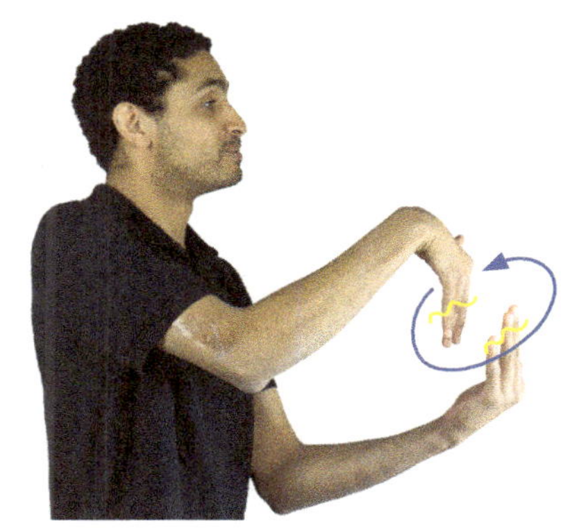

24. WHO
    "L" bended handshape on your chin while the one finger bends repeatedly.

25. WHAT
    both "5" open handshapes facing up away from your body & shake back and forth.

26. HOW

1. Both "5" bended handshapes knuckles touching in front of your body, then turn over outward away from your body.

2. It means how do you do that?

27. WHERE

"1" handshape facing outward and shakes back & forth repeatedly.

28. WHY

1. "middle finger" handshape near your temple bends repeatedly.

2. "Y" fingers" handshape near your temple middle 3 fingers bend repeatedly to form a "Y".

3. "Y" handshape touches your temple and moves downward while middle 3 fingers touch the palm once.

29. WHICH

Both "10" handshapes move up & down alternalting away from your body repeatedly.

30. WHEN

1st "1" handshape in front of yourself stays still while the 2nd "1" handshape moves in a half circle then touches the tip of the 1st "1" handshape's finger once.

31. YES

"S" handshape moves up and down repeatedly.

32. NO

"3" closed handshape facing outward and move fingers & thumb together once.

CHAPTER

3 Feelings

1. HAPPY
   Both "5" closed handshapes on your chest moves upward and in a circular motion repeatedly.

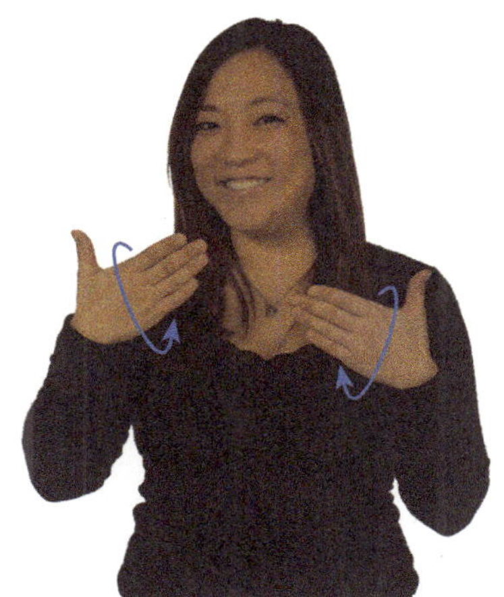

2. SAD
   Both "5" closed handshapes in front of your face move downward once.

3. **GROUCHY**
   "5" bended handshape squeezing in front of your face bends repeatedly.

4. **LOVE**
   Both "S" handshapes cross each other on your chest once.

5. **I LOVE YOU**
   Fingerspell "I-L-Y" to form one sign.

6. HATE
   Both "8" handshapes away from your body flick once.

7. LIKE
   "Middle finger & thumb" handshape sideways on your chest moves far outward away from your body to form "8" handshape once.

8. DON'T LIKE
   "Middle finger & thumb" handshape sideways on your chest moves away from your body and pinches together and flick downward once.

9. **PLEASE**
   "5" closed handshapes on your chest moves in a circular motion continually.

10. **LAUGH**
    1. Both "L" handshapes. pointer fingers on the sides of your mouth and thumb out move repeatedly towards ears as in "smile".

2. Both "5" open handshapes. 1st "5" bended handshape facing up while the 2nd "5" bended handshape facing down and moving back and forth alternately and repeating.

11. FRIENDLY

Both "5" open handshapes near your cheek move backward and wiggling fingers repeatedly.

12. CRY

Both "1" handshapes on the upper cheek under eyes move and change to "1" handshapes downward repeatedly.

13. SORRY

"A" handshape on your chest moves in a circular motion continually.

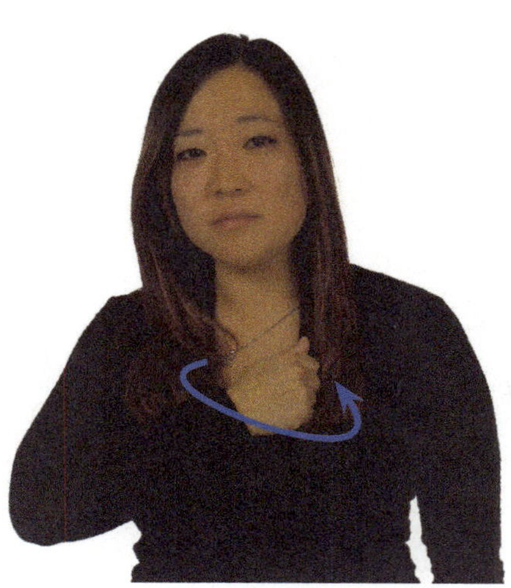

14. ANGRY

Both "5" bended handshapes bend on your chest move sideways outward once quickly.

15. BOILING
1st "5" closed handshape facing down stays still and the 2nd "5" open handshape under the 1st "5" handshape wiggling your fingers near your stomach.

16. BLOWUP
1st "S" handshape facing sideways while the 2nd "5" open handshape on the top of 1st "S" handshape moves upward quickly.

17. PEACE
Both "5" handshapes palm touching each other and turn over and separate sideways from your body.

18. FEAR

Both "5" open handshapes facing outward near your shoulder move downward slightly.

19. AFRAID

Both "5" open handshapes facing yourself near the chest moves and becomes "5" handshapes.

20. SUFFERING

"A" handshape on your chin moves back & forth repeatedly.

21. PATIENT

"A" handshape's thumb on your chin moves downward shortly once.

22. GRIEF

1. Both "A" handshapes touching each other near your chest turn over once.

2. Both "S" handshapes facing down in front of yourself while the 2nd "S" handshape moves downward once.

23. SHOCKED

1. 1st "5" handshape's finger on the upper side of your temple and change to both "5" open handshapes move downward once.

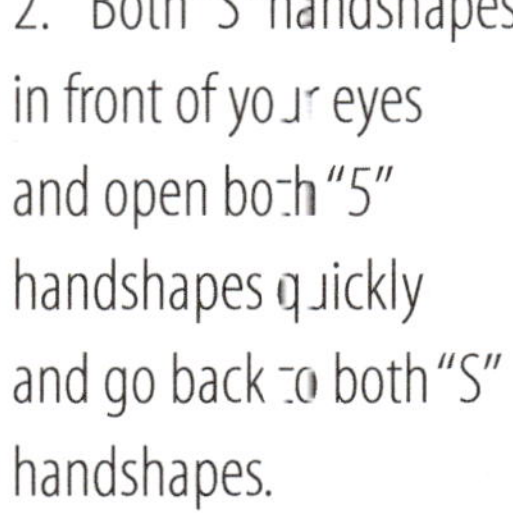

2. Both "S" handshapes in front of your eyes and open both "5" handshapes quickly and go back to both "S" handshapes.

24. FEEL

"Middle finger" handshape on your chest moves in a circular motion continually.

25. PITY

1. Both "middle finger" handshapes away from your body move up & down continually.

2. "Middle finger" handshape away from your body moves up & down continually.

26. **FEEL HURT**
"Middle finger" handshape on your chest moves outward once.

27. **EXCITED**
Both "middle finger" on your chest move up and outward alternating continually.

28. THRILLED
Both "middle finger" handshapes on your chest move upward and curve outward once.

29. EMOTION
Both "E" handshapes on your chest move upward alternating continually.

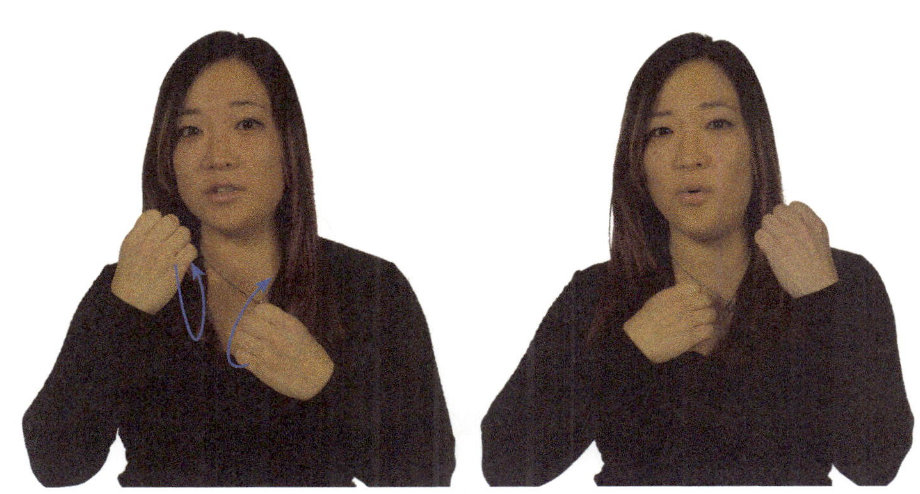

30. DISAPPOINTED
"1" handshape touches on your chin once.

31. DISCOURAGED
Both "middle finger" handshapes on your chest move downward once.

32. DEPRESSED
Both "5" open handshapes on your chest move downward once.

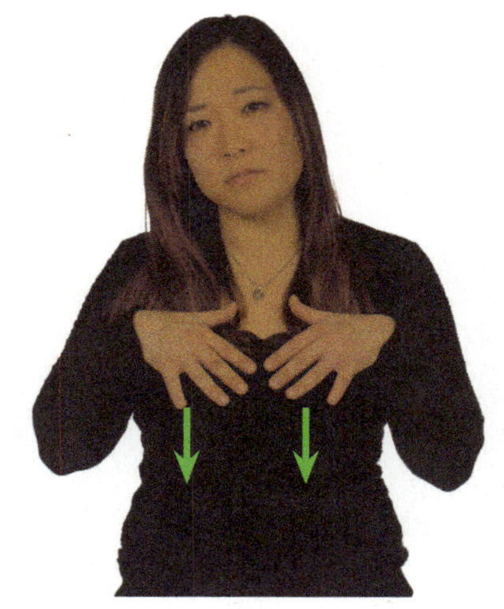

33. LONELY
"1" handshape on your chin moves down repeatedly.

34. INSPIRED

Both "S" handshapes on your chest move upright and change to both "5" handshapes once.

35. EAGER

Both "5" handshape's palms touching each other and rub them back and forth repeatedly.

36. FRUSTRATED

Both "B" handshapes with backside of finger touching chin alternating repeatedly.

37. HUMBLE

1st "5" closed handshape facing down stays still while the 2nd "B" handshape's fingers move from your chin under "5" closed handshape once.

38. SHY

"5" bended handshape on the side of your chin moves upward and over once.

39. EMBARRASS

Both "5" open handshapes in front of your face move alternating continually.

40. BLUSH

1. "1" handshape on your chin "sign red" then change to both "S" handshapes move upward to open "5" handshapes once.

2. Both "A" handshapes on both sides of your chin move upward and turn to "L" once.

41. FLIRT

Both "5" open handshapes: 2 thumbs touching each other facing outward while "5" handshapes wiggle continually.

42. KISS

1. "O" closed handshape near your mouth moves toward ear.

2. "O" closed handshape touches on your chin.

43. KIND

"5" bended handshapes alternate over "5" bended handshape once or twice.

44. MEAN

Both "E" handshapes touching each other. 1st "E" handshape stays still while 2nd "E" handshape moves downward once.

45. WANT

Both "5" bended handshapes facing upward and move toward your body once.

46. DON'T WANT

Both "5" bended handshapes facing up then turn over downward once.

47. WISH

"C" bended handshape on your chest moves downward slightly once.

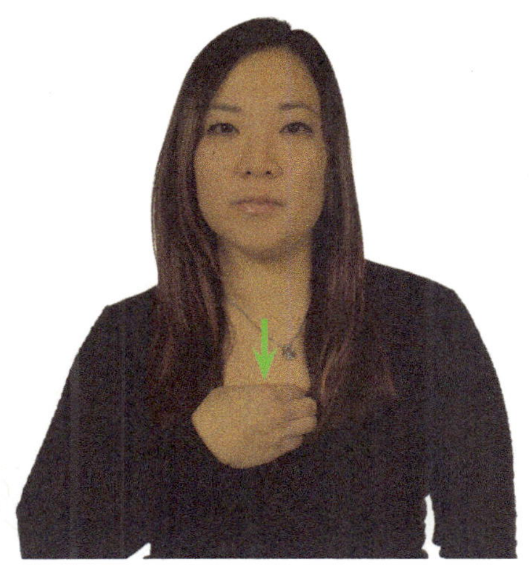

48. PREFER

"Middle finger" handshape taps on your chin repeatedly.

49. FAVORITE

1. "Middle finger" taps on your chin repeatedly

2. "V" bended handshape's finger tips tap on the side of your temple repeatedly.

50. COMFORTABLE

1st "5" bended handshape facing down while the 2nd "5" bended handshape on the top of 1st "5" bended handshape move alternating continually.

51. SATISFIED

1st "B" closed handshape on the chest stays still while the 2nd "B" handshape above the 1st "B" handshape on the chest once.

52. RELIEVED

Both "B" handshapes same as above move downward once.

53. COMPLAIN

"5" bended handshape taps on your chest repeatedly.

54. PRIDE

"A" handshape facing down on your chest moves upright once.

55. BRAG

Both "10" handshapes on each side of your hip move back and forth alternating repeatedly.

56. SELFISH

Both "3" handshapes palms facing down fingers move and bend toward your body once.

57. STINGY

1st "5" closed handshape facing up while the 2nd "5" bended handshape on the top of 1st "5" closed handshape's palm and bends moving toward your body repeatedly (to show the act of scratching palm).

58. JEALOUS

1. "J" handshape on your chin near your mouth moves sideways once.

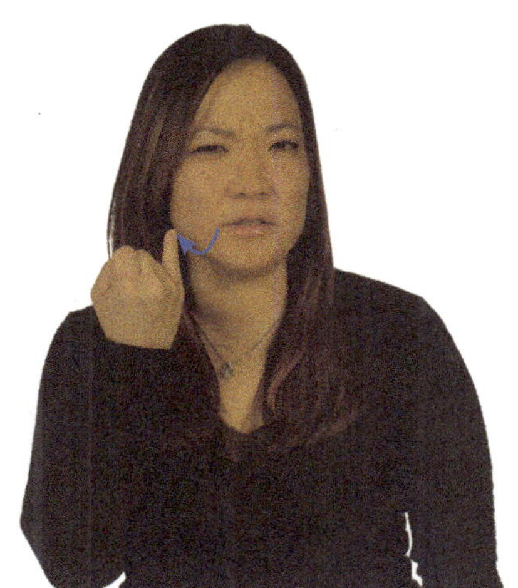

59. GUILTY

"G" handshape facing outward on the upper shoulder hits your shoulder once or repeatedly.

60. CONFESS

Both "5" closed handshapes on your chest move outward once.

61. TEND

Both "middle finger" handshapes on your chest move outward once.

62. REVENGE

1. 1st "L" closed handshape stays still while the 2nd "L" closed handshape touch each other and bounce back once.

2. 1st "L" closed handshape stays still while the 2nd "L" closed fingers handshape on your nose moves downward and touches the 1st "L" once and bounces back.

63. UNFAIR

1st "F" handshape sideways stays still while the 2nd "F" handshape touches on the tip of 1st "F" handshape moves downward once.

64. BRAVE

Both "5" bended handshapes on your chest move outward and change to "S" handshape once.

65. INSULT

1. "1" handshape on the side of your body moves upward once.

2. "1" handshape away from your body moves toward yourself once.

CHAPTER

4 Mind

1. BRAIN

   "1" bended finger handshape taps on the top of your head repeatedly.

2. MIND

   "1" bended finger handshape taps on the top of your head once.

3. KNOW

"5" closed handshape touches on your forehead once.

4. DON'T KNOW

"5" closed handshape on your forehead turns downward away from your forehead.

5. THINK

"1" handshape taps on your forehead once.

6. STILL THINKING

Both "O" closed handshapes in front of your forehead and moves alternating continually.

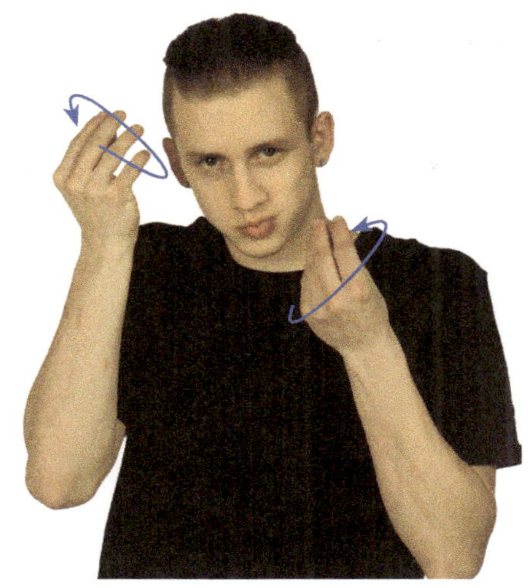

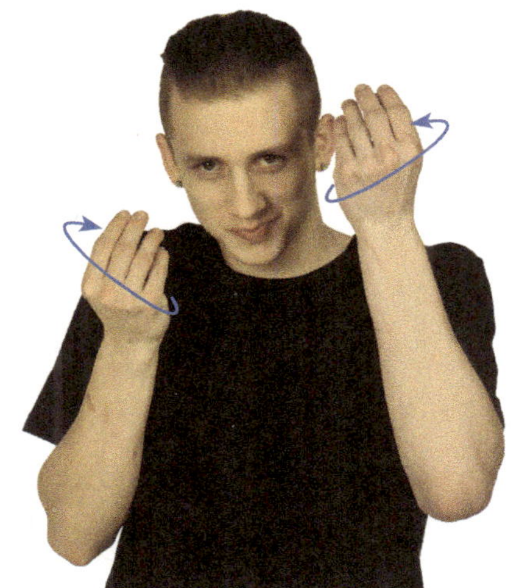

7. MEMORIZE

1. "1" handshape taps on the forehead and change to "S" away from your face once.

2. Variation of "Memorize"

8. REMEMBER
   1st "A" handshape facing sideways stays still while the 2nd "A" handshape's thumb taps on your forehead and moves down and touches the 1st "A" handshape's thumb once.

9. WONDER
   Both "1" handshapes palm facing yourself in front of your face move alternating continually.

10. REASON
    "R" handshape in front of your forehead and moves circular motion continually.

11. IT'S UP TO YOU

"1" handshape taps on your forehead and changes to "10" handshape away from your face once.

12. FORGET

"5" closed handshape sideways on your forehead moves sideways to "A" handshape once.

13. SMART

1. "Middle finger" handshape taps on your forehead and twists away from your face once.

2. "1" handshape taps on your forehead and moves upward once.

14. GENIUS

1. 1st "C" handshape on your forehead while the 2nd "C" handshape touches or near the 1st "C" handshape once.

NOTE: You can use only 1 hand as a variation.

2. "L" bended handshape's finger taps on your forehead then both finger and thumb close together and move outward once.

15. STUPID

1. "V" handshape sideways taps on your forehead repeatedly.

2. 1st "V" handshape facing sideways on your forehead stays still while the 2nd "V" handshape touches the 1st "V" handshape once.

16. DUMB

"A" handshape facing yourself taps on your forehead once.

17. WISE

"X" handshape in front of your forehead moves up and down repeatedly.

18. LOGICAL

"L" handshape in front of your forehead moves circular motion continually.

19. COMMON SENSE

"C" handshape taps on your forehead and change to "S" once.

20. **PHILOSOPHY**
"P" handshape in front of your forehead moves up and down repeatedly.

21. **IDEA**
Little finger handshape facing yourself on the side of your forehead moves upward once.

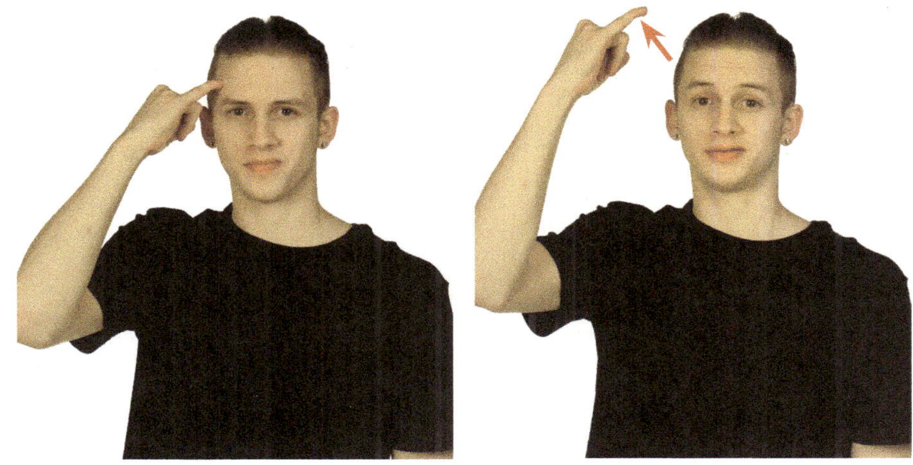

22. **SURPRISE**
Both "L" closed handshapes near your eyes and change to open "L" handshapes upward once.

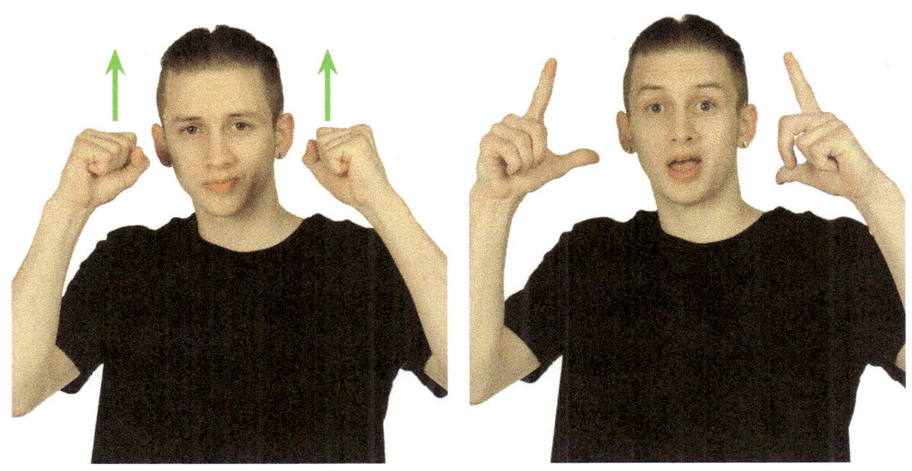

23. HOPE

1. Both 1st finger handshape's one on your temple and the other away from your face then change to both "5" closed and bended handshapes away from your body move down at the same time once.

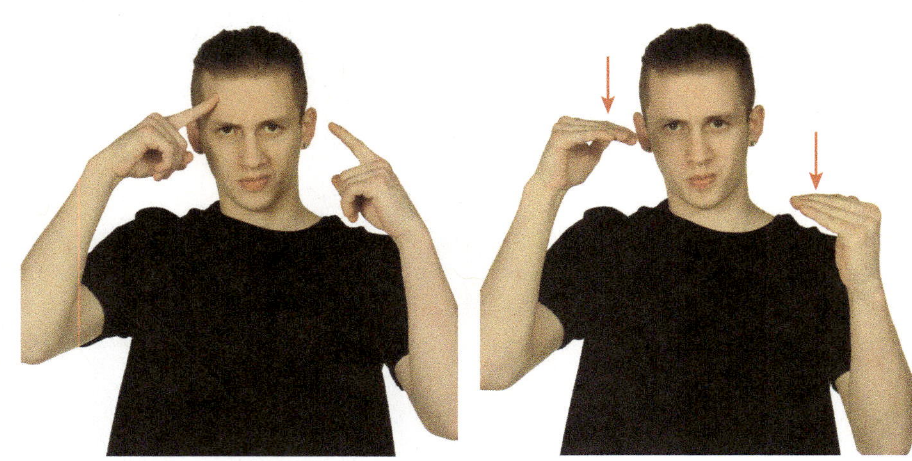

2. Both "R" handshapes away from your body move forward and backward repeatedly.

3. (No picture) 1st "5" bended handshape near the side of your head while the 2nd "5" handshape away from your body move down at the same time once.

24. OPINION
"O" handshape in front of your forehead moves up and down repeatedly.

25. BELIEVE
"1" handshape taps on your forehead and change to "5" bended handshape clasps the 2nd "5" bended handshape once.

26. DON'T BELIEVE
"10" Handshape's thumb under your chin moves outward once then sign "believe" as above.

27. AGREE

1. 1st "1" handshape facing sideways stays still while the 2nd "1" handshape taps on your forehead then moves down to the 1st handshape's level and twist both "1" handshapes downward once.

2. Variation of "Agree"

28. DISAGREE

1st "1" handshape in front of yourself while the 2nd "1" handshape taps on your forehead once moves downward sideways touches on the tip of the 1st "1" handshape. Then both "1" handshapes move away from each other once.

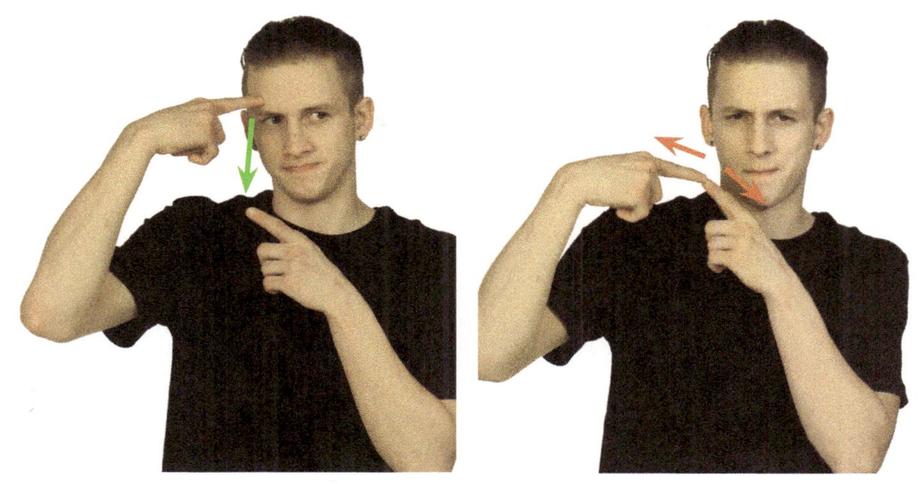

29. UNDERSTAND

1. "S" handshape facing yourself on the side of your head changes to "1" handshape flick once.

2. "S" handshape facing yourself on the side of your head changes to "1" handshape flick repeatedly.

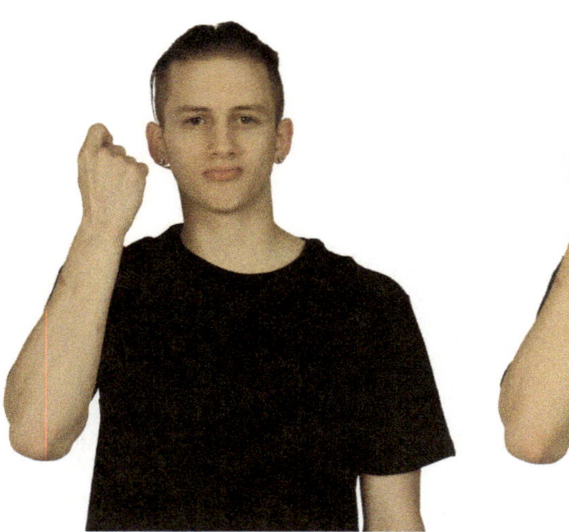

30. **MISUNDERSTAND**

"V" handshape facing sideways on the side of your temple flips over once.

31. **WORRY**

Both "5" closed handshapes in front of your forehead move alternating continually.

32. DOUBT

"V" bended handshape facing yourself in front of your eyes moves out and down quickly once.

33. DECIDE

1. 1st "1" handshape on your forehead moves and changes to both "F" handshapes downward once.

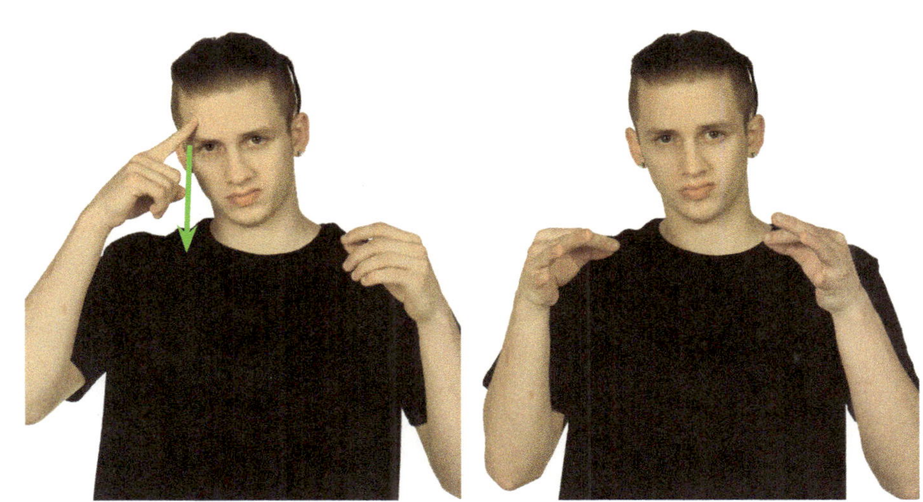

2. Both "F" handshapes facing down away from your body move downward once.

34. ATTENTION

Both "5" closed handshapes sideways on each side of your head move back and forth repeatedly.

35. FOCUS

Both "5" closed handshapes sideways on each side of your head and move outward once.

36. THEORY

"T" handshape on the side of your head moves upward like a swirl.

37. FANTASY

1. Both "F" handshapes on the side of your forehead move upward like a swirl continually.

2. "F" handshape on the side of your forehead moves upward like a swirl.

38. STUBBORN

"5" closed handshape's thumb facing forward on the side of your forehead while "4 fingers" moves downward once.

39. REBEL

"S" handshape's arm facing yourself moves and twists outward once.

40. GOAL

1st "1" handshape in front of your body stays still at your forehead height while the 2nd "1" handshape sideways on side of your face moves to touch the fingertip of the 1st "1" handshape once.

41. GUESS

"C" handshape in front of your face changes to "S" once.

42. HABIT

1. 1st "5" closed handshape facing down in front of your body while the 2nd "5" closed handshape crosses at the wrist of the 1st "S" handshape and changes both "5" closed handshapes to "S" handshapes while moving downward at the same time once.

43. TRADITION

1. 1st "S" handshape facing down in front of your body stays still while the 2nd "T" handshape on top of the 1st "S" handshape moves down once.

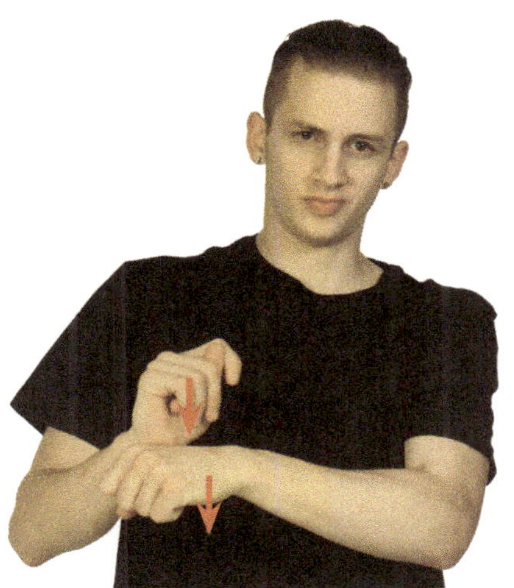

2. Both "T" handshapes above your shoulder move both "T" handshapes above your should move downward once.

44. INFORM YOU

1. Both "O" closed handshapes in front of your face move toward your face and change to "5" handshapes at the same time.

2. Both "O" closed handshapes facing yourself move outward and change to "5" open handshapes at the same time once.

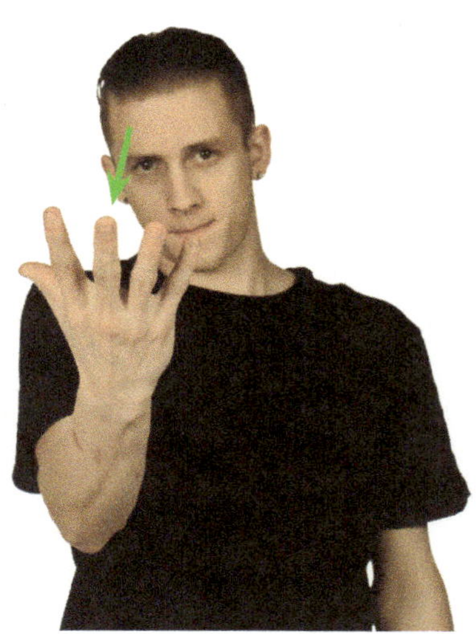

45. PUZZLED

"X" handshape taps on top of your forehead once.

46. VERY PUZZLED

"4" bended handshape facing outward taps on top of your forehead once.

47. SUSPECT

"X" handshape facing yourself taps on your forehead and your finger moves up and down repeatedly.

48. RESPECT

"R" handshapes in front of your forehead moves outward once.

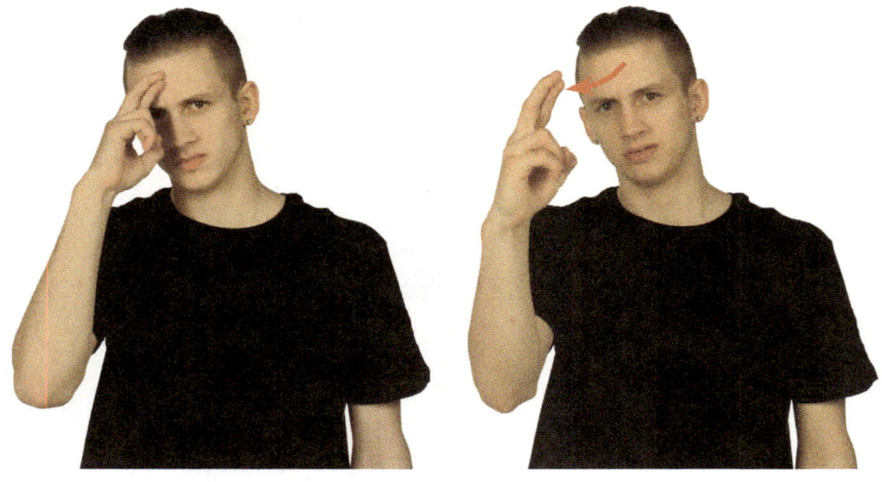

49. VERY RESPECTFUL

Both "R" handshapes in front of your forehead move outward and upward once.

50. HONOR

"H" handshape in front of your forehead moves outward once.

51. VERY HONORED

Both "H" handshapes in front of your forehead move outward and upward once.

52. FAITH

1. 1st "F" handshape facing sideways in front of yourself stays still while the 2nd "1" handshape taps on your forehead and changes to "F" handshape facing sideways moves downward and touches on the top of the 1st "F" handshape once.

2. 1st "F" handshape facing in front of yourself sideways stays still while the 2nd "F" touches on the top of the 1st "F" handshape once.

53. PICTURE

1st "5" closed handshape facing sideways stays still while the 2nd "C" handshape on the side of your temple moves downward and touches the 1st "5" closed handshape's palm.

54. INVENT

"B" open handshape on your forehead moves upward once.

55. VISUAL

Both "S" handshapes touching each other in front of your forehead move sideways once and change to both "5" open handshapes away from your head once.

56. EGOTISTIC

Both "L" bended handshapes with pointer fingers touching your temples and move outward once.

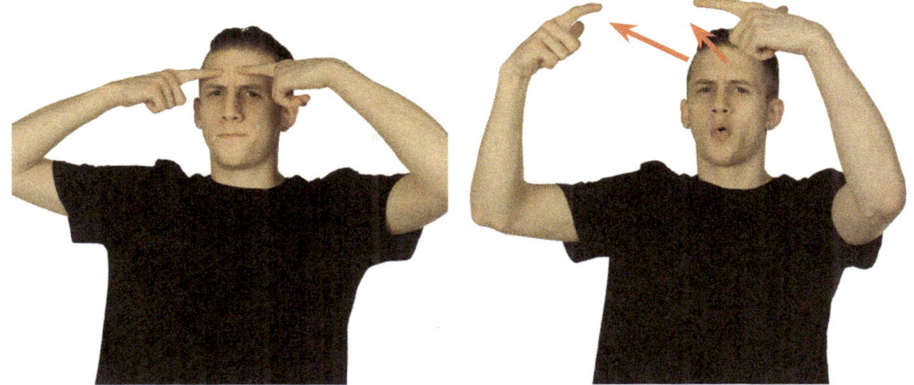

57. OPEN MINDED

Both "B" handshapes sideways in front of your forehead. Fingertips touching each other then move out sideways once.

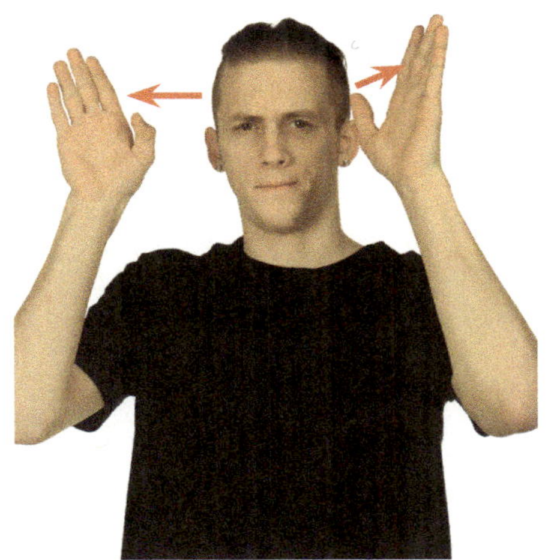

58. NARROW MINDED

Both "B" handshapes sideways away from side of your face and move inward and touch the tip of your fingers once.

59. WHY, BECAUSE

1. "I-L-Y" handshape on the side of your head and two middle fingers move up and down repeatedly.

2. "Middle finger" handshape on the side of your head while the middle finger moves up and down repeatedly.

3. "Y"bended handshape on the side of your head and middle 3 fingers move up and down repeatedly.

60. BRAINSTORMING, CREATIVE

Both "4" handshapes on each side of your head move like a swirl upward and alternating.

61. IMAGINATION

Both "I" handshapes on each side of your head move like a swirl upward and alternating.

CHAPTER

5 Time, Year and Calendar

1. TIME

   1st "S" handshape facing down in front of yourself stays still while the 2nd "X" handshape's finger taps on your wrist repeatedly.

2. DAY

   1st "5" closed handshape facing down in front of yourself while the 2nd "D" handshape's elbow rests on the top of the 1st "5" closed handshape. "D" handshape moves down once.

3. YEAR

1st "S" handshape facing sideways in front of yourself stays still while the 2nd "S" handshape moves around the 1st "S" handshape and touches on the top of 1st "S" handshape once.

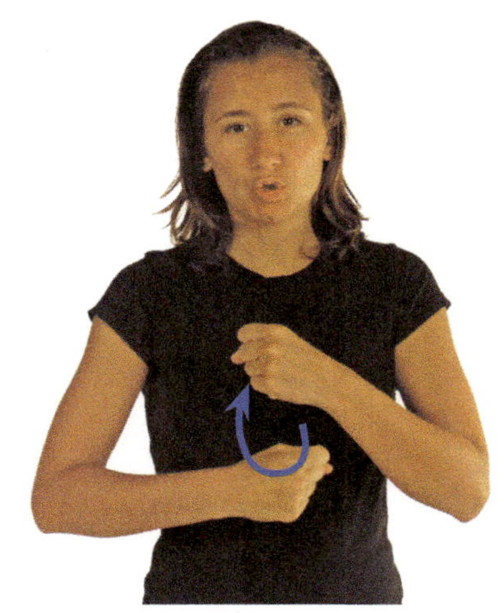

4. NEXT YEAR

1st "S" handshape facing sideways in front of yourself stays still while the 2nd "S" handshape on the top of 1st "S" handshape moves forward away from your body and changes to "1" handshape once.

5. LAST YEAR

1st "S" handshape facing sideways in front of yourself stays still while the 2nd "S" handshape on the top of 1st "S" handshape moves backward and changes to "1" handshape once.

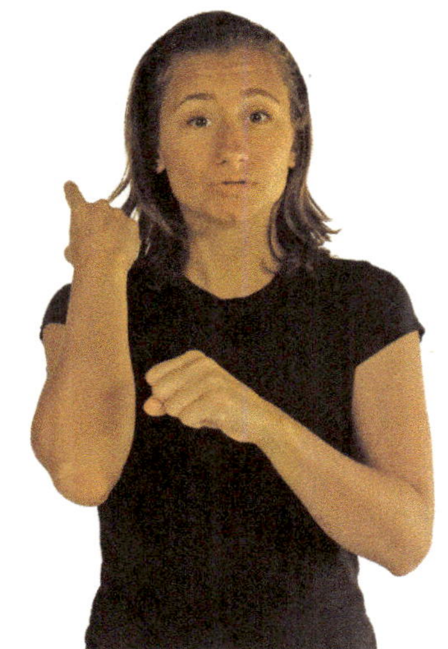

6. WEEK

1st "5" closed handshape facing sideways in front of yourself stays still while the 2nd "1" handshape's fingers touching the 1st "5" handshape's palm and slides from thumb side to finger side once.

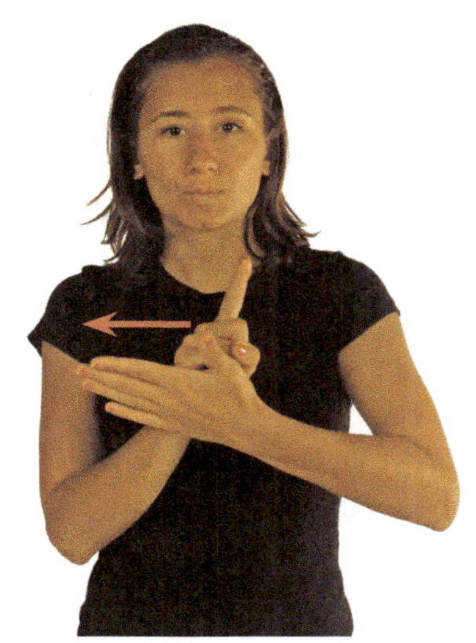

7. NEXT WEEK

1. 1st "5" closed handshape facing sideways in front of yourself stays still while 2nd "1" handshape's fingers touching the 1st "5" handshape's palm and slides from thumb side then moves in front of the 1st "5" handshape once.

2. Variation of "Next Week"

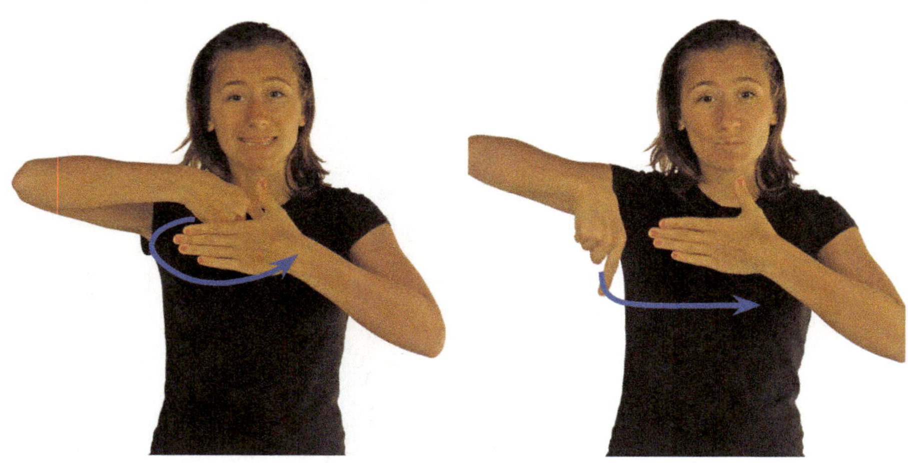

8. LAST WEEK

1st "5" closed handshape facing sideways in front of yourself stays still while the 2nd "1" handshape's fingers touching the 1st "5" handshape's palm and slides from thumb side then moves backward away from palm once.

9. MONTH

1st "1" handshape facing away from your body stays still while the 2nd "1" handshape sideways moves downward once (knuckles touching).

10. MONTHLY

1st "1" handshape facing away from your body stays still while the 2nd "1" handshape sideways moves downward repeatedly (knuckles touching).

11. LAST MONTH

1st "1" handshape facing away from your body stays still while the 2nd "1" handshape sideways with knuckles touching moves down once and becomes a "5" handshape and moves backwards once.

12. NEXT MONTH

1. 1st "5" closed handshape facing sideways in front of yourself stays still while the 2nd "5" closed handshape touches the 1st "5" closed handshape's palm then moves up and over the top of the 1st "5" closed handshape once and sign "month" as above.

2. 1st "1" handshape facing away from your body stays still while the 2nd "1" handshape sideways with knuckles touching moves down once with exaggerated movement.

13. DAILY

"A" handshape on your jaw moves from ear to chin repeatedly.

14. MORNING

1st"5"closed handshape facing sideways in front of yourself stays still while the 2nd"5" closed handshape facing upward the 1st"5" closed handshape touches the inner elbow and the 2nd"5" closed handshape bends and moves upright palm facing yourself once.

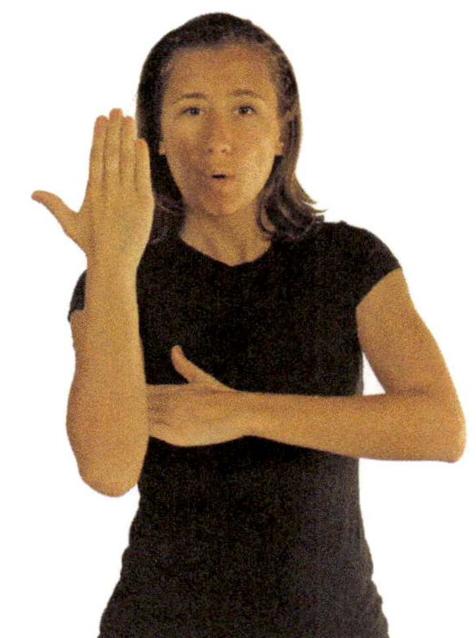

15. NOON

1st"5" closed handshape facing down in front of yourself stays still while the 2nd"5" closed handshape's elbow facing sideways touches on the top of the 1st"5" closed handshape's fingers once.

16. AFTERNOON

1st"5" closed handshape facing down, in front of yourself, stays still while the 2nd"5" closed handshape's elbow on the 1st"5" bended handshape's fingers facing down halfway away from yourself once.

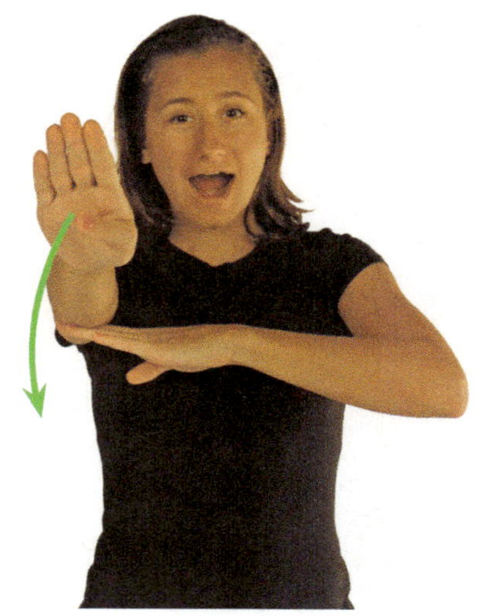

17. NIGHT

1st "5" closed handshape facing down, in front of yourself, stays still while the 2nd "5" bended handshape bends over the 1st "5" closed handshape once.

18. EVERY MORNING

1st "5" closed handshape facing down in front of your self stays still while the 2nd "5" closed handshape's inner elbow slides from your 1st "5" closed handshape's elbow to your hand.

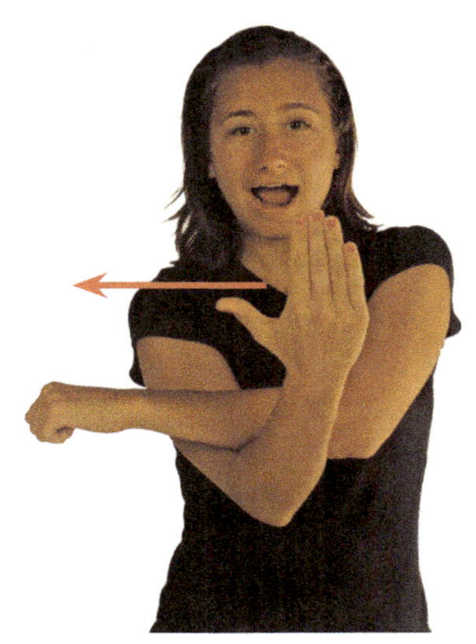

19. EVERY AFTERNOON

1st "S" handshape facing down in front of yourself stays still while the 2nd "5" handshape's inner elbow slides from the middle of your 1st "S" handshape's arm to your hand.

20. EVERY NIGHT

1st "5" closed handshape facing sideways, in front of yourself, stays still while the 2nd "5" bended handshape moves across the 1st "5" closed handshape's arm toward fingers.

21. OVERNIGHT/ALL NIGHT

1st "5" handshape facing sideways in front of yourself stays still and the 2nd "5" closed handshape facing away from yourself rests on the 1st "5" closed handshape's fingers then the 2nd "5" closed handshape folds over the 1st "5" closed handshape once to rest under your elbow

22. OVERSLEPT

1. 1st "5" closed handshape facing down, in front of yourself, stays still while the 2nd "F" handshape moves from your elbow upward.

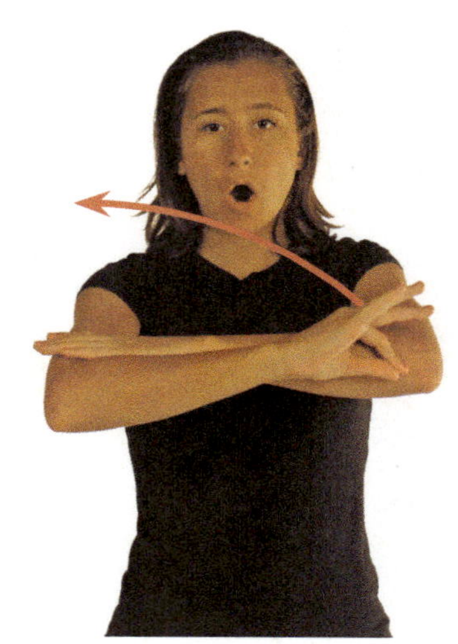

Chapter 5 Time, Year and Calendar 111

2. 1st "5" handshape facing down, in front of yourself, stays still and the 2nd "F" handshape moves under the 1st "5" handshape's arm upward.

23. SUNRISE

1. 1st "5" closed handshape facing down, in front of yourself, stays still while the 2nd "C" handshape moves from the 1st "5" handshape's elbow upwards to noon once.

 Chapter 5 Time, Year and Calendar 112

2. 1st"5" closed handshape facing down, in front of yourself, stays still while the 2nd "O" handshape moves from the 1st "5" handshape's elbow upwards to noon once.

24. SUNSET

1. 1st"5" closed handshape facing down, in front of yourself, stays still while the 2nd "C" handshape moves from the 1st"5" handshape's elbow downwards once.

2. 1st"5" closed handshape facing down, in front of yourself, stays still while the 2nd "O" handshape moves from the 1st"5" handshape's elbow downwards once.

25. EARLY

1. Both "L" handshapes on your chest near shoulders move forward once. For instance: pulling forward on suspenders/overall.

2. 1st "5" closed handshape facing down, in front of yourself, stays still while the 2nd "middle finger" handshape touches on the top of the 1st "5" closed handshape moves forward once.

26. TODAY

1. Both "Y" handshapes palm up stays still then change "Day" sign as above.

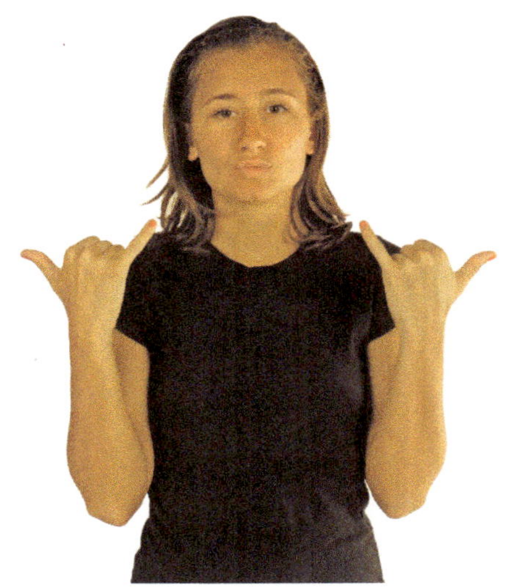

2. Both "Y" handshapes palms facing up move up and down repeatedly.

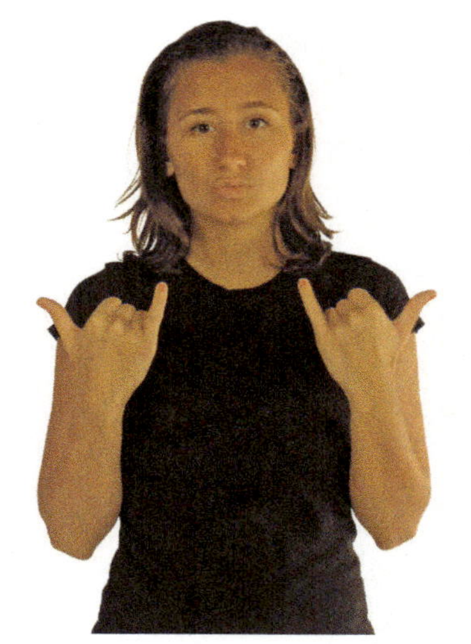

27. NOW

Both "Y" handshapes palms facing up move down once.

28. TOMORROW

"A" handshape on your cheek moves forward once.

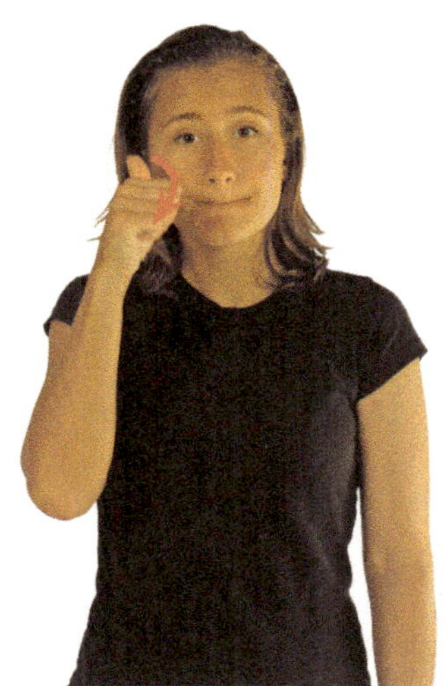

29. YESTERDAY

"A" handshape on your cheek moves backward towards your ear once.

30. **TWO DAYS AGO**

"2" handshape. "1" finger touches your cheek flips toward ear once.

31. **THREE DAYS AGO**

"3" handshape. Thumb on your cheek flips toward ear once.

32. **FUTURE**

"5" closed handshape near side of your forehead moves forward once extending arm fully.

33. WILL

"5" closed handshape near side of your forehead moves forward slightly.

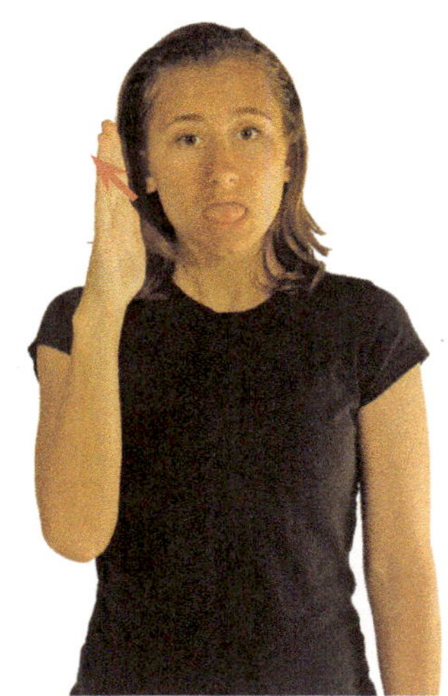

34. HOUR

1. 1st "5" closed handshape facing sideways stands upright and the 2nd "1" handshape on the 1st "5" closed handshape's palm and moves clockwise once.

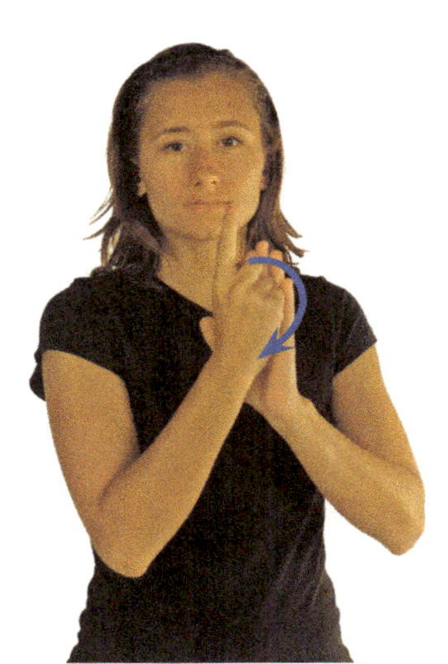

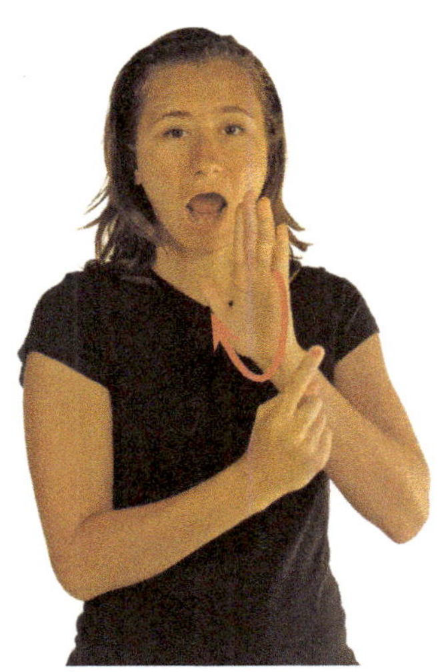

2. Variation of "Hour"

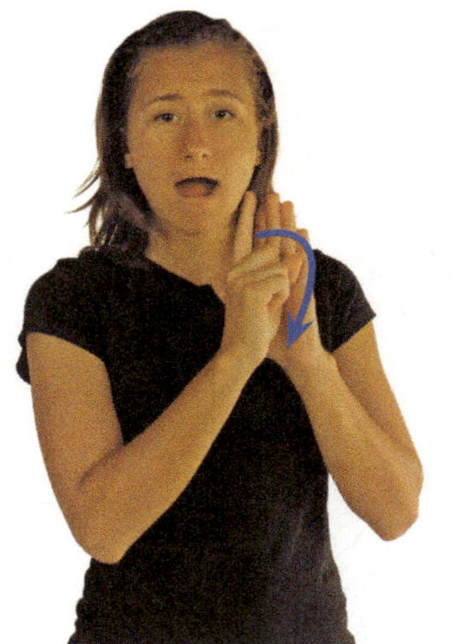

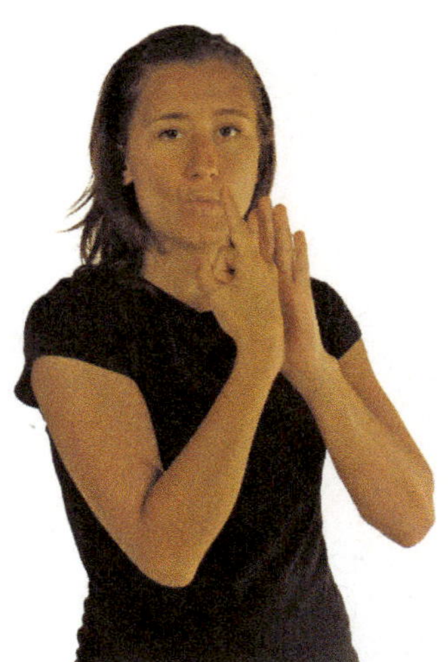

35. HALF HOUR

1st "5" handshape facing sideways stays still while the 2nd "1" handshape touches on the palm of the 1st "5" handshape moves downward once.

36. MINUTE

1. 1st "5" closed handshape stands upright and the 2nd "1" handshape on the 1st "5" closed handshape and moves twice slightly.

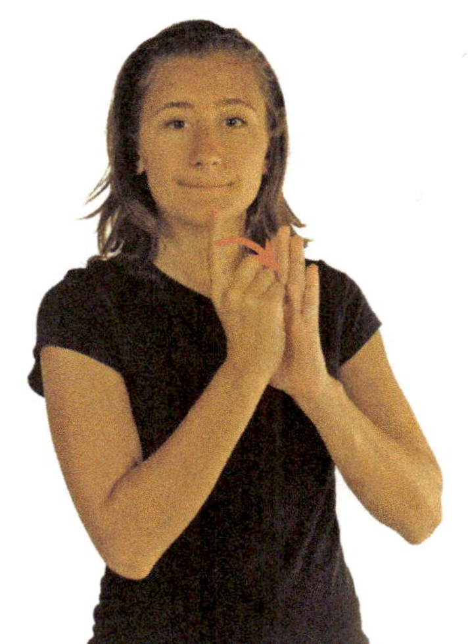

2. Variation of "Minute"

37. SUNDAY

Both "5" closed handshape upright palms outward above head and moves downward once.

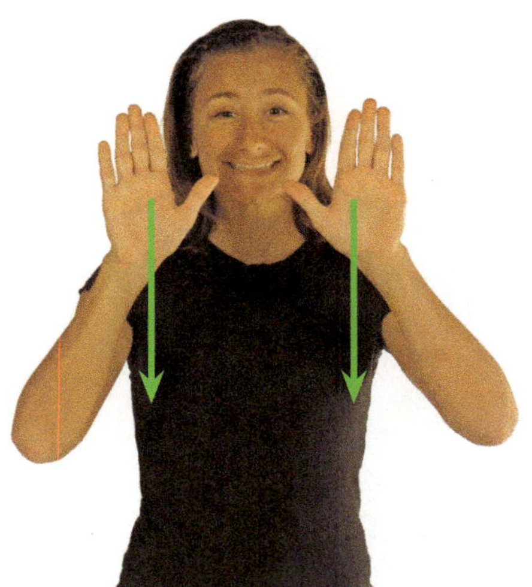

38. MONDAY

"M" handshape facing yourself moves in a circular motion.

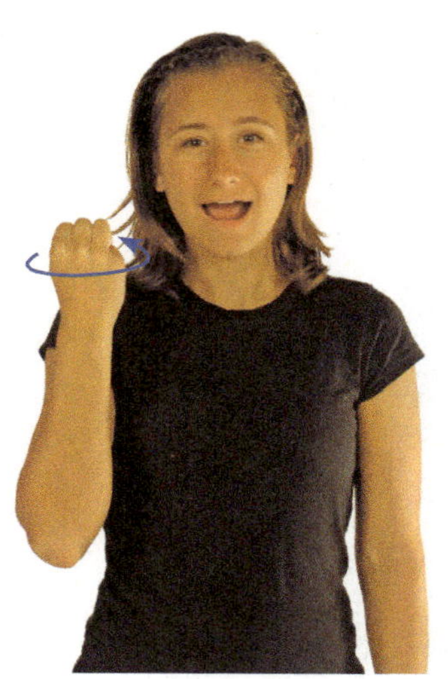

39. TUESDAY

"T" handshape facing yourself moves in a circular motion.

40. WEDNESDAY

"W" handshape facing yourself moves in a circular motion.

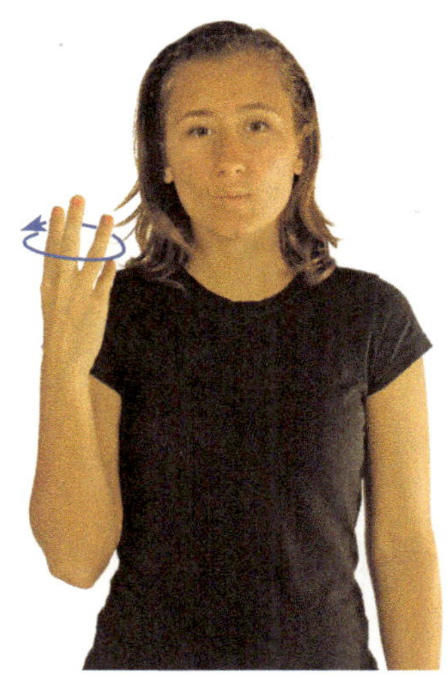

41. THURSDAY

"H" handshape facing yourself moves in a circular motion.

42. FRIDAY

"F" handshape facing yourself moves in a circular motion.

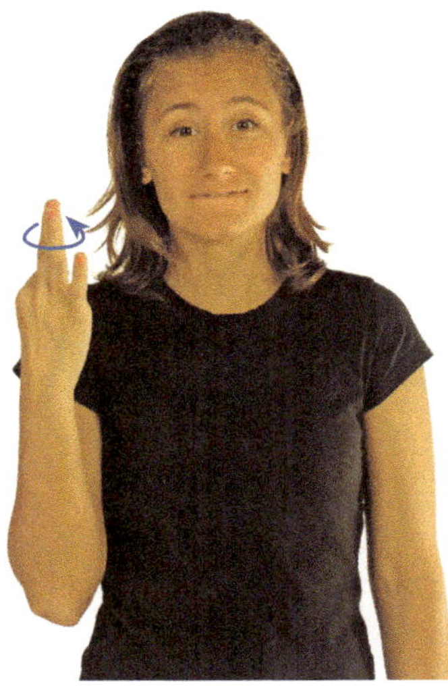

43. SATURDAY

"S" handshape facing yourself moves in a circular motion.

44. JANUARY

Fingerspell J-A-N.

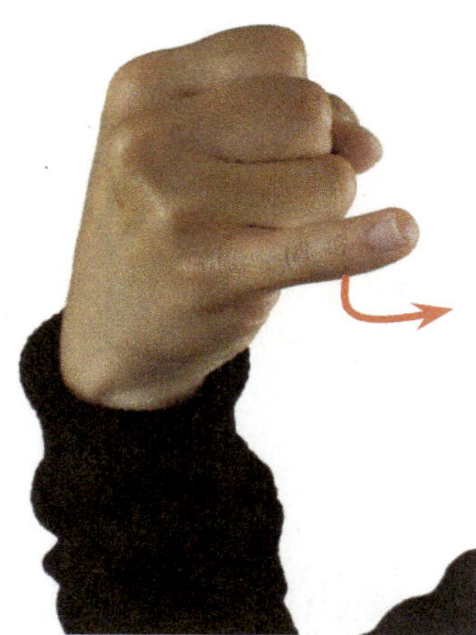

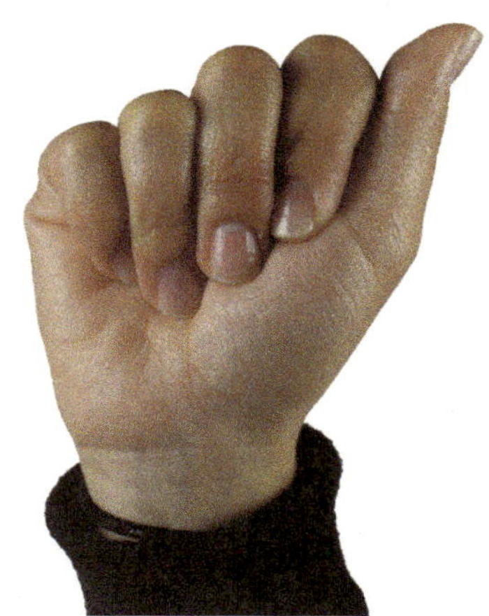

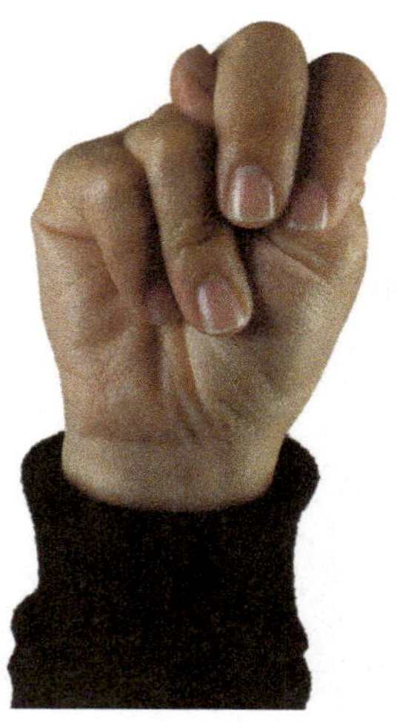

45. FEBRUARY

Fingerspell F-E-B.

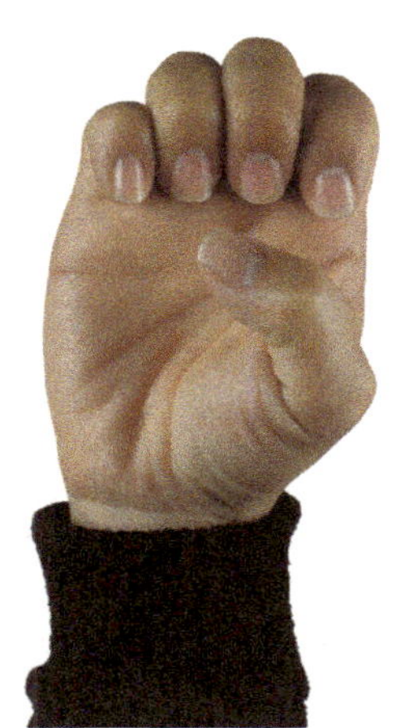

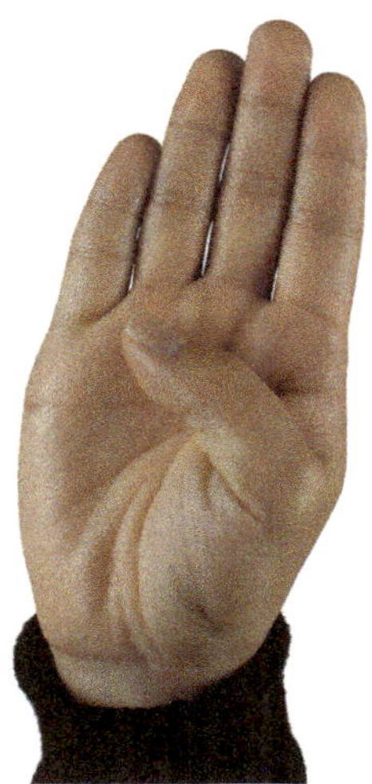

46. MARCH

Fingerspell M-A-R-C-H.

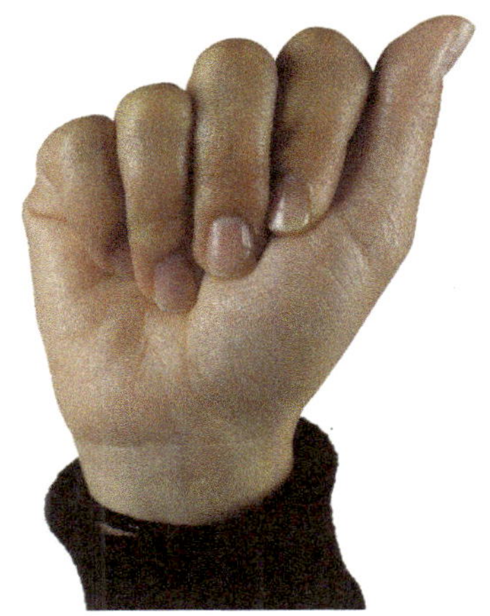

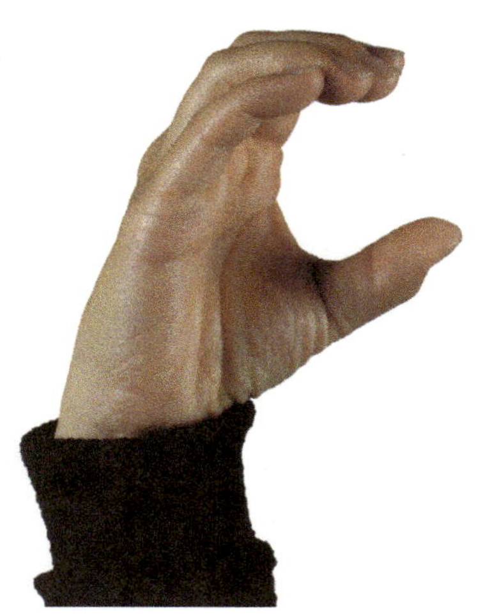

47. APRIL

Fingerspell A-P-R-I-L.

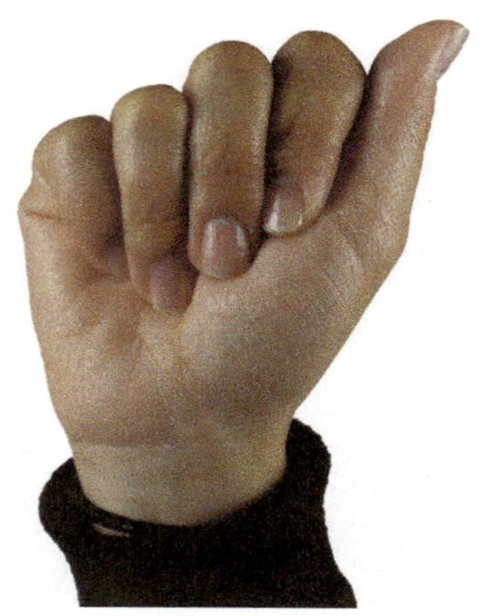

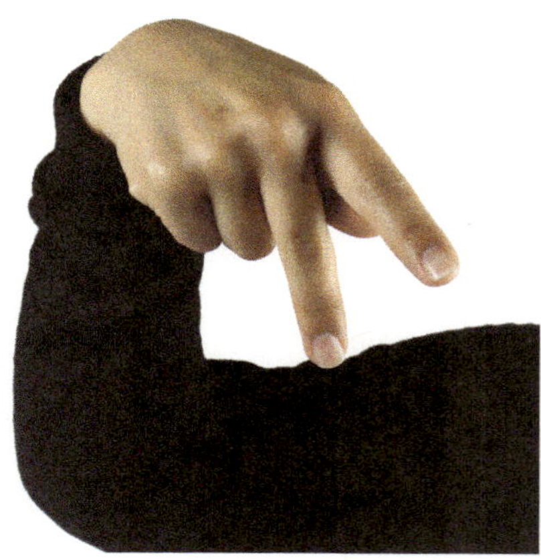

48. MAY

Fingerspell M-A-Y.

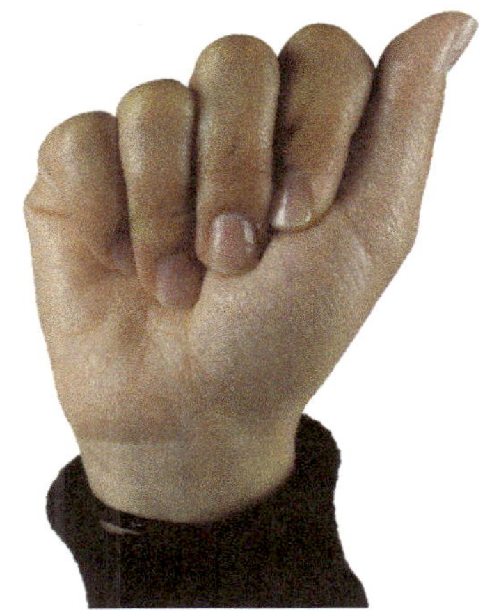

49. JUNE

Fingerspell J-U-N-E.

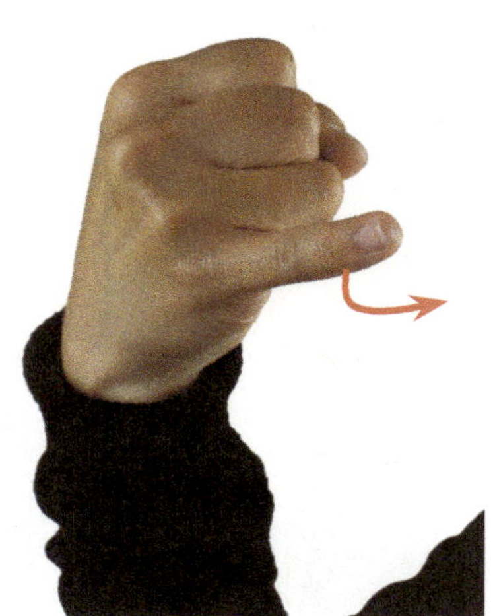

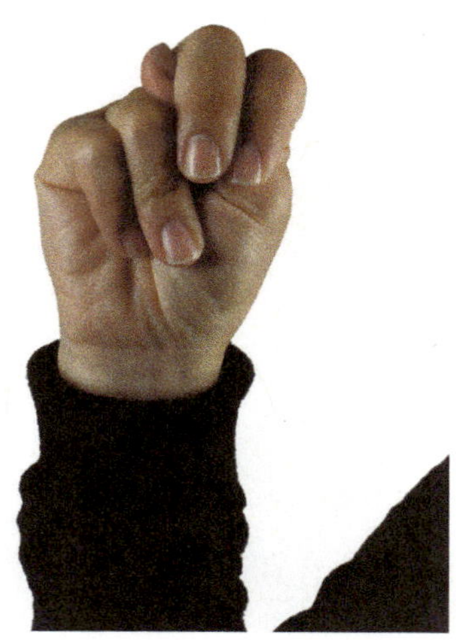

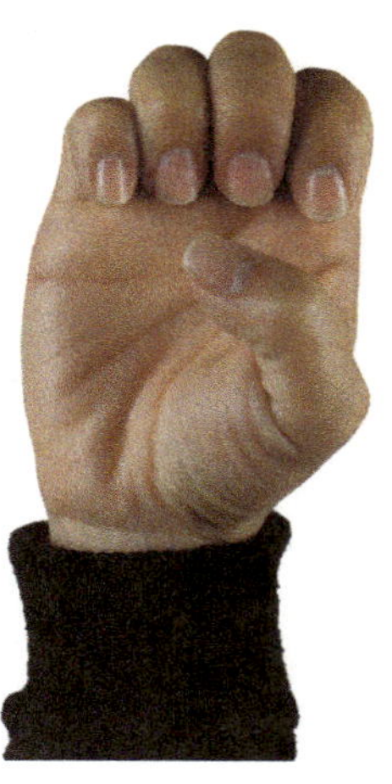

50. JULY

Fingerspell J-U-L-Y.

51. AUGUST

Fingerspell A-U-G.

52. SEPTEMBER

Fingerspell S-E-P-T.

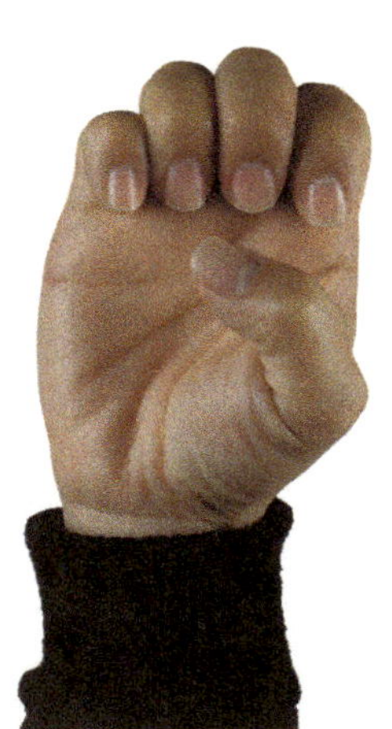

53. **OCTOBER**

Fingerspell O-C-T.

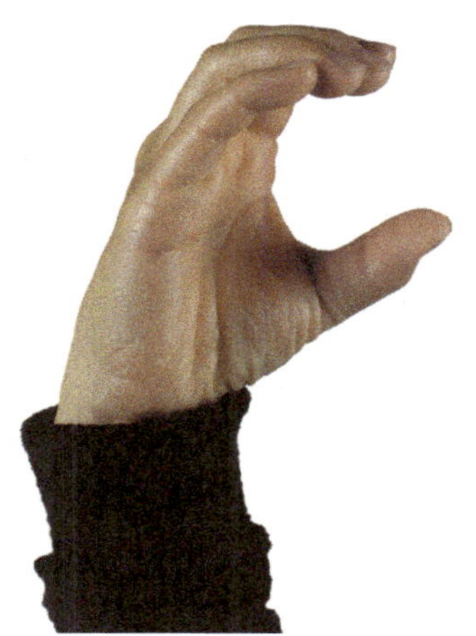

54. **NOVEMBER**

Fingerspell N-O-V.

55. DECEMBER

Fingerspell D-E-C.

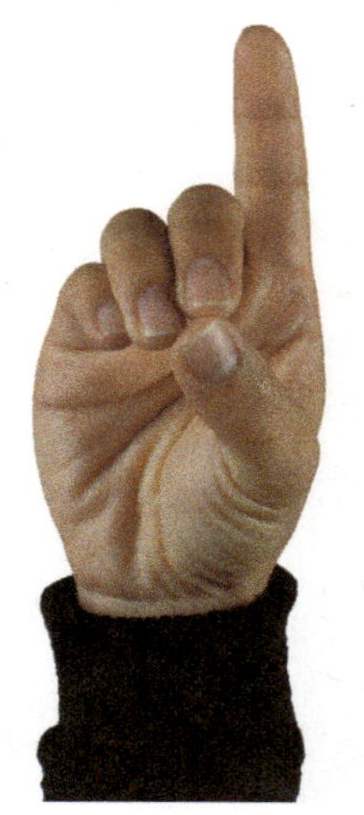

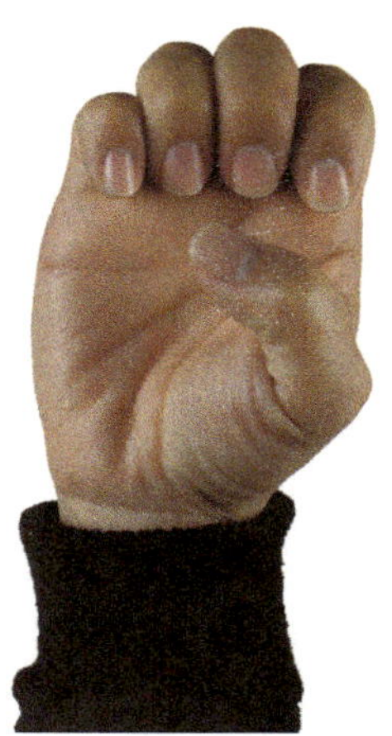

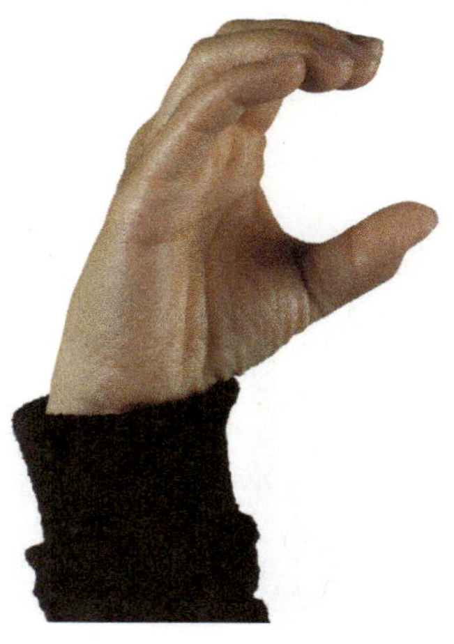

CHAPTER

6 Colors

1. RED

   "1" handshape on your chin moves up and down once or repeatedly.

2. PURPLE

   "P" handshape away from your body and shakes "P" handshape back and forth repeatedly.

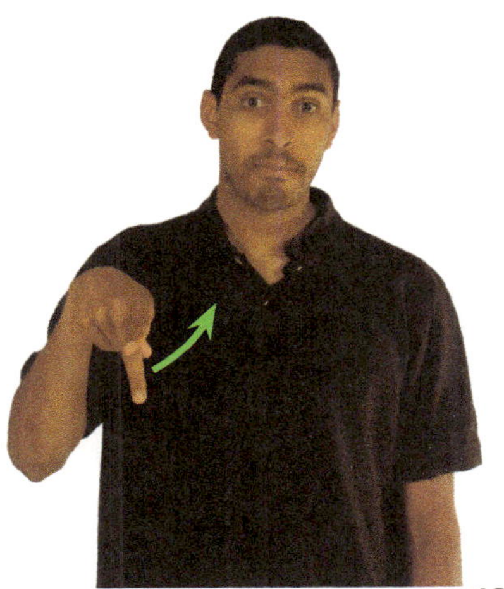

3. GREEN
"G" handshape away from your body twists back and forth repeatedly.

4. BLUE
"B" handshape away from your body and twists back and forth repeatedly.

5. WHITE
"5" closed handshape facing yourself on your chest moves outward to "O" closed handshape once.

6. BLACK

"1" handshape sideways on your forehead moves from side to side once.

7. GRAY

Both "5" open handshapes touch each other and move back and forth repeatedly.

8. ORANGE

"C" handshape in front of your mouth and squeezes to "S" handshape repeatedly.

9. **YELLOW**

"Y" handshape away from your body shakes back and forth repeatedly.

10. **GOLD**

"1" handshape on your ear moves downward and changes to "Y" handshape once.

11. **SILVER**

"1" handshape on your ear moves downward and changed to "5" handshape once.

12. TAN

"T" handshape on your cheek moves downward once.

13. BROWN

"B" handshape on your cheek slides down slightly once.

14. PINK (no picture)

"K" handshape's third finger facing sideways taps on your chin up and down repeatedly.

CHAPTER

7 Animals

1. ANIMAL
   Both "5" handshape's fingertips on both sides of your chest move sideways repeatedly.

2. CAT
   "F" handshape on your dimple near your mouth moves outward repeatedly.

3. DOG

   1. "K" handshape away from your body moves the middle finger rapidly.

   2. "5" handshape slap your upper thigh then moves outward and changes to a "snap" once.

4. COW

   "Y" handshape's thumb on the side of your temple moves back and forth repeatedly.

5. HORSE
"H" and "thumb" handshape on the side of your temple while "H" handshape moves back and forth repeatedly.

6. DONKEY
"5" closed handshape on the side of your forehead fingers move downward repeatedly.

7. GOAT
"S" handshape facing yourself on your chin moves upward and changes to "v" handshape facing yourself on your forehead once.

8. SHEEP

   1st "5" handshape facing up stays still while the 2nd "V" handshape facing up on the 1st "5" handshape's inner arm and moves back and forth from wrist to elbow on the 1st "5" handshape like a shearing scissors repeatedly.

9. BUFFALO

   "Y" handshape facing you on your forehead rocks back and forth repeatedly.

10. PIG

    "5" closed handshape facing down under your chin move fingers up and down repeatedly.

11. RABBIT

1. Both "H" handshapes. 1st "H" handshape facing yourself stays still while the 2nd "H" handshape facing yourself on the thumb of the 1st "H" handshape. Both "H" handshapes move back and forth repeatedly.

2. Both "H" handshapes touch on both side of your head and move back & forth repeatedly.

12. SQUIRREL

Both "V" bended handshapes facing each other and touching repeatedly.

13. LION

"5" bended handshape's fingers facing down on the top of your head moves from forehead to back of your head once.

14. TIGER

Both "5" bended handshapes on both of your cheeks move outward once.

15. GIRAFFE

"C" handshape sideways with fingertips facing you in front of your neck move hand upward to front of your head once (for example: long neck).

16. BEAR

Both "5" open and bended handshapes cross on your chest and "5" handshapes bend on your chest repeatedly.

17. MONKEY

Both "5" bended handshapes facing up and inward on both sides of your ribs and move up and down repeatedly.

18. DEER

Both "5" open handshapes facing forward on each side of your head move upward slightly once (for example: to show antlers).

19. MOOSE

Both "5" open handshapes facing forward on each side of your head move upward bigger than deer once.

20. CARIBOU

Both "5" open handshapes facing forward on each side of your head move forward curved once.

21. ELEPHANT

"5" closed handshapes with fingers pointing down wrist under your nose moves downward like a slide once (for example: to show long trunk).

22. FROG

"V" bended handshape facing down under your chin flicking repeatedly.

23. TURTLE

1st "5" closed handshape facing down while 2nd "A" handshape placed under the "5" bended handshape's thumb touching palm. Thumb on "A" hand moves up and down repeatedly (for example: to show head in shell).

24. SEA TURTLE

1st "5" closed handshape facing down stays still while the 2nd "5" closed handshape on top of the 1st "5" closed handshape. Both thumbs move circular motion continually.

25. FISH

"5" closed handshape facing sideways wiggles away from your body (for example: to show swimming).

26. DOLPHIN

1. "D" handshape facing down in front of your chest moves up & down (for example: to show swimming).

2. "R & thumb" handshape facing yourself in front of your chest moves up and down (for example: to show swimming).

27. WHALE

1st "5" closed handshape facing down while the 2nd "Y" handshape rests on the top of 1st "5" closed handshape's arm and then moves up, down, and backward (for example: to show swimming).

28. SHARK

1. Variation of "Shark"

2. Variation of "Shark"

3. Variation of "Shark"

29. **SKUNK**

"K" handshape facing down with your fingertips on the top of your forehead moves toward back of your head.

30. BIRD

"G" handshape facing outward on top of your mouth, thumb and finger moves up and down repeatedly (for example: to show chirping).

31. CHICKEN

1. Same sign as above "bird."

2. 1st "5" closed handshape facing up away from your body while the 2nd "G" handshape facing outward on top of your mouth moves downward and touches the palm of 1st "5" closed handshape (to show eating from the palm).

32. DUCK

3″ closed handshape's wrist on the top of your mouth, thumb and fingers move up and down repeatedly.

33. GOOSE

1st "5" closed handshape facing up stays still while the 2nd "3" closed handshape on top of the 1st "5" closed handshape's inner arm moves up and down while moving toward wrist.

34. TURKEY

1. "Q" handshape facing down on your chin moves downward and touches on your upper chest (for example: to show rooster's cruncle/wattle).

2. "Q" handshape facing down on your chin moves sideways repeatedly.

35. EAGLE

"X" handshape facing away from your face on top of your nose once.

36. OWL

Both "O" handshapes in front of your eyes move up and down repeatedly.

37. MOUSE

"1" handshape facing sideways on your nose moves downward slightly and repeatedly.

38. RAT

"R" handshape facing sideways on your nose moves downward slightly once.

39. FOX

"F" handshape facing sideways on your nose moves up and down repeatedly.

40. KANGAROO

1. Both "5" bended handshapes facing down in front of your chest move outward once.

2. Kangaroo

Both "8" handshapes facing down in front of your chest move outward and flick once.

41. CAMEL

"5" bended handshape facing down away from your body moves like curve (for example: shape of camel's humps).

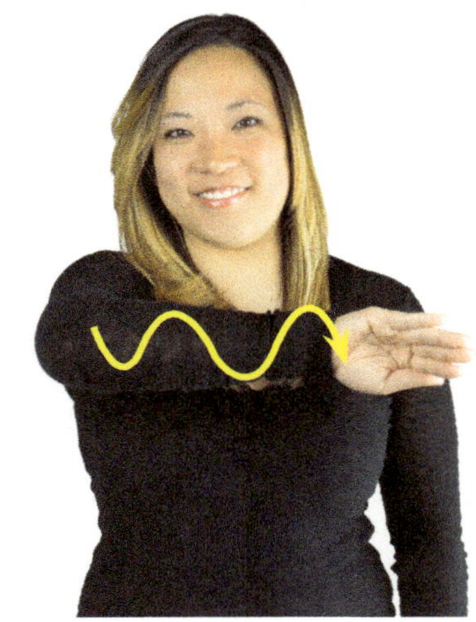

42. WOLF

"5" open handshape facing yourself on your nose and moves down and outward turns in to "5" closed handshape bringing all fingers together once away from your face (for example: as if grabbing your nose).

43. SNAKE

1. "V" bended handshape facing down under your chin moves outward like a swirl (for example: to show a slithering snake's tongue).

2. 1st "5" closed handshape facing down stays still while the 2nd "1" handshape under the 1st "5" closed handshape moves like zigzag.

44. BUTTERFLY

Both "5" handshapes lock at thumbs lock each other in front of your chest facing yourself move back and forth like wings moving.

45. BEE

"8" closed handshape touches on your cheek and changes to "B" handshape slab on your cheek once.

46. MOSQUITO

1. Same as "bee" above.

2. Both "S" handshapes. 1st "S" handshape on your nose stays still while 2nd "S" handshape touches on end of the 1st "S" handshape moves downward like drill.

3. "G" handshape on your nose moves back and forth slightly and repeatedly.

47. BUGS

"3" bended handshape facing sideways on your nose. 1st "thumb" on your nose while "V" bended handshape moves repeatedly.

48. WORM

1st "5" closed handshape facing sideways away from your body stays still while the 2nd "1" handshape touches on the palm of the 1st "5" closed handshape moves while the "1" finger moves up and down sideways (like a worm wiggling).

49. INSECT

Both "5" handshapes facing down your thumbs cross each other while the fingers wiggle forward.

50. ALLIGATOR

1st "5" closed handshape facing up away from your body stays still while the 2nd "5" closed handshape facing down away from your body touches on the top of 1st "5" closed handshape moves up and down repeatedly (for example: as in a large mouth opening).

51. CROCODILE

1st "5" bended handshape facing up away from your body stays still while the 2nd "5" bended handshape facing down away from your body touches on the top of 1st "5" bended handshape moves up and down repeatedly (for example: as in a large mouth opening).

52. GORILLA

Both "A" handshapes on your chest move outward alternating continually (for example: like beating on chest).

53. HIPPO

Both "1 finger & little finger" handshapes. 1st "1 finger & little finger" handshape facing up stays still while the 2nd "1 finger & little finger" handshape facing down touches the tips of first finger and little finger. Both fingers move up and down at the same time repeatedly (for example: looks like hippo's teeth).

54. PENGUIN

Both "5" closed handshapes on each side of your hips palms facing down and move back and forth repeatedly.

55. ZEBRA

1st "5" handshape in front of yourself and the 2nd "5" handshape in front of your chest move the opposite direction from each other (for example: to show stripes).

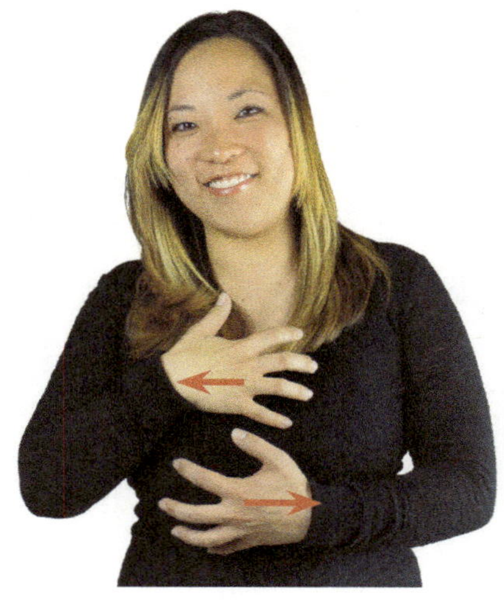

56. BULL

"Y" handshape facing outward taps on your forehead once.

57. BAT

Both "X" handshapes facing yourself cross each other on your chest while both bended fingers tap on your chest once or repeatedly.

58. DINOSAUR

1. 1st "5" closed handshape facing down stays still while the 2nd "D" handshape facing sideways moves up and down repeatedly (for example: like a walking "D").

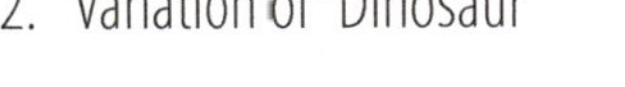

2. Variation of "Dinosaur"

59. SEAL

1. Both "5" closed handshapes cross at wrist and palm of hands touch each other repeatedly.

2. (no picture)
Both "5" closed handshapes cross at wrist and back of hands touch each other repeatedly (opposite from above).

60. RACOON

Both "V" handshapes sideways and facing yourself in front of your eyes move outward and close at the same time once.

61. ROOSTER

"3" open handshape on your forehead moves back and forth repeatedly.

CHAPTER

8 Food

1. VEGETABLES
   "V" handshape. First finger on your chin moves sideways repeatedly.

2. GARLIC
   "X"bended handshape on the side of your nose moves twisting repeatedly.

3. ONION
   "X" bended handshape near your eye moves twisting repeatedly.

4. POTATO
   1st "S" handshape facing down stays still while the 2nd "V" bended handshape taps on the top of the 1st "S" handshape repeatedly.

5. MUSHROOM
   1st "1 "handshape facing up stays still while the 2nd "5" bended handshape on the top of the "1" handshape moves up and down repeatedly.

6. GREEN ONION

Sign "green" in chapter 6 then change to the "onion" sign as above.

7. CARROT

1. "S" handshape on side of your chin while your mouth moves like you are eating at the same time.

2. 1st "1" handshape in front of yourself while the 2nd "10" handshape facing sideways thumb moves up and down on the 1st "1" handshape repeatedly.

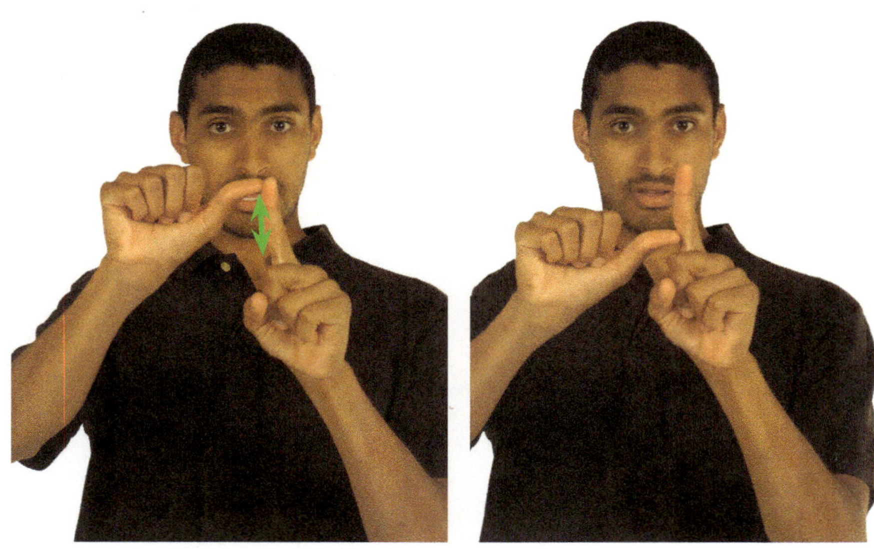

8. CORN

1. "1" handshape facing down in front of your mouth twists back and forth and moves from one side of your mouth to the other.

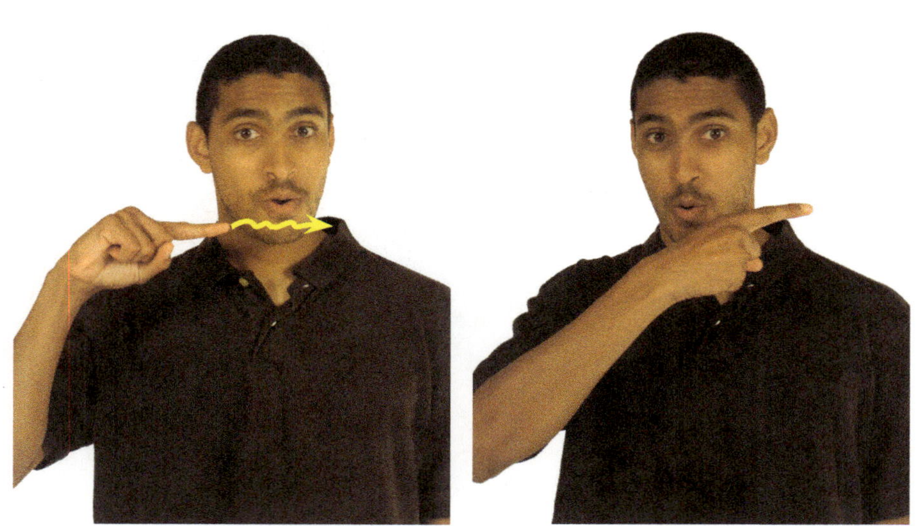

2. Both "1" handshapes facing each other in front of your mouth turn over alternating.

9. SALAD

Both "5" bended handshapes facing up away from your body move in a circular motion repeatedly (to show tossing a salad).

10. PUMPKIN

1st "S" handshape facing down in front of yourself stays still while the 2nd "8" handshape flicks on the top of the 1st "S" handshape repeatedly.

11. WATERMELON

"W" handshape facing sideways on your chin moves back and forth repeatedly then changes to the sign of "pumpkin" as above.

12. TOMATO

1. 1st "1" handshape facing sideways in front of yourself stays still while the 2nd "1" handshape on your chin moves downward and touches the 1st "1" handshape's fingertips once (for example: to show slicing).

2. 1st "O" closed handshape facing sideways in front of yourself stays still while the 2nd "1" handshape on your chin moves downward and touches the 1st "O" closed handshape's fingertips once (for example: to show slicing).

13. WATER
"W" handshape facing sideways on your chin moves back and forth repeatedly.

14. POP, SODA
1st "S" handshape facing sideways in front of yourself stays still while the "middle finger" shandshape moves inside the 1st "S" handshape then moves up and changes to "5" handshape quickly then moves back and down and hits palm onto 1st "S" handshape.

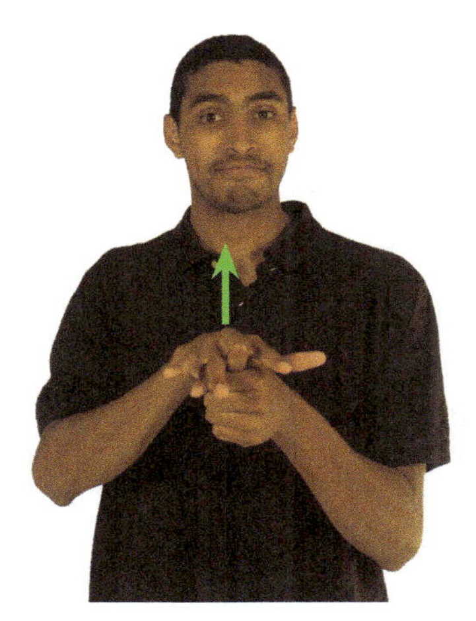

15. WINE

"W" handshape sideways on your cheek moves in a circular motion continually.

16. WHISKEY

Both "1 finger and little finger" handshapes touch each other and bounce up and down repeatedly.

17. BEER

"B" handshape facing sideways on the side of your chin moves up & down once or repeatedly.

18. JUICE

"J" handshape away from your body moves the shape of "J" once or repeatedly.

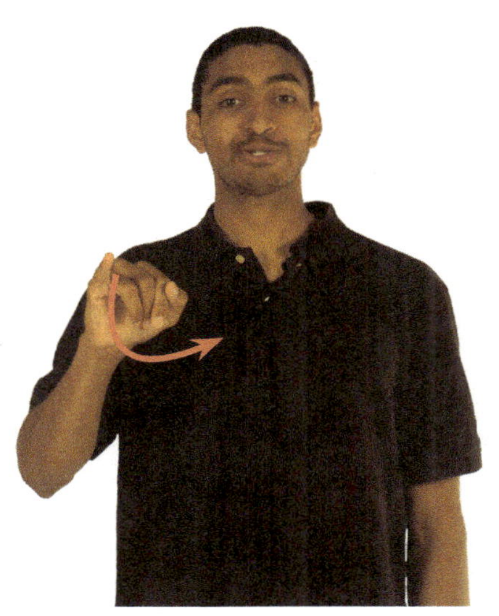

19. MILK

"S" handshape away from your body squeezes repeatedly.

20. TEA

1st "S" handshape facing sideways stays still while the 2nd "9" handshape touches inside the "S" handshape moves in a circular motion continually.

21. COFFEE

1st "S" handshape facing sideways stays still while the 2nd "S" handshape on top of the 1st "S" handshape moves in a circular motion continually.

22. BUTTER

1st "5" closed handshape facing up stays still while the 2nd "3" closed handshape brushes on the palm of the 1st "5" closed handshape repeatedly.

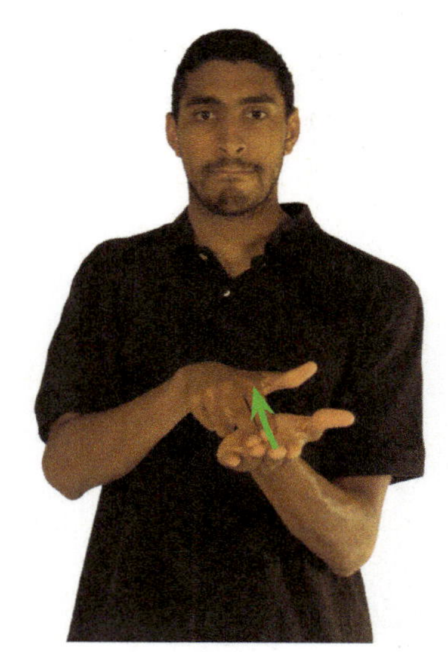

23. CHEESE

1st "5" closed handshape facing up in front of yourself while the 2nd "5" closed handshape is facing down touching and pressing and twisting against each other repeatedly.

24. CREAM

1st "5" closed handshape facing up in front of yourself stays still while the 2nd "5" bended handshape on top of the 1st "5" closed handshape's palm moves down and changes to "A" handshape.

25. ICE CREAM

"S" handshape facing sideways in front of your mouth moves up & down repeatedly (for example: to show licking ice cream cone).

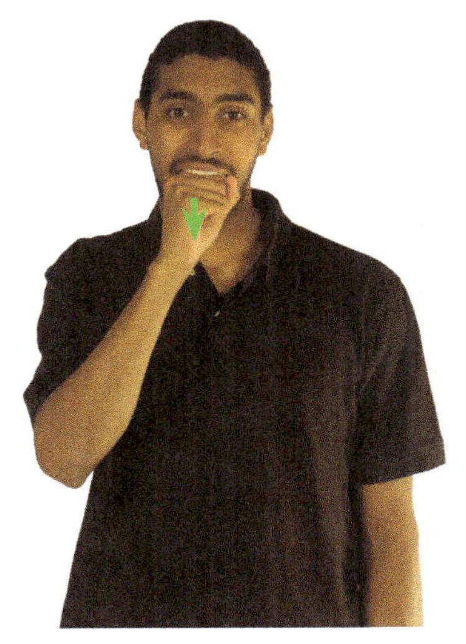

26. **SOUR CREAM**

"1" handshape on your chin moves twisting once then add the sign of "cream" as above.

27. **EGG**

Both "H" handshapes in front of yourself cross at your fingers and move down outward once.

28. BACON

Both "H" handshapes facing down in front of yourself fingertips touching each other then wiggle fingers and move outward like swimming.

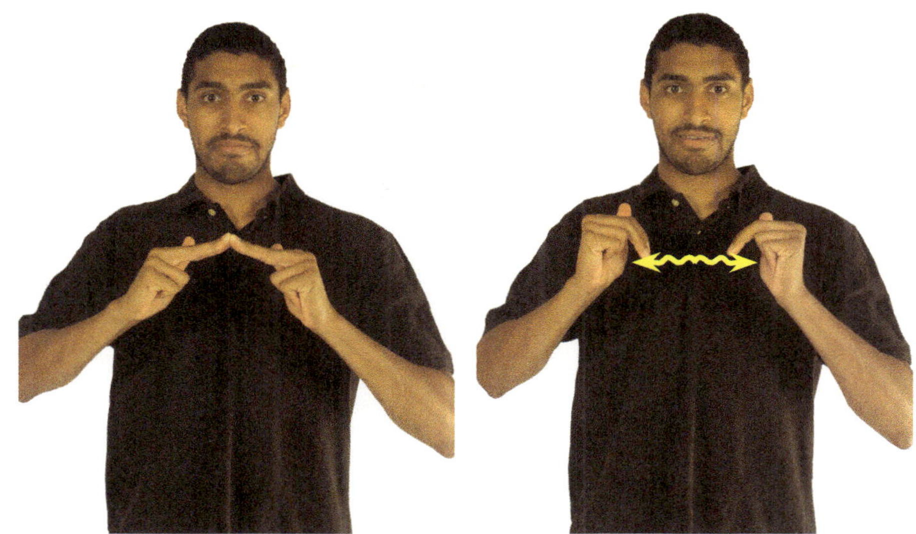

29. MEAT, STEAK

1st "5" closed handshape facing down in front of yourself stays still while the 2nd "8" handshape squeezes the skin/muscle between 1st and thumb once.

30. SAUSAGE, HOT DOG

Both "S" handshapes touch each other in front of your body and squeeze repeatedly while moving outward.

31. TACO

1st "C" handshape facing up in front of yourself stays still while the 2nd "5" closed handshape sits in between the 1st "C" handshape's thumb & fingers then moves up and down repeatedly.

32. BURRITO

Both "5" bended handshape facing sideways in front of yourself like the shape of "G" move back and forth.

33. HAMBURGER

1st"5" bended handshape facing up in front of yourself while the 2nd"5" bended handshape facing down and both hands clasps each other and turn over.

34. CHEESEBURGER

Sign with"cheese" as above then sign of"hamburger" as above.

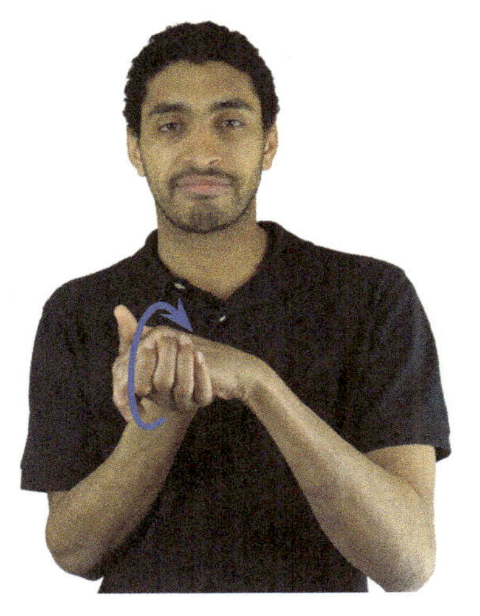

35. SANDWICH

1. Both "5" closed and bended handshapes' fingers on top of each other in front of your mouth.

2. Both "5" closed handshapes facing sideways in front of your mouth like the shape of "G" both handshapes's fingers move up and down repeatedly.

36. CHICKEN

1. Same sign as "bird" in chapter 7.

37. TURKEY

1. Same sign as "turkey" in chapter 7.

2. Variation of "Turkey"

38. DUCK

Same sign as "duck" in chapter 7.

39. FISH
    Same sign "fish" in chapter 7.

40. SHRIMP
    "X" handshape facing down in front of yourself wiggle finger and moves sideways repeatedly.

41. LOBSTER
    Both "V" handshapes facing down move fingers back and forth sideways repeatedly (to show pinchers).

42. CRAB

Both "O" closed handshapes facing down fingers touch thumbs repeatedly.

43. CEREAL

1. "1" handshape facing down on your chin wiggle finger and move sideways repeatedly.

2. 1st "5" curved handshape facing up stays still while the 2nd "5" curved handshape touches on the top of 1st "5" curved handshape's palm then moves upward near your mouth (for example: like scoop/spoon).

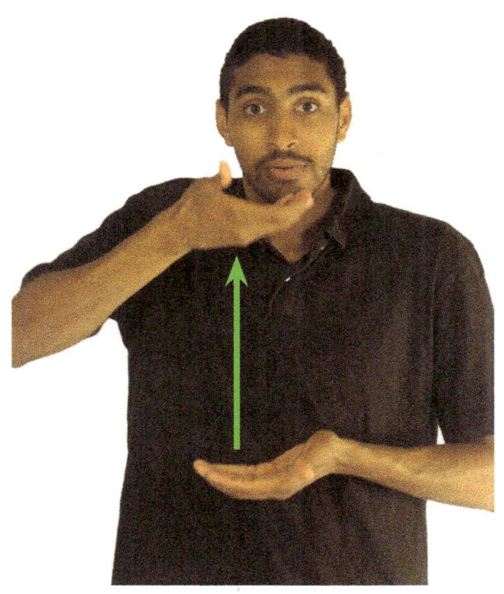

44. PEAR

1st "O" closed handshape facing down stays still while the 2nd "5" bended handshape closes around the fingers of the 1st "O" closed handshape then slides out and becomes an "O" closed handshape.

45. PINEAPPLE

1. "K" handshape on the side of your cheek moves twisting repeatedly.

2. "F" handshape in front of your eye moves up and down repeatedly.

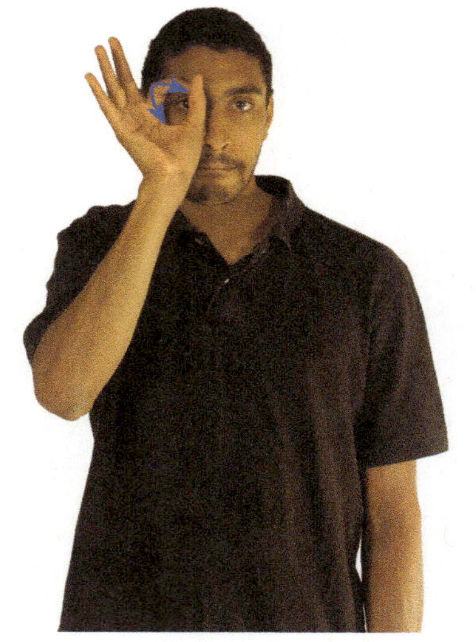

46. APPLE

"X" handshape's knuckle on the side of your cheek twists repeatedly.

47. LEMON

"L" handshape's thumb taps on your chin while "L" handshape's finger moves up and down repeatedly.

48. DRESSING, SAUCE

"10" handshape facing down in front of yourself moves in a circular motion continually.

49. CANDY

"1" handshape on the side of your lower cheek moves twisting repeatedly.

50. CHOCOLATE

1st "5" closed handshape facing down away from your body stays still while the 2nd "C" handshape on the top of the 1st "5" closed handshape moves in a circular motion continually.

51. DONUT

1. 1st "5" closed handshape facing sideways while the 2nd "thumb and "R" handshape place thumb on the palm of the 1st "5" closed handshape move "R" upward once.

2. Both "R" handshapes away from your body fingertips touch each other and move backward like a circle once (to form a circle/donut).

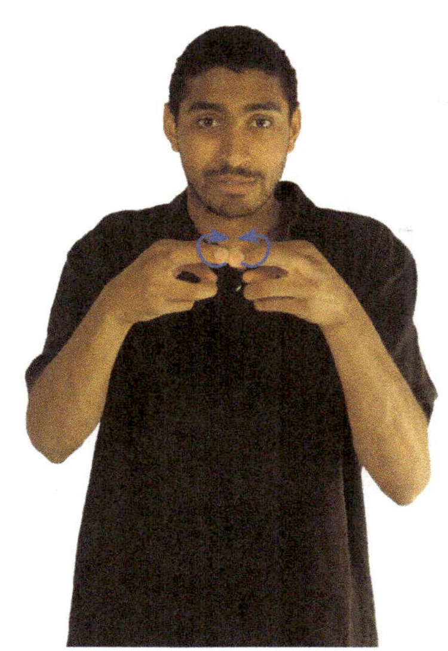

52. SUGAR

1. "3" closed handshape on your chin bends up and down repeatedly.

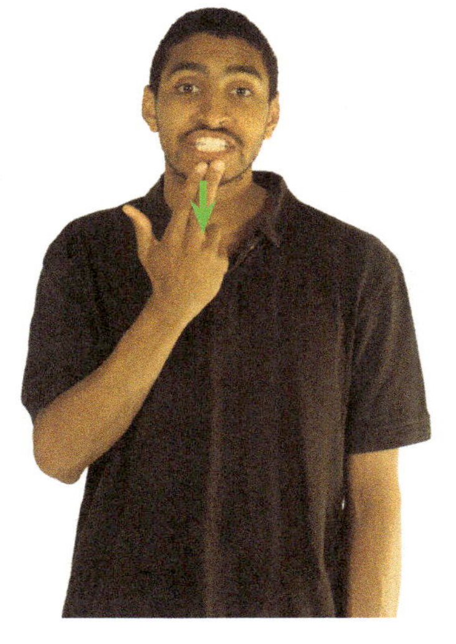
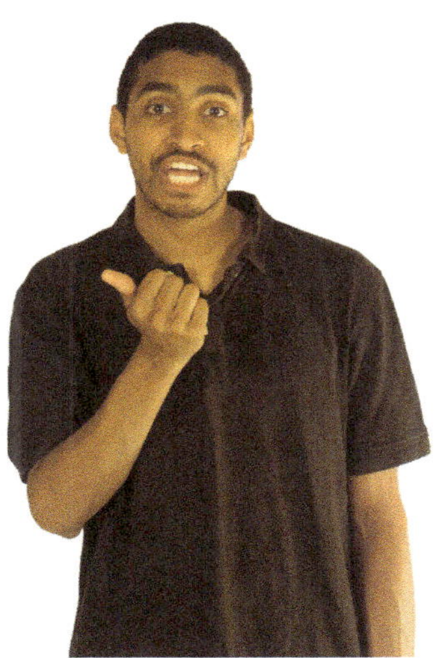

2. "5" closed handshape on your chin bends up and down repeatedly

53. BROWN SUGAR

Sign of "brown" in chapter 6 then sign of "sugar" as above.

54. BREAD

1st "5" closed handshape facing sideways in front of yourself while the 2nd "5" bended handshape on the front of the 1st "5" closed handshape moves down once (as in slicing).

55. TOAST

1st "5" closed handshape facing sideways in front of yourself stays still while the 2nd "V" handshape touches on the back of 1st "5" closed handshape then moves to the other side and touches the "5" closed handshape's palm once.

56. VANILLA (LIQUID)

1st "5" closed handshape in front of yourself stays still while the 2nd "V" handshape facing down on the top of the 1st "5" closed handshape moves in a circular motion.

57. SALT

1st "V" handshape facing down in front of yourself while the 2nd "V" handshape on the top of the 1st "V" handshape and wiggle fingers up and down at the same time alternating.

58. PEPPER

"F" handshape facing down away from your body moves up and down repeatedly.

59. SPICY

"A" handshape's wrist on your chin moves outward then changes to "5" open handshape and wiggle fingers.

60. GRAVY, GREASE

1st "5" closed handshape facing sideways in front of yourself stays still while the 2nd "8" handshape touches on the bottom of both sides of the 1st "5" closed handshape moves downward repeatedly.

61. PIZZA

1. "L" bended handshape facing up to your mouth (for example: like taking a bite).

2. Fingerspell both "ZZ"

3. Fingerspell p-zz-a (for example: use "V" handshape to show Z's at the same time).

62. SPAGHETTI

Both "I" handshapes facing sideways touch each other and move outward like a spiral.

63. PEACH

"5" closed handshape facing sideways taps on your upper cheek and slides down and brings fingers & thumb together once.

64. SOUP

"5" closed handshape facing up in front of yourself stays still while the 2nd "U" handshape facing moves from palm up to your mouth once or repeatedly.

CHAPTER

9 Clothes

1. HAT
   "5" closed handshape facing down taps on the top of your head repeatedly.

2. CAP
   "A" handshape facing sideways in front of your forehead moves forward and backward repeatedly.

3. **JACKET, COAT**
   Both "10" handshapes on both sides of your upper chest moves downward once.

4. **LEATHER JACKET**
   "5" curved handshape facing sideways taps on your upper chest and moves in a circular motion repeatedly then changes to both "10" handshapes on both sides of your upper chest moves downward once.

5. WINDBREAKER JACKET

"5" open handshapes facing sideways in front of yourself move back and forth sideways repeatedly then sign "jacket" as above.

6. GLOVES

1st "5" closed handshape facing down away from your body stays still while the 2nd "5" closed handshape touches on the top of the 1st "5" closed handshape then the 1st "5" closed handshape moves and touches on the top of the 2nd "5" handshape alternating.

7. SHIRT
   "F" handshape facing down taps on the top of your shoulder repeatedly.

8. SKIRT
   Both "5" curved handshapes on each side of your hips move downward once.

9. PANTS

Both "5" closed handshapes's fingers touch on both upper thighs and move upward and bend repeatedly.

10. SHORTS

Both "5" closed handshapes facing sideways touch on both thighs and slide outward repeatedly.

11. TIE

"U" handshape facing yourself touches on your lower neck moves downward once.

12. BOWTIE

Both "S" handshapes cross each other at the wrists on the top of your upper chest change to "V" handshapes once. (to show the shape of a bowtie)

13. SHOES

Both "S" handshapes facing down bounce off each other repeatedly.

14. SOCK

Both "1" handshapes facing down rubbing against each other alternating repeatedly.

15. HIGH HEELS

Both "I" handshapes facing down away from your body move up and down alternating repeatedly.

16. BOOTS

Both "B" handshapes facing down away from your body bounce off each other repeatedly.

17. BATHING SUIT, SWIMMING SUIT

Both "B" handshapes facing down away from your body touch each other then move outward and fingerspell S-U-I-T.

18. PAJAMA
Fingerspell P-J.

19. BACKPACK

1. Both "10" handshapes on top of your shoulders move down slightly once or repeatedly.

2. (No picture) Both "C" handshapes tap on your upper chest and move forward and backward repeatedly.

20. PURSE, BAG

"S" handshape facing down away from your side of your body moves up and down slightly and repeatedly (to show carrying a purse).

21. BUTTON

"F" handshape sideways on your chest moves and bounces downward.

22. ZIPPER

1st "L" closed handshape touches on your stomach while the 2nd "L" closed handshape touching on the tip of the 1st "L" closed handshape moves upward once (to show that you zipped your jacket/coat).

23. DRESS

Both "5" open handshape's palms facing yourself in front of your body move downward once.

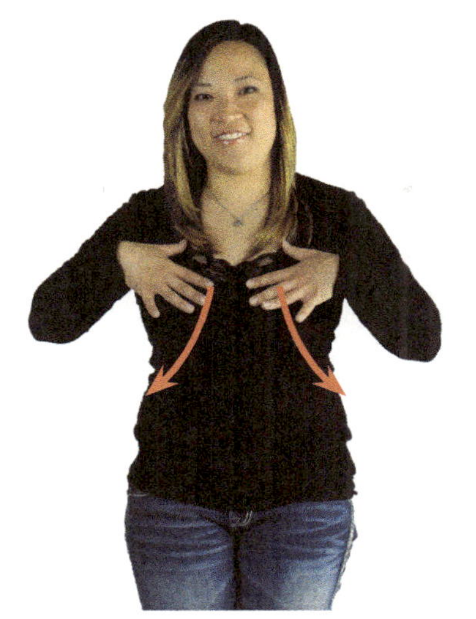

CHAPTER

10 Sports

1. ARCHERY
   1st "S" handshape facing sideways away from your body stays still while the 2nd "S" handshape facing sideways touches the 1st of the "S" handshape pulls away (like pulling the arrow towards to your shoulder) then changes to "V" bended handshape sideways flicks once.

2. CHAMPIONSHIP
   1st "1" handshape facing sideways away from your body stays still while the 2nd "5" open and bended handshape touches on the top of the 1st "1" handshape once.

3. DANCE

1st "5" closed handshape facing up in front of yourself stays still while the 2nd "V" handshape pointing down on top of 1st "5" closed handshape moves back and forth repeatedly.

4. SWIMMING

Both "B" handshapes facing down away from your body touch each other then move outward repeatedly.

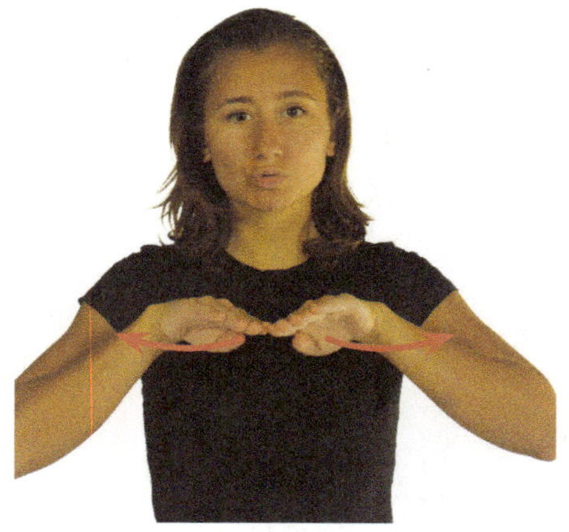

5. FOOTBALL

Both "5" opened handshapes facing each other fingers come together and apart repeatedly.

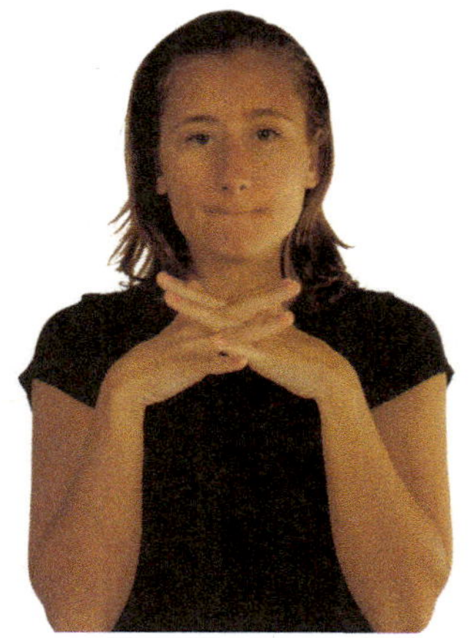

6. BASEBALL
   1st "S" handshape facing sideways stays still on the side of your shoulder while the 2nd "S" handshape facing sideways on the top of the 1st "S" handshape both hands move forward (to show hitting a ball).

7. SOFTBALL
   Both "5" open handshapes facing sideways touch the tips of both fingertips once or repeatedly.

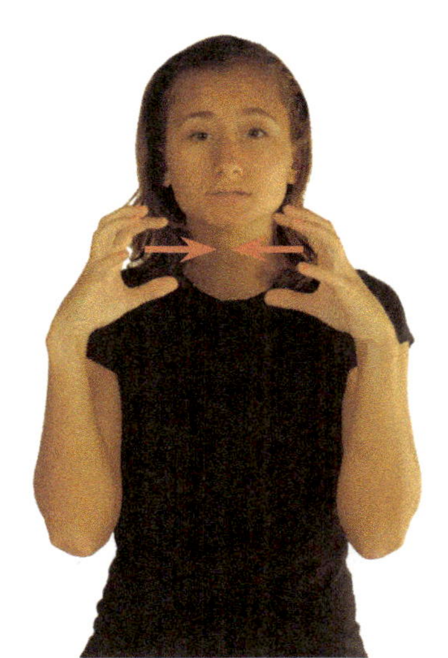

8. HOCKEY
   1st "5" closed handshape facing up stays still while the 2nd "X" handshape's knuckle slides on the palm of the 1st "5" closed handshape repeatedly.

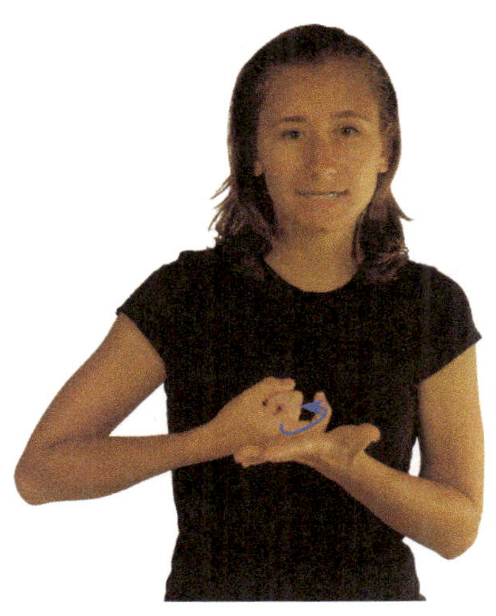

9. KAYAKING

   Both "S" handshapes facing down on each side of your body rock side to side repeatedly.

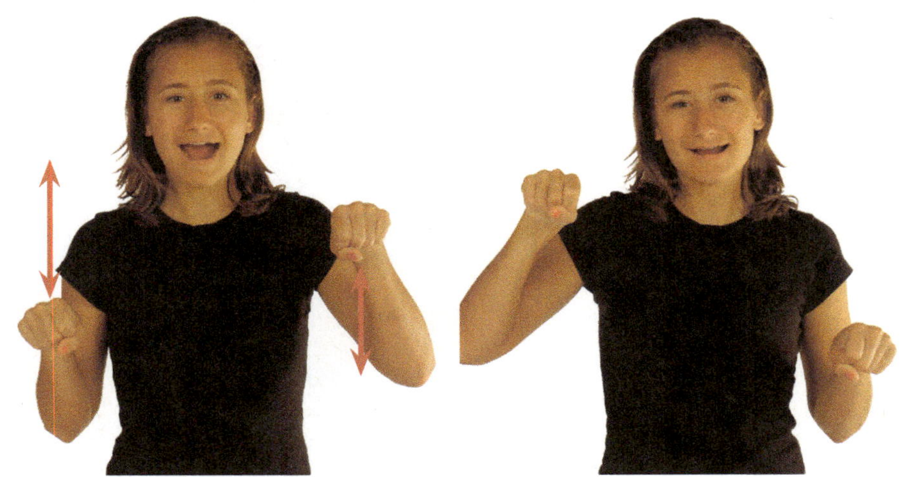

10. CANOEING

    1st "S" handshape facing sideways on the left side of your rib while the 2nd "S" handshape facing sideways near the 1st "S" handshapes move backward then reverses when you sign on the other side of your rib repeatedly.

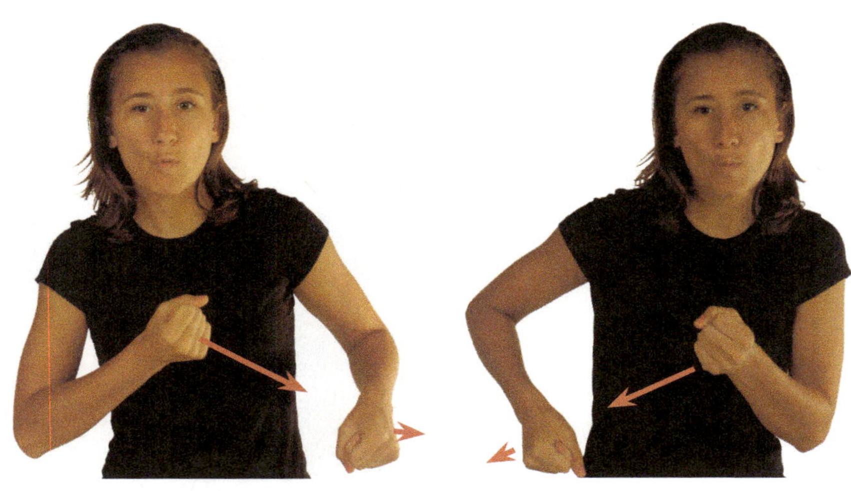

11. GYMNASTICS

    1st "U" handshape facing sideways in front of yourself while the 2nd "U" handshape facing sideways touches moves around and under the 1st "U" handhsape ending with the back of your hand touching your finger once.

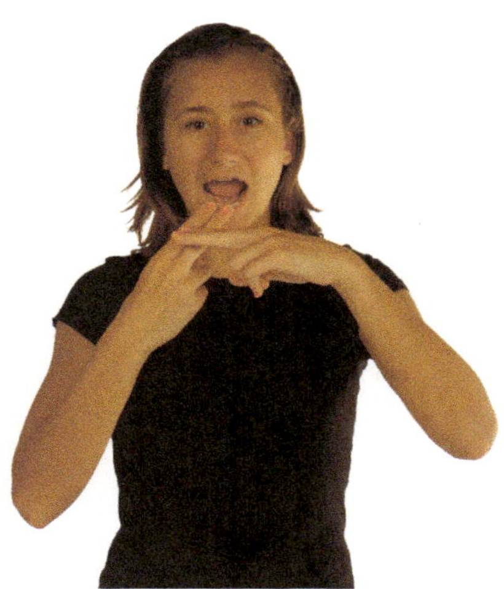

12. HUNTING

1. Both "H" handshapes away from your body pointing like you use your gun move up and down slightly & repeatedly.

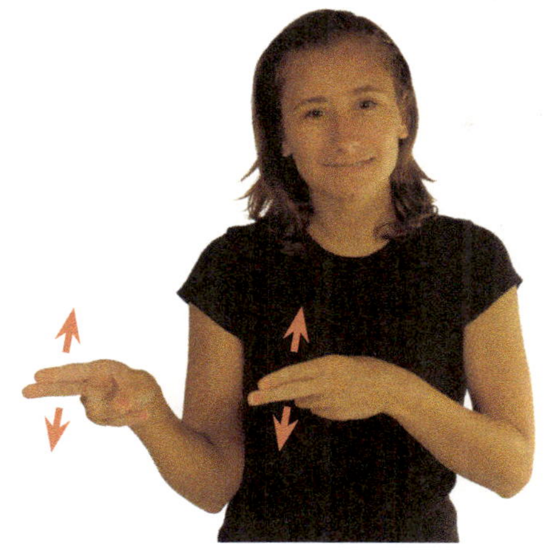

2. Both "H & Thumb" handshapes away from your body pointing like you use your gun move up and down slightly & repeatedly.

13. TENNIS

"S" handshape or "L" closed handshape away from your body moves back and forth sideways repeatedly.

14. PING PONG

"A" handshape away from your body moves back and forth sideways short and quick movements repeatedly.

15. RACQUET

"R" handshape away from your body moves sideways back and forth repeatedly.

16. ICE SKATING

Both "X" handshapes facing up away from your body move back and forth alternating repeatedly.

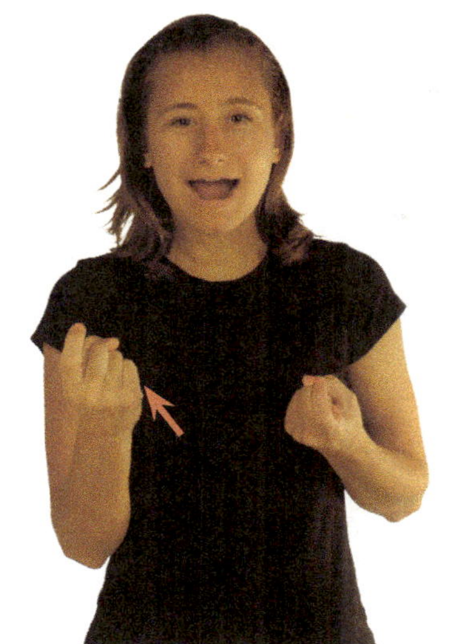

17. ROLLERBLADE

Both "B" handshapes facing each other away from your body move back and forth alternating repeatedly.

18. ROLLERSKATING

Both "V" bended handshapes facing up away from your body move back and forth alternating repeatedly.

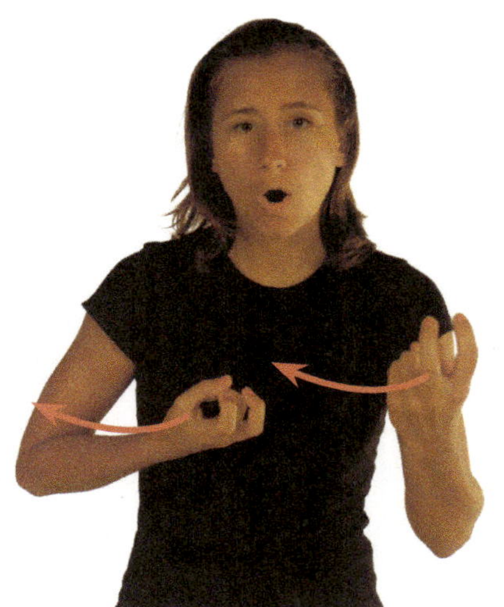

19. DIVING

1st "5" closed handshape facing down in front of yourself while the 2nd "V" handshape facing down touches on the top of the "5" closed handshape's fingers move up then downward once. (To showing diving from a board.)

20. BASKETBALL

1. Both "5" handshapes sideways away from your body move up and down repeatedly.

2. Both "3" handshapes sideways away from your body move up and down repeatedly.

21. SURFING

1st "5" closed handshape facing down while the 2nd "V" handshape facing down on the top of the 1st "5" closed handshape moves up and down in a circular motion.

22. SNOWBOARDING

1. Both "5" closed handshapes facing down in front of your body touch fingertips and move up & down repeatedly.

2. (no picture) Both "5" closed handshapes facing down in front of yourself move together back and forth. Shown in the video.

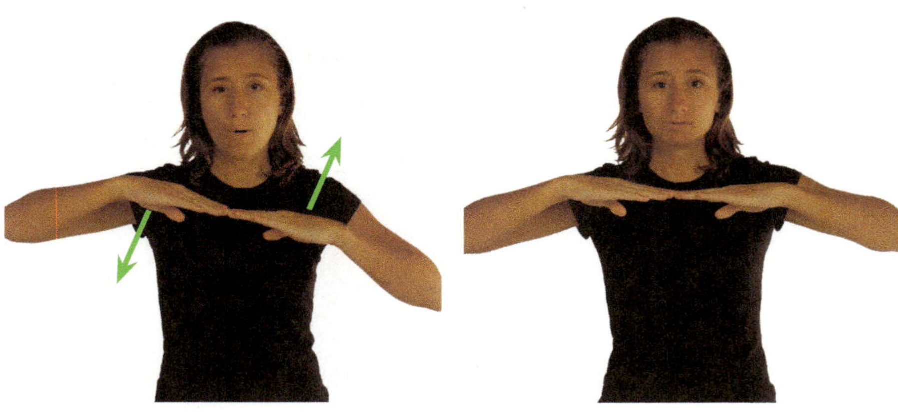

23. CLIMBING

Both "5" open and bended handshapes facing forward away from your body move upward alternating repeatedly (to show climbing).

24. BICYCLE

Both "S" handshapes facing down away from your body move in an alternating circular motion (to show pedaling a bike).

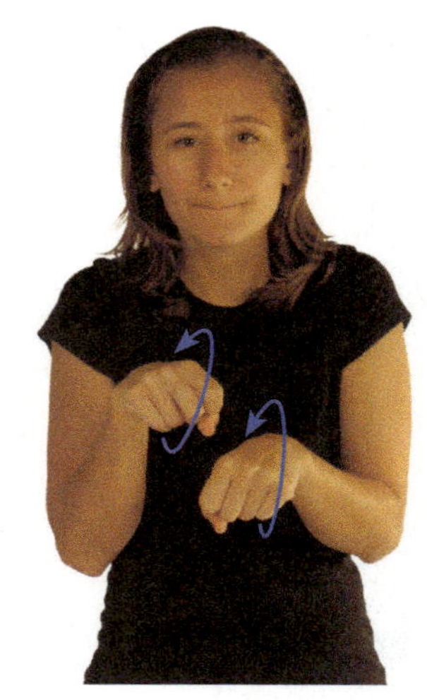

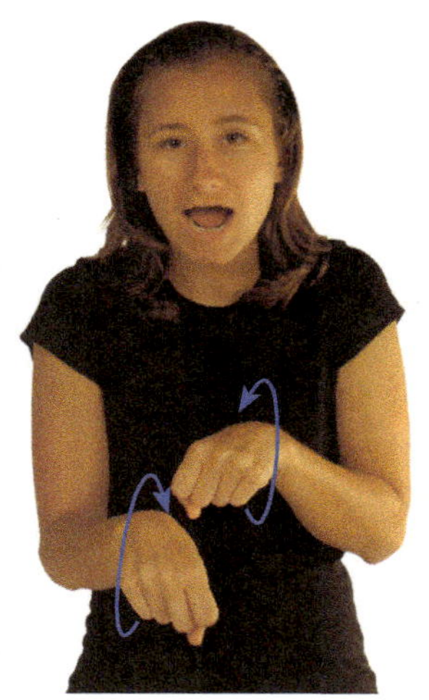

25. WRESTLING

1. Both "5" open handshapes facing each other fingers come together and move back and forth repeatedly.

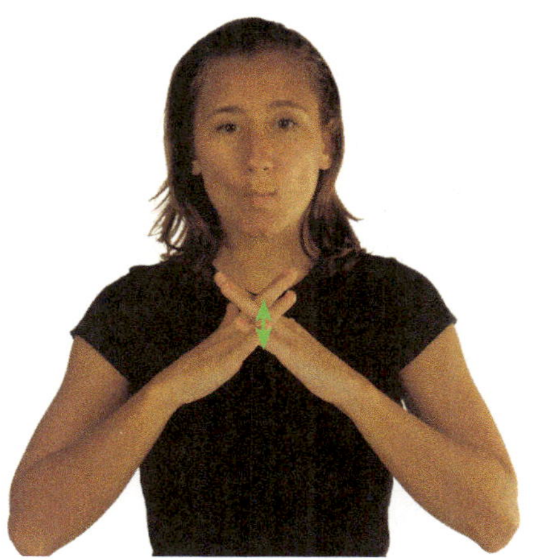

2. Both "5" open handshapes facing each other fingers clasp together and bend wrist sideways repeatedly.

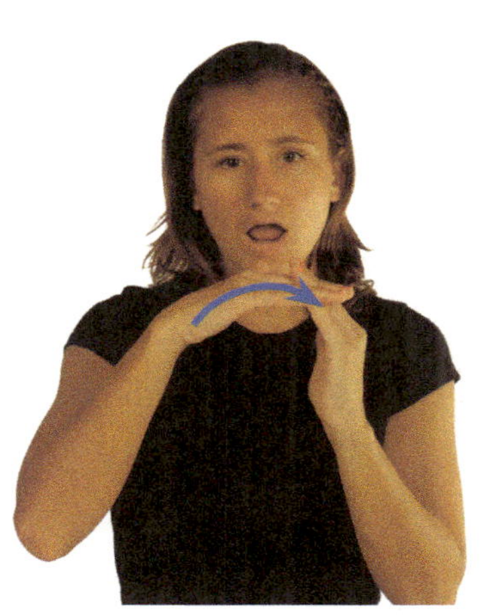

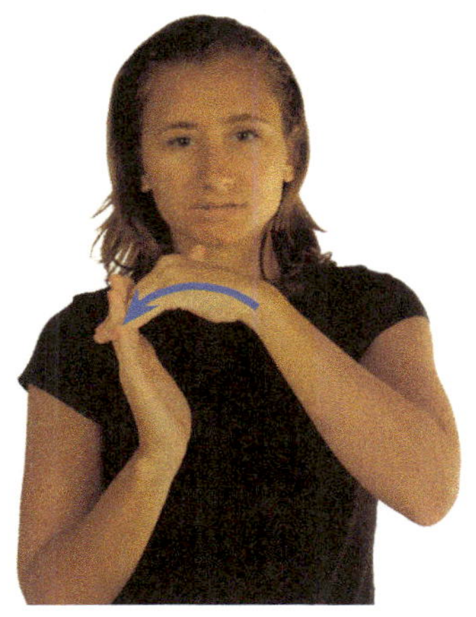

26. BOXING

Both "S" handshapes sideways away from your body move alternating back and forth continually (to show punching).

27. **KARATE**
    Both "B" handshapes facing sideways away from your body move alternating repeatedly (to show hand chop).

28. **TAEKWONDO**
    1st "S" handshape facing down in front of yourself while the 2nd "S" handshape facing up near your rib moves forward and punches outward while pulling the 1st "S" handshape moves backward once.

29. RACING

Two "A" handshapes facing sideways touch each other and move forward and backward repeatedly.

30. HORSE RACING

Sign "horse" in Chapter 7 then sign "racing" as above.

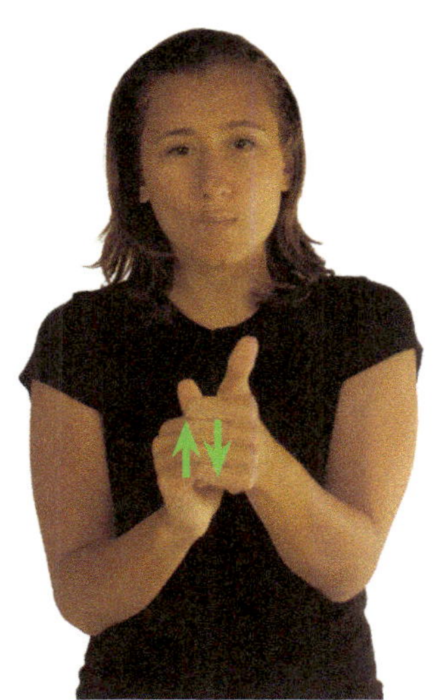

31. GOLF

1st "A" handshape facing sideways near your stomach stays still while the 2nd "A" handshape facing sideways moves sideways (to show playing golf).

32. SOCCER

1st "B" handshape facing sideways in front of yourself away from your body while the 2nd "B" handshape facing sideways kicks the first "B" handshape repeatedly.

33. JUGGLING

Both "5" closed handshapes facing up move upward and change to "5" open handshapes alternating and repeatedly.

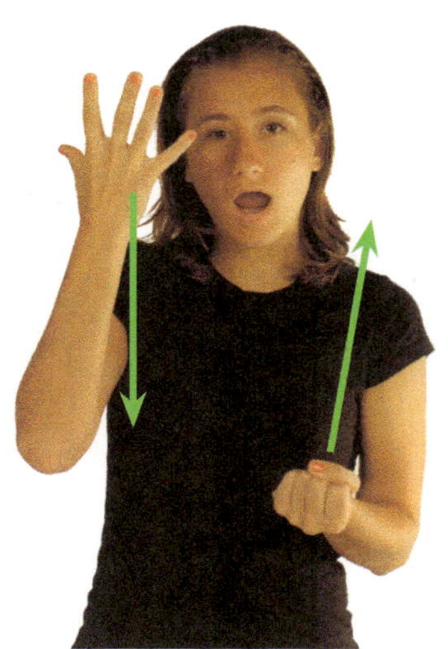

34. FISHING

1st "A" handshape facing sideways stays still on the side of your shoulder while the 2nd "A" handshape facing sideways on the top of the 1st "S" handshape both hands move forward and backward repeatedly.

35. VOLLEYBALL

1. Both "8" handshapes move upward and change to "5" opened handshapes repeatedly.

2. Both "5" closed handshapes move upward repeatedly.

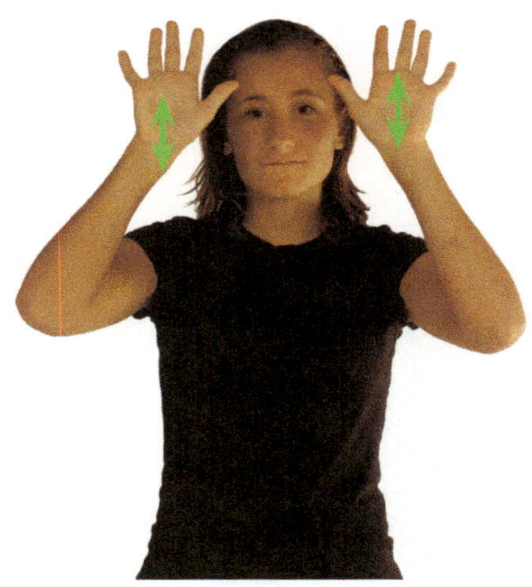

36. SAILING

1st "1" handshape touches the palm of the 2nd "5" closed and bended handshape.

37. SKIING

Both "X" handshapes facing up away from your body move downward once.

38. CC SKIING

Fingerspell C-C then sign "skiing" as above.

39. RUNNING/TRACKING

1st "L" bended handshape sideways stays still while the 2nd "L" bended handshape's finger touches the 1st "L" bended handshape's thumb both handshapes curl and move forward and backward repeatedly.

40. WEIGHT LIFTING

Both "S" handshapes facing move up and down repeatedly.

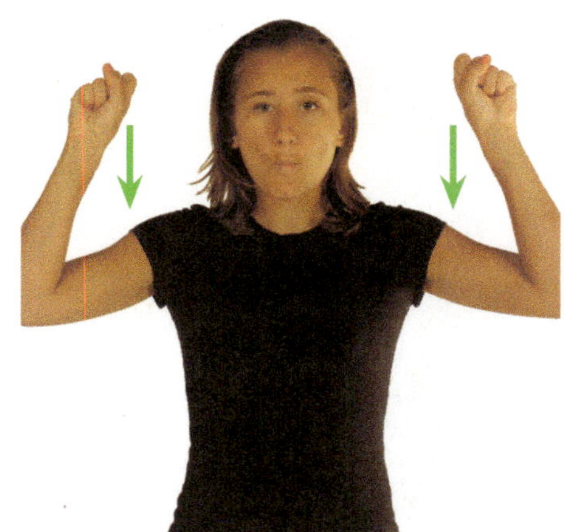

41. OLYMPIC

Both "9" handshapes link together then turns over repeatedly (to show links in a chain).

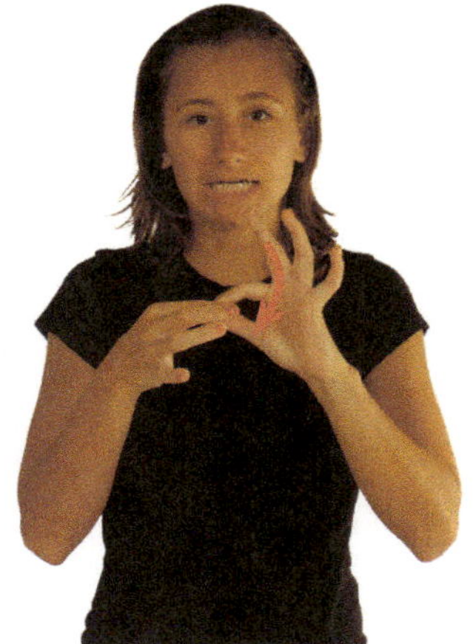

42. DOG RACING

1. Sign "dog" in Chapter 7 then sign "racing" as above.

2. Variation of "Dog Racing"

43. MOTORCYCLE RACING

1st "S" handshape facing down stays still while the 2nd "S" handshape twists up and down repeatedly (to show accelerating).

44. BOWLING

1. "5" open and bended handshape facing up moves back near your rib moves forward repeatedly.

45. PARACHUTING

1st "1" handshape facing sideways away from your body while the 2nd "5" open and bended handshape on the top of the 1st "1" handshape and move both handshapes downward.

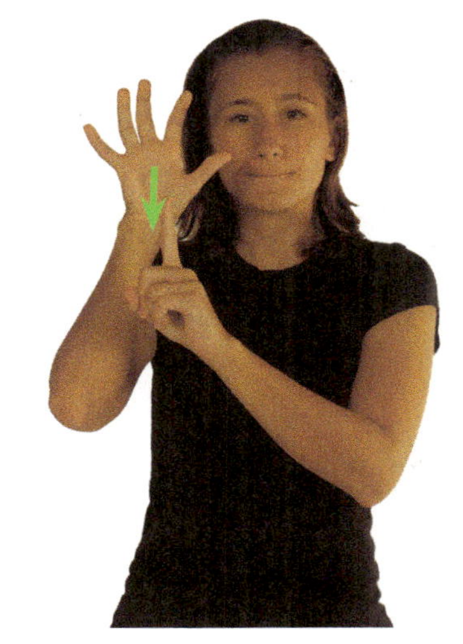

46. POOLTABLE

1st "V" bended handshape facing down away from your body stays still while the 2nd "A" handshape facing sideways show holding a pool stick moves back & forth repeatedly.

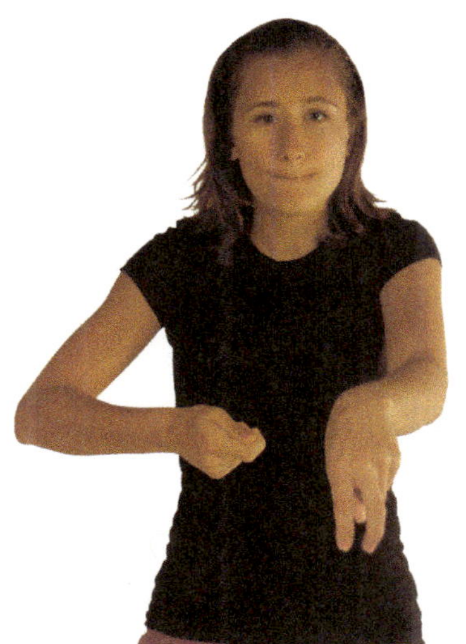

47. ROWING

Both "S" handshapes facing down away from your body move back ward and up then move down and forward continually.

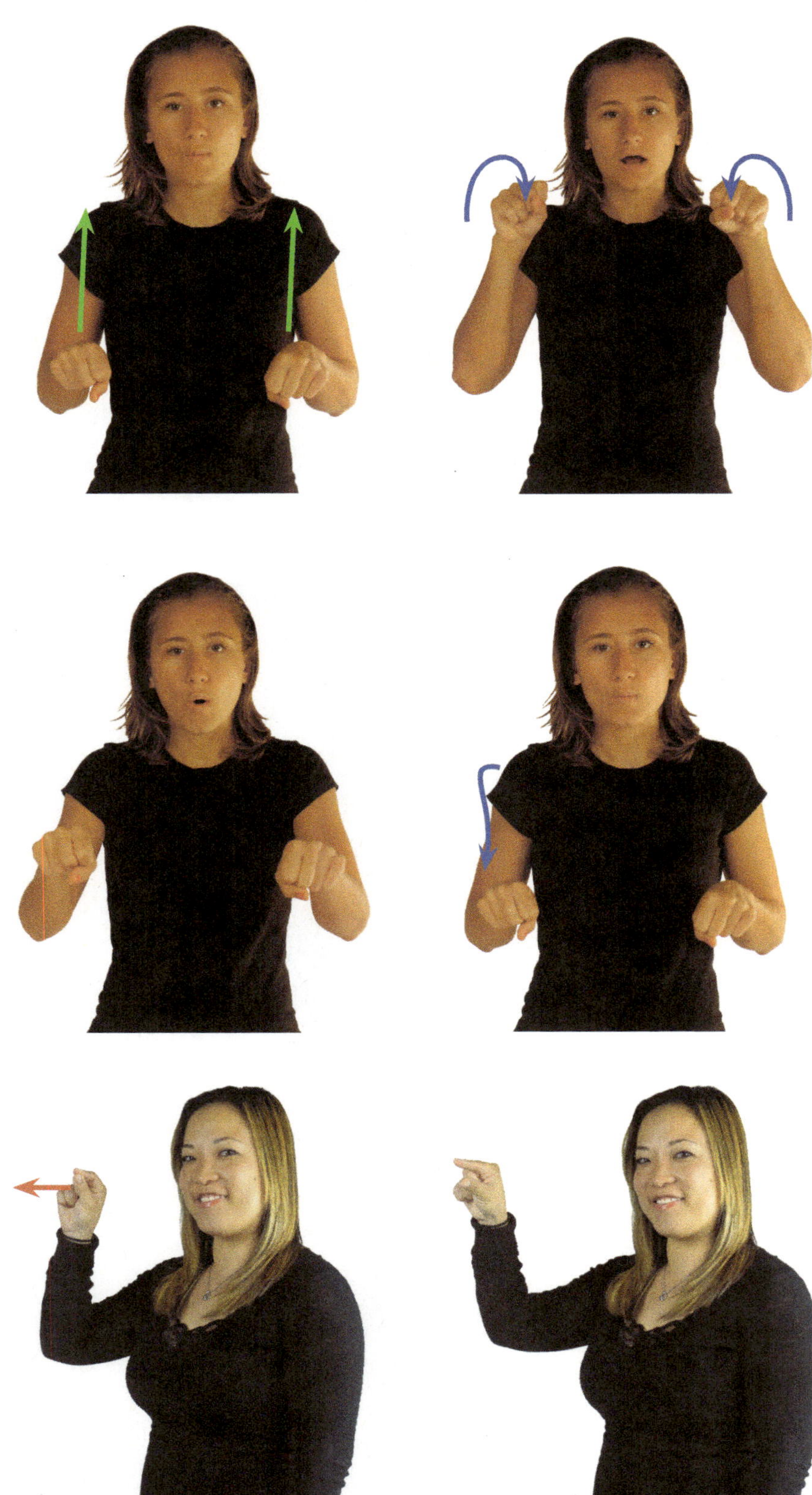

48. DARTS

"L" closed handshape facing sideways moves outward and open like playing a dart.

CHAPTER 11 Furniture

1. FURNITURE
   "F" handshape away from your body moves sideways repeatedly.

2. DRESSER
   Both "5" bended handshapes facing up away from your body pull backward toward your body once.

3. CHAIR

1st "H" bended handshape facing down stays still while the 2nd "H" bended handshape on the top of the 1st "H" handshape moves up and down repeatedly.

4. ROCKING CHAIR

Both "3" handshapes facing sideways move backward and forward like rocking a chair repeatedly.

5. TABLE

1st "5" closed handshape facing down in front of yourself stays still while the 2nd "5" closed handshape facing down in front of yourself on the top of the 1st "5" closed handshape moves up and down repeatedly.

6. CABINET

   Both "S" handshapes facing sideways away from your body move backward and outward once (to show you open the cabinet/door). Explanation: Some Deaf and Hard of Hearing people sign with "S" handshapes and others sign with "A" handshapes. Both of them are correct.

7. SOFA, COUCH

   1st "H" handshape facing down stays still while the 2nd "H" bended handshape once then change to both "C" handshapes facing down touch each other then move away sideways once.

8. LAMP

"5" closed handshape near your head opens to "5" opened handshape once.

9. CLOSET

1st "1" handshape facing sideways in front of yourself stays still while the 2nd "X" handshape taps the 1st "1" handshape 2 or 3 times. Then sign "cabinet" as above.

10. TELEVISION

Fingerspell T-V.

11. CLOCK

1st "5" handshape facing down stays still while the 2nd "X" handshape taps on the top of the 1st "5" handshape then changes to both "C" handshapes away from your face like the shape of clock once.

12. BED

Both "5" closed handshapes palms touching then rest your face against the back of your hand once.

13. BEDROOM

Sign "bed" as above then both "5" closed handshapes facing sideways away from your body move like the shape of a box once.

14. RESTROOM

1. "T" handshape facing forward moves back and forth repeatedly.

2. "R" handshape facing down moves sideways once.

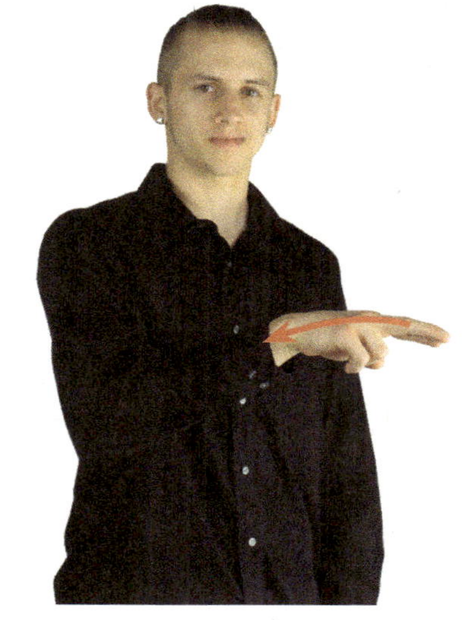

15. SHOWER

"S" handshape facing down above your head and changes to "5" open handshape repeatedly.

16. BATH TUB

Both "A" handshapes facing yourself on your chest move up and down repeatedly and change both to "5" closed and curved handshapes facing up touch each other and move outward sideways.

17. RECREATION ROOM

1. Both "5" closed handshapes facing sideways on your chest one above the other and move in a circular motion continually then both "5" closed handshapes facing sideways away from your body move like the shape of a box once.

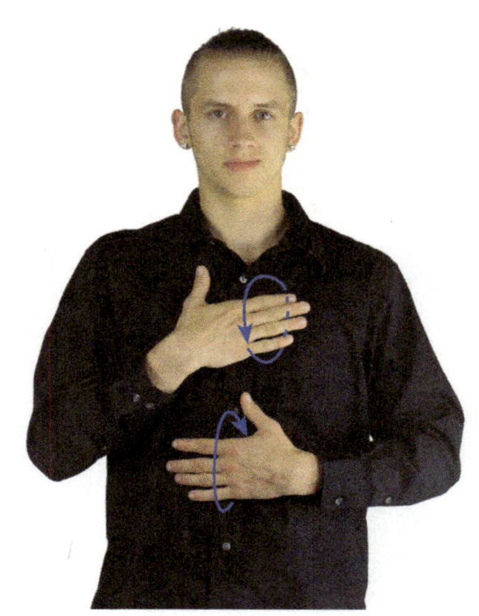

2. Both "Y" handshapes facing sideways shakes back and forth repeatedly then both "5" closed handshapes facing sideways away from your body move like the shape of a box once.

18. LIVING ROOM

"5" handshape's thumb on your chest moves upward in a circular motion continually then both "5" closed handshapes facing sideways away from your body move like the shape of a box once.

19. FAMILY ROOM

Both "F" handshapes start with thumbs touching each other move around and ends with little fingers touching then both "5" closed handshapes facing sideways away from your body move like the shape of a box once.

20. KITCHEN

1. "K" handshape moves back and forth repeatedly.

2. 1st "5" closed handshape facing up in front of yourself stays still while the 2nd "K" handshape on the 1st "5" closed handshape's palm moves back and forth sideways repeatedly.

21. DINING ROOM

"O" closed handshape's fingers on your mouth moves forward and backward repeatedly turn to 1st "5" closed handshape facing down in front of yourself stays still while the 2nd "5" bended handshape bends over the 1st "5" closed handshape once. Then change to both "5" closed handshapes facing sideways away from your body move like the shape of a box once.

22. SUNROOM

"O" handshape away from your head changes to "5" open handshape then changes to both "5" closed handshapes facing sideways away from your body move like the shape of a box once.

23. OFFICE

Both "O" handshapes facing down move like the shape of a box once.

24. LAUNDRY

1. 1st "5" open handshape facing up while the 2nd "5" open handshape facing down and move twisting movement repeatedly.

2. "1 finger and little finger" handshape's 1 finger points on your temple and twists repeatedly.

25. GARAGE

1st "5" closed handshape facing down stays still while the 2nd "3" handshape facing sideways moves under the 1st "5" closed handshape once.

26. SINK

Both "5" closed and curved handshapes facing up touch each other and move outward sideways.

27. MIRROR

"5" closed and curved handshape in front of your face moves side to side repeatedly.

28. FAUCET

Both "S" handshapes facing down away from your body move backward toward your body once (to show turning on a faucet).

29. TOWEL

1st "S" handshape near your hip stays still while the 2nd "S" handshape above your shoulder and both "S" handshapes move back and forth alternating and repeatedly.

30. SOAP

1st "5" closed handshape facing up stays still while the 2nd "5" closed and bended handshape's fingers tap on the palm of 1st "5" bended handshape moves in a circular motion repeatedly.

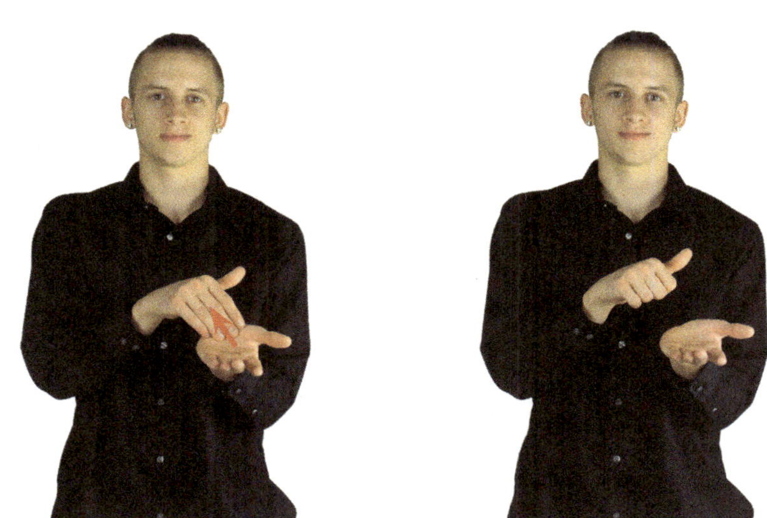

31. SHAMPOO

Both "5" bended handshapes on both sides of your head moves forward and backward repeatedly (to show scrubbing your hair).

32. VACUUM CLEANER

Both "A" handshapes facing sideways away from your body move upward and downward repeatedly (to show vacuuming).

CHAPTER

12 Nature and Environment

1. FALL

   1st "5" handshape sideways and halfway down stays still while the 2nd "B" handshape brushes your elbow of the 1st "5" handshape moves downward repeatedly.

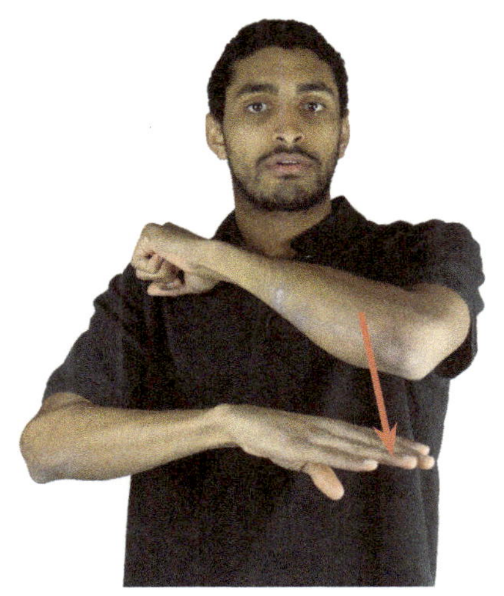

2. WINTER

   Both "S" handshapes facing sideways away from your body move in and out in an opposite direction repeatedly.

3. SPRING

1st "C" handshape facing down in front of yourself stays still while the 2nd "O" handshape facing up moves inside the bottom of the "C" handshape and moves up and changes to "5" open handshape once.

4. SUMMER

"X" handshape on your forehead moves sideways once.

5. RAIN

Both "5" bended handshapes facing down above your shoulders move up and down repeatedly.

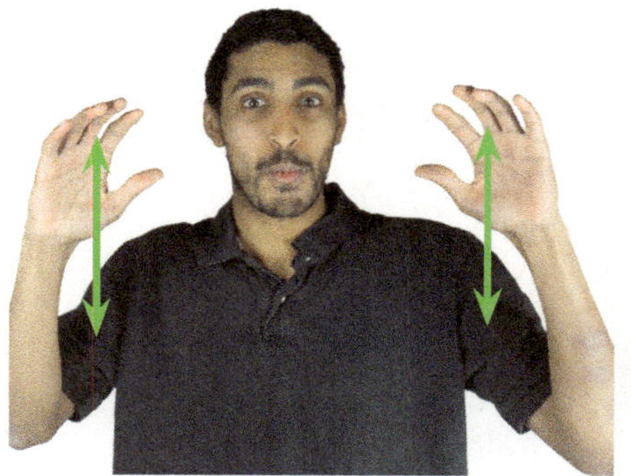

6. EARTHQUAKE

   1st "5" bended handshape facing down while the 2nd "F" open handshape touches the 1st "5" bended handshape's wrist and moves forward and backward once then change both to "S" handshapes facing down away from your body shakes repeatedly.

7. HURRICANE

   1. Both "L" handshape's facing sideways in front of yourself, thumbs touch on top of each other and move pointer fingers back and forth (to show swirling). *Variation can include hands moving forward while pointer fingers are moving.

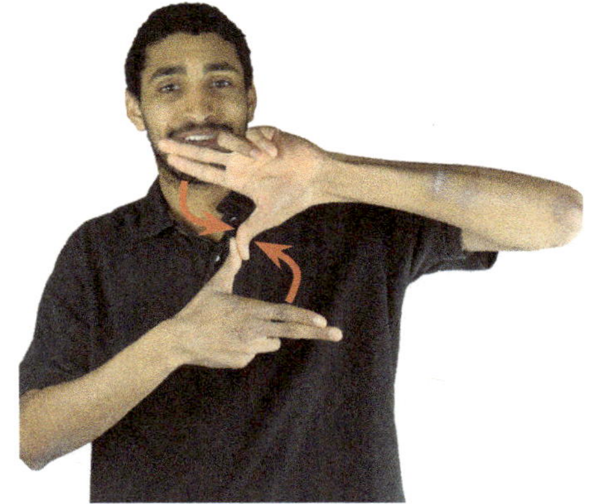

8. FLOOD

"W" handshape facing sideways on your chin moves forward and backward repeatedly then sign both "5" open handshapes facing down move from bottom upward once.

9. TORNADO

1. Both "middle finger" handshapes touch each other and move upward and downward at the same time like a spiral motion.

2. Both "middle finger" handshapes touch each other and move forward at the same time.

3. "1" handshape moves downward like a spiral motion.

10. ENVIRONMENT

1. 1st "1" handshape facing sideways in front of yourself stays still while the 2nd "E" handshape sideways touches the 1st "1" handshape moves around halfway once.

2. 1st "1" handshape away from your body stays still while the 2nd "O" closed handshape touches on the 1st "1" handshape's finger and moves around halfway and changes to "5" handshape once.

3. 1st "1" handshape away from your body stays still while the 2nd "5" open handshape touches on the 1st "1" handshape and moves around once.

11. LAND

Both "5" closed and bended handshapes in front of yourself touch each other and move downward then change both to "5" closed handshapes facing down and outward once.

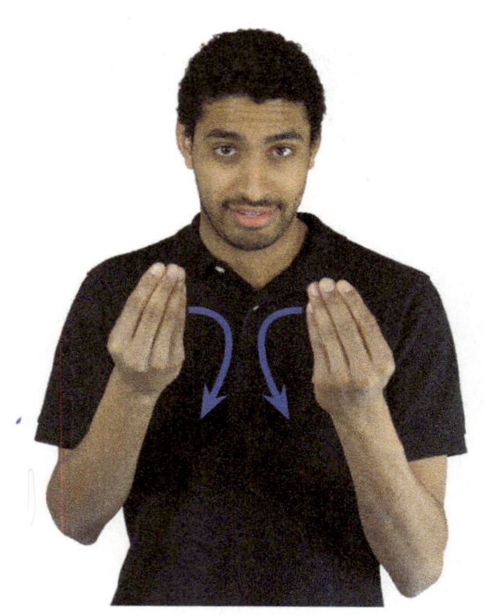

12. BEACH

1. 1st "5" closed and bended handshape facing down away from your body stays still while the 2nd "O" closed handshape moves towards the 1st "5" closed handshape then changes to "5" open handshape repeatedly.

2. 1st "5" closed and bended handshape facing down in front of yourself stays still while the 2nd "O" closed handshape moves toward and touches the 1st "5" handshape then changes to "5" open handshape repeatedly.

13. OCEAN

1. "W" handshape facing sideways on your chin and changes to both "5" closed and bended handshapes facing down away from your body move like ocean's movement repeatedly.

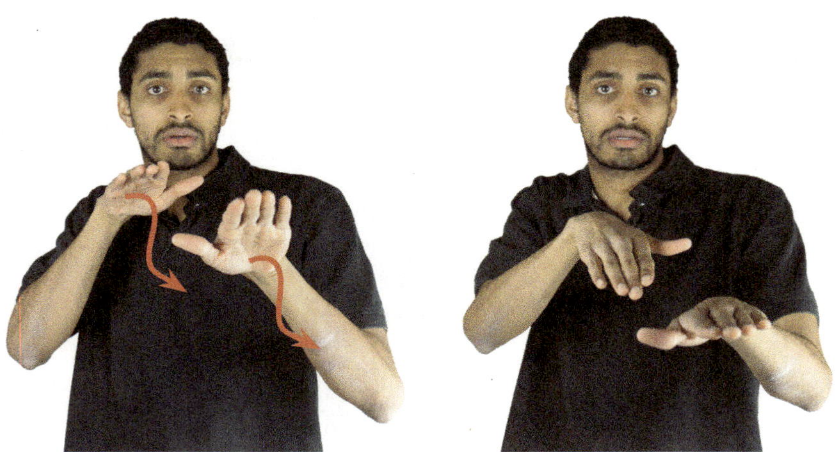

2. Both "O" handshapes facing down and sideways away from your body move like ocean's movement repeatedly.

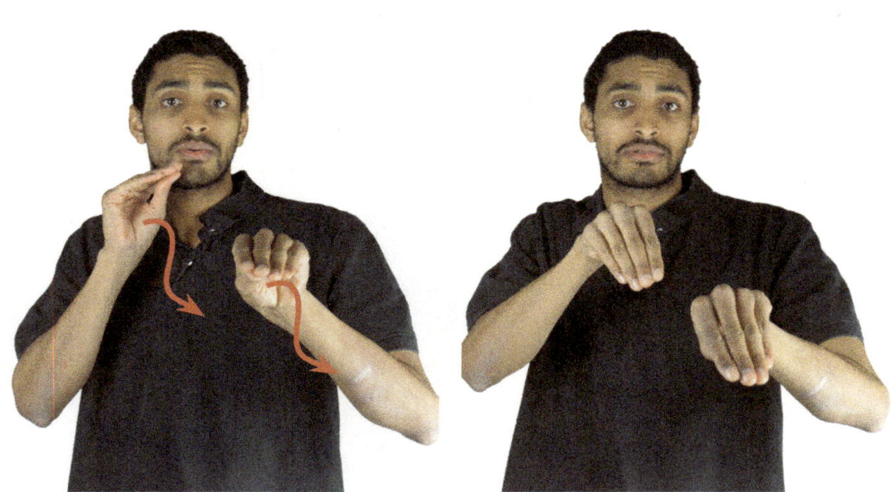

3. Variation of "Ocean"

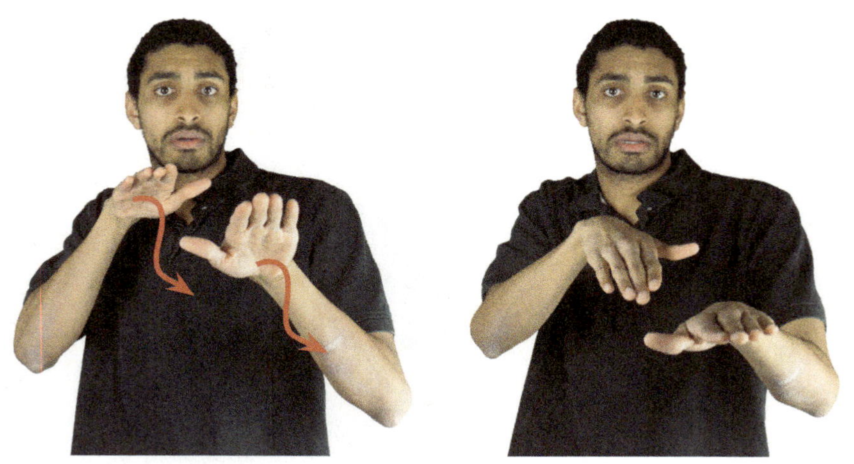

14. RIVER

1. Both "5" open handshapes facing down away from your body move forward like rapid water.

2. 1st "W" handshape facing sideways on your chin and changes to sign "river" as above.

3. "W" handshape facing sideways on your chin and changes to both "5" closed handshape facing sideways move forward like the shape of a stream.

15. TREE

1st "5" closed handshape facing down while the 2nd "5" open handshape's elbow on the top of the 1st "5" handshape's fingers shakes back and forth repeatedly.

16. GREEN HOUSE

Sign "green" in Chapter 6 then changes to both "5" closed handshape's fingers facing sideways in front of your face touch each other and move downward like the shape of the house once.

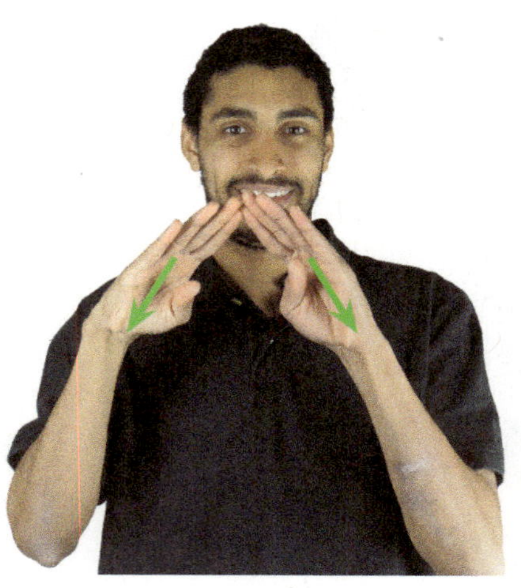

17. SKY

"5" closed handshape facing down above your head moves from one side to the other side once.

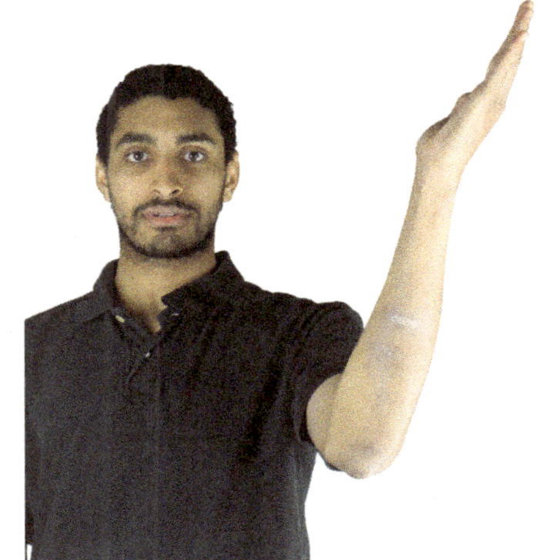

18. CLOUD

1st "5" open handshape facing up stays still while the 2nd "5" open handshape facing down above the 1st "5" open handshape and moves like a swirl.

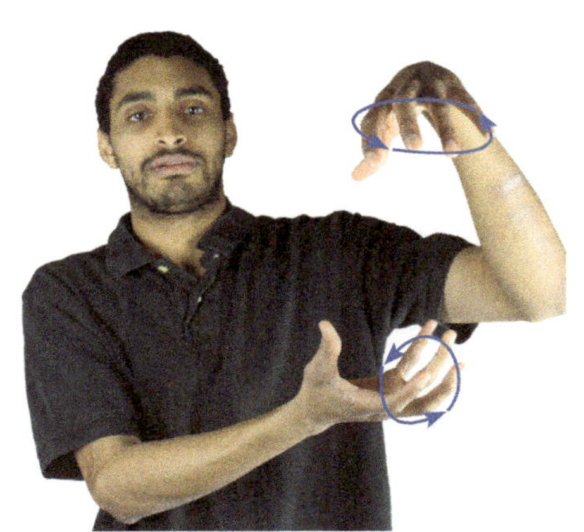

19. SUN

1. "C" handshape touches on the upper part of your temple moves upward once.

2. "O" hand shape above your head moves around then changes to "5" open handshape moves downward toward your head once.

20. MOON

"L" bended handshape on your temple moves upward once.

21. WORLD

1. Both "5" open handshapes facing forward thumb and pointer fingers touching each other then moves around and touch little fingers together once.

2. Both "W" handshapes facing sideways touch on top of each other and move around each other once.

22. NATURE

1st "S" handshape facing down in front of yourself stays still while the 2nd "H" handshape facing down moves in a half-circle then touches on the top of the 1st "S" handshape once.

23. UNIVERSE

Both "U" handshapes facing sideways touch on top of each other and move around each other once.

24. STAR

Both "1" handshapes facing forward away from your body touch each other and moves up and down alternating repeatedly.

25. GALAXY

Sign "star" as above then sign "sky" as above.

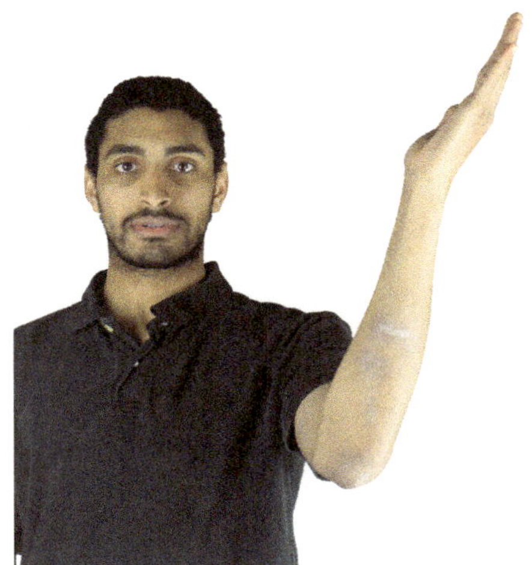

26. WATER

"W" handshape facing sideways on your chin moves back and forth repeatedly.

27. ICE

Both "5" open handshapes facing down away from your body bend fingers and move hands toward yourself once.

28. SNOW

1. Both "5" open handshapes facing down fingers touch on your shoulders then move up and out the fingers wiggle as hands move downward once.

2. Sign "white" in Chapter 6 then sign "snow" as above once.

3. Both "5" open handshapes facing forward away from yourself and move zigzag while you wiggle your fingers.

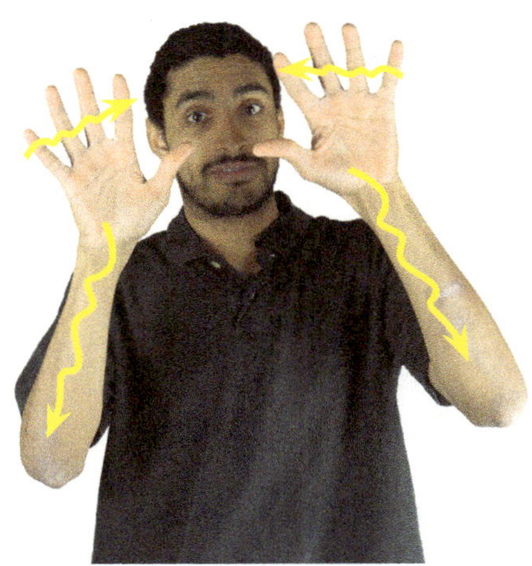

29. WINDY

Both "5" open handshapes facing sideways away from your body move from one side to the other side quickly repeatedly. *Use face expression.

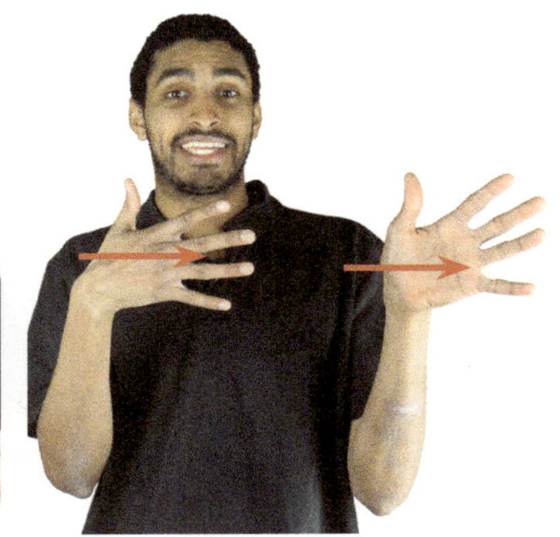

30. BREEZE

Sign "windy" as above but sign slowly.

31. RAINBOW

Both "4" handshapes touch on each other's fingertips then top hand moves from one side to the other side once (to show the shape of a rainbow).

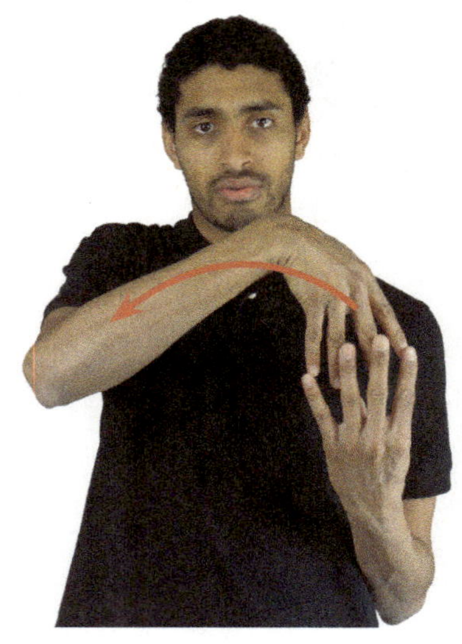

32. THUNDERSTORM

"1" handshape on your ear then changes to both "S" handshapes facing down in front of your body shake back and forth.

33. LIGHTNING

"1" handshape facing forward starts above your head and moves downward like a swirl once.

34. FOUNTAIN

1st "C" handshape facing down in front of yourself stays still while the 2nd "O" handshape moves inside the bottom of the "C" handshape then moves up and over while changing to "5" open handshape once.

35. ISLAND

1st "S" handshape facing down stays still while the 2nd "little finger" handshape on the top of the 1st "S" handshape moves in a circular motion.

36. HILL

"5" closed & curved handshape facing down moves up and down like the shape of a hill.

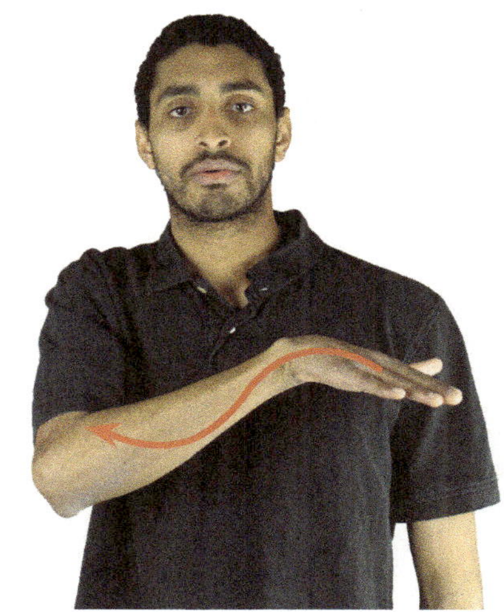

37. VALLEY

Both "B" handshapes facing down move from head height downward with the back of your hands facing each other and comes together at your thumbs (to show the shape of a curve).

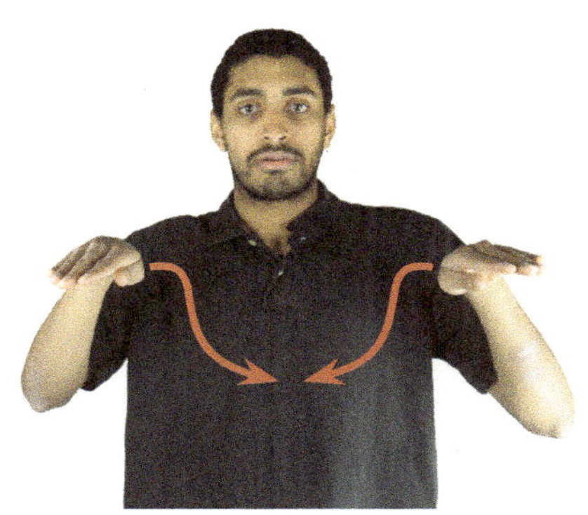

38. GRASS

"5" open and bended handshape facing up touches under your chin moves forward and backward slightly.

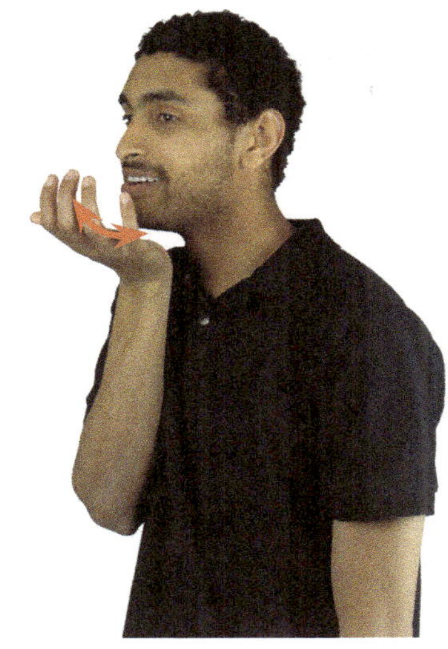

39. HAY

"5" open handshape facing up touches under your chin moves forward and backward slightly.

40. FARM

1. "5" open handshape's thumb under your chin moves from one side to the other side once.

2. 1st "5" closed handshape facing sideways stands halfway while the 2nd "5" closed handshape's fingers rubs the 1st "5" handshape's elbow in a circular motion continually.

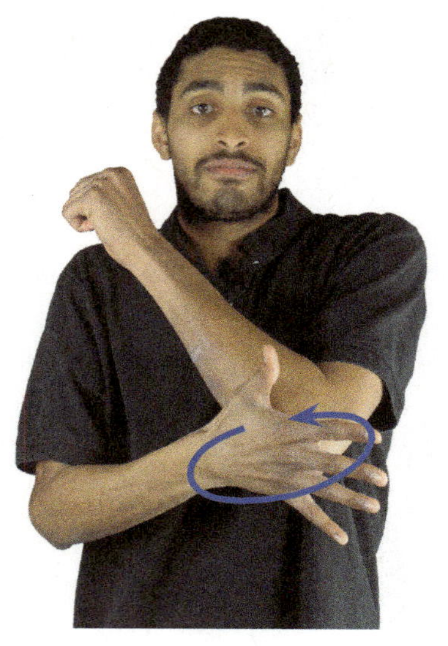

41. HARVEST

1st "S" handshape facing sideways holding stays still while the 2nd "A" handshape moves under the 1st "S" handshape from one side to the other side once (to show harvesting).

42. VOLCANO

Sign "fountain" as above, but use facial expression.

43. WATERFALL

"W" handshape facing sideways on your chin then change to both "5" open handshape and wiggle fingers as your hands move downward (to show water falling).

44. EQUATOR

Both "E" handshape's thumbs touch each other then move around and stop when little fingers touch once.

45. MOUNTAIN

1st "S" handshape facing down stays still while the 2nd "S" handshape facing down on top of the 1st "S" handshape both move upward at the same time and change to "5" open handshapes once.

CHAPTER

13 Opposites

1. BIG
   Both "L" bended handshapes facing down move away from each other at the same time once.

2. LITTLE
   Both "5" closed handshapes facing each other move back and forth slightly.

3. CHEAP
1st "5" closed handshape facing sideways stays still while the 2nd "B" handshape brushes on the palm of the 1st "5" closed handshape once.

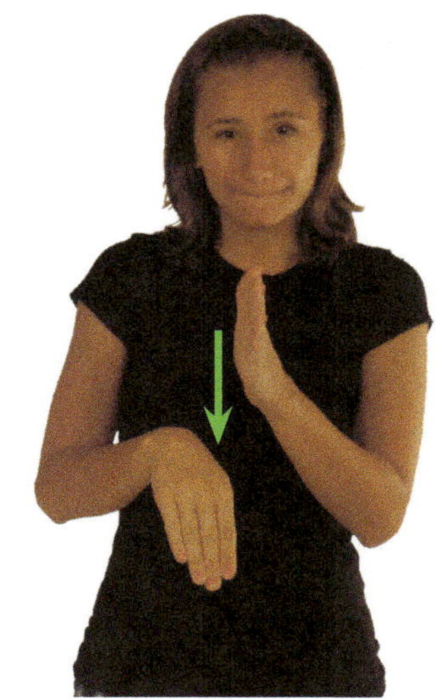

4. EXPENSIVE
1st "5" closed handshape facing up stays still while the 2nd "O" handshape's fingers touch the palm of the 1st "5" closed handshape moves upward and changes to a "5" open handshape facing down once.

5. CLEAN

   1st "5" closed handshape facing up stays still while the 2nd "5" handshape facing down slides against the 1st "5" handshape moving sideways once.

6. DIRTY

   "5" open handshape facing down under your chin stays still while wiggling your fingers.

7. EASY

   1st "5" closed and bended handshape facing sideways in front of yourself stays still while the 2nd "5" closed & bended handshape's fingers brush against the 1st "5" handshape's fingers repeatedly.

8. DIFFICULT
   Both "V" bended handshapes sideways in front of yourself touch each other at your knuckles and move up and down repeatedly.

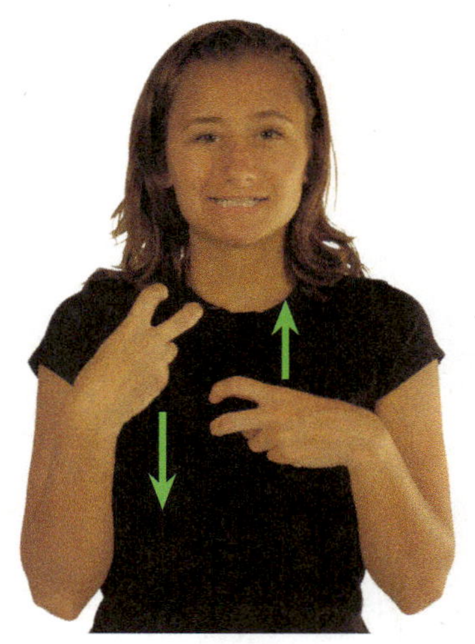
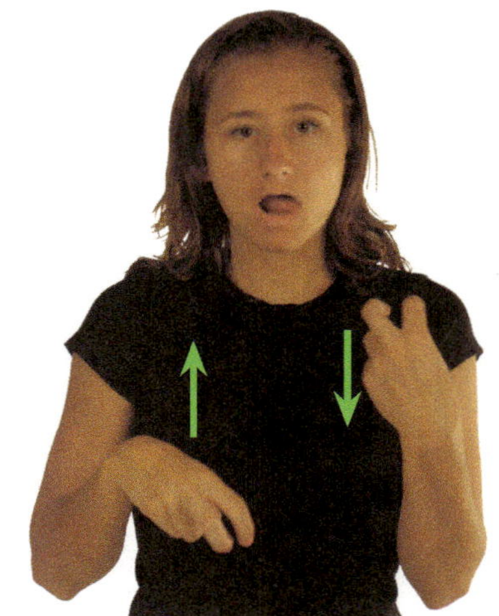

9. FAR
   1. 1st "A" handshape facing sideways stays still while the 2nd "A" handshape facing sideways touches the 1st "A" handshape's knuckles and moves upward once.

   2. "1" handshape points upward once.

10. NEAR

1st "5" closed and curved handshape facing yourself while the 2nd "5" closed and curved handshape moves toward to the 1st "5" closed and curved handshape's palm once.

11. FAST

Both "L" handshapes facing sideways away from the side of your body, moves backward while curling your pointer fingers once (to show shooting).

12. SLOW

1st "5" closed handshape facing down stays still while the 2nd "5" closed handshape facing down on top of the 1st "5" closed handshape moves from fingers backward once.

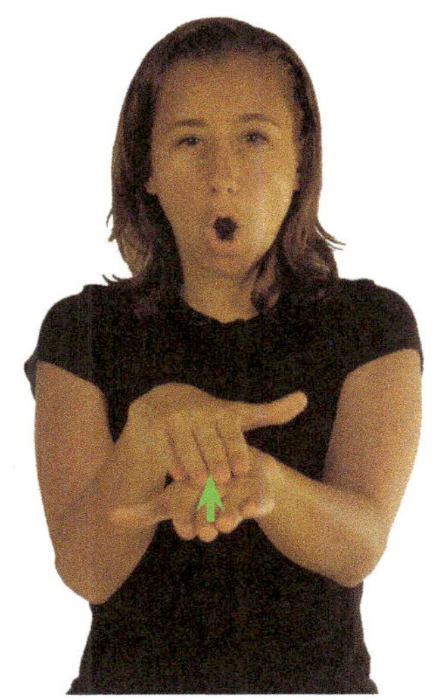

13. FAT (OBESE)

Both "5" open and curved handshapes facing sideways and down on each side of your body and move outward while using facial expression.

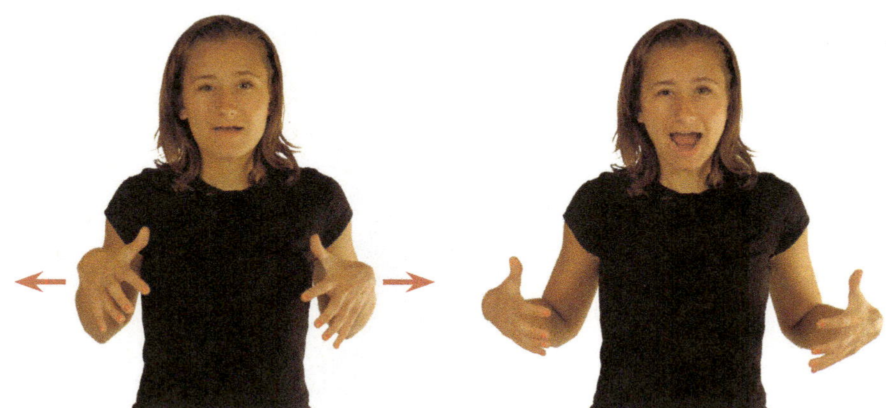

14. THIN

1. "L" bended handshape's finger and thumb moves from your neck down once.

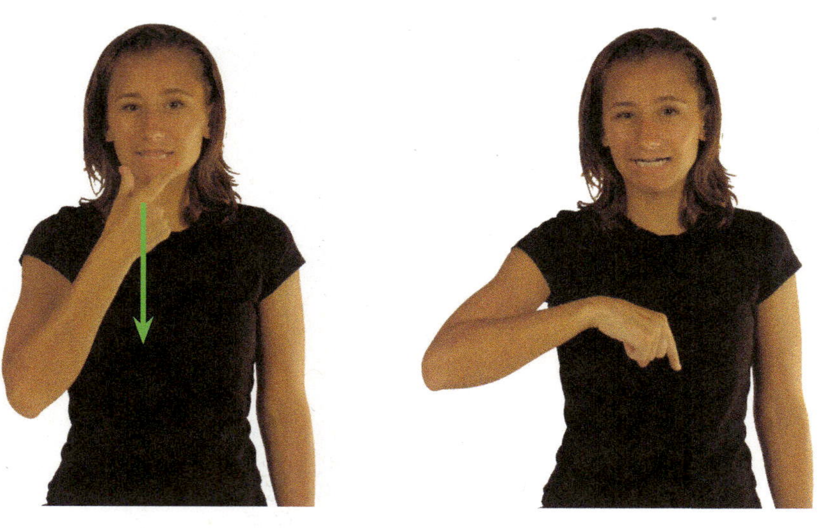

2. Both "little finger" handshapes touch each other and move up and down (away from each other) at the same time while using facial expression once.

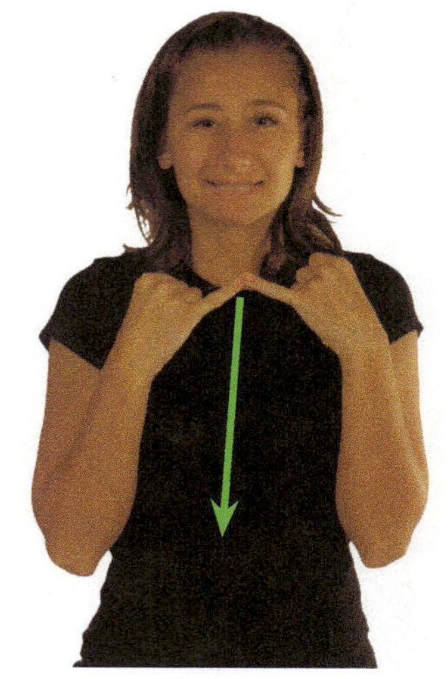

15. FULL

1st "S" handshape facing sideways in front of yourself stays still while the 2nd "5" open handshape facing down slides across the 1st "S" handshape sideways once.

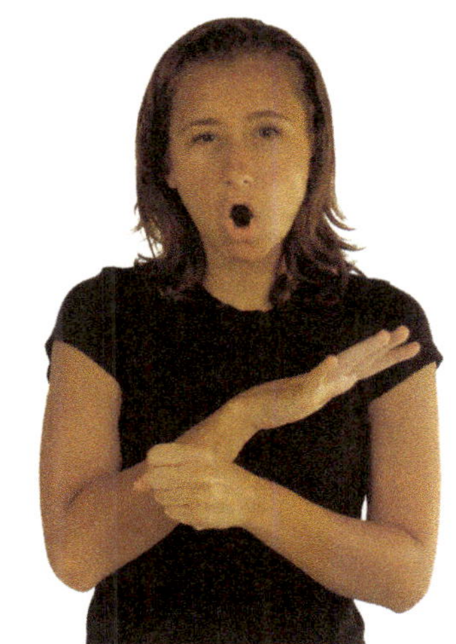

16. EMPTY

1st "5" closed handshape facing down stays still while the 2nd "middle finger" handshape touches on top of the 1st "5" handshape moves outward repeatedly.

17. GOOD

"5" closed handshape on your chin moves outward once.

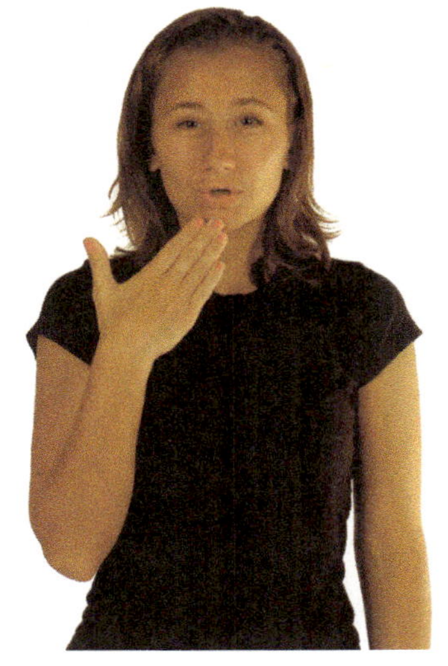
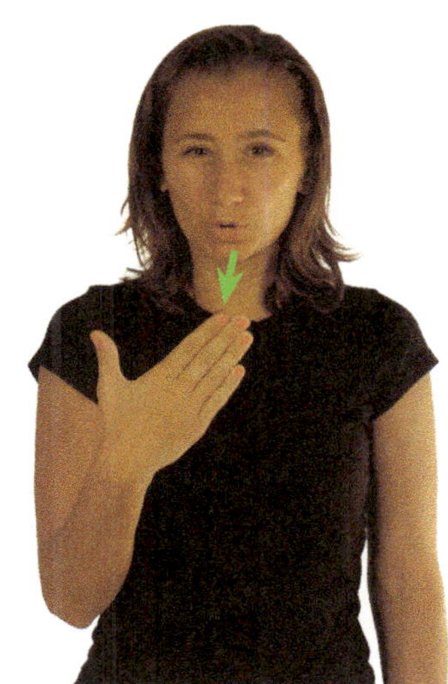

18. BAD

"5" closed handshape on your chin moves out and turns down once.

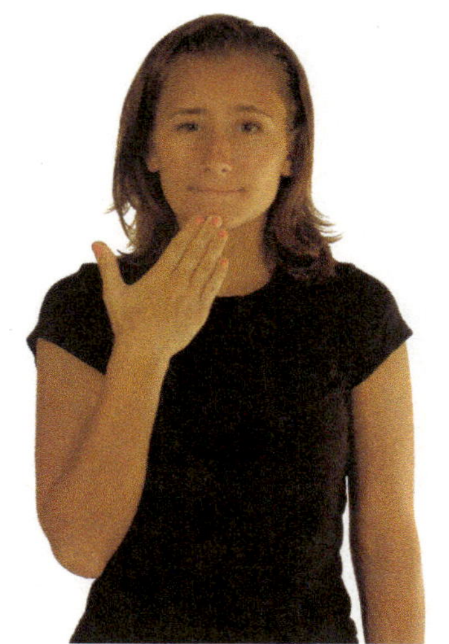

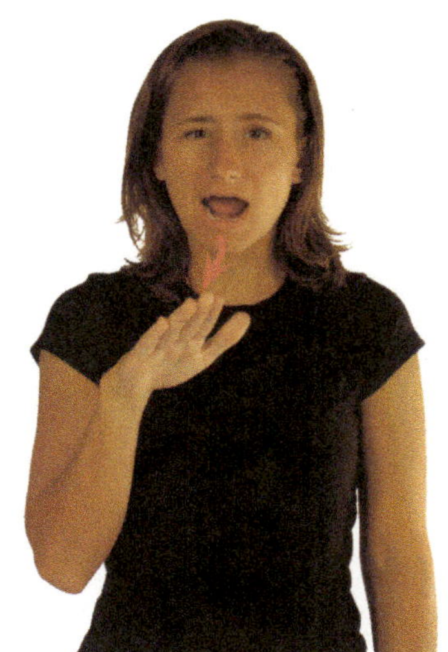

19. HAPPY

Both "5" handshapes hit on your chest and move in a circular motion continually.

20. SAD

Both "5" open handshapes in front of your face move downward once.

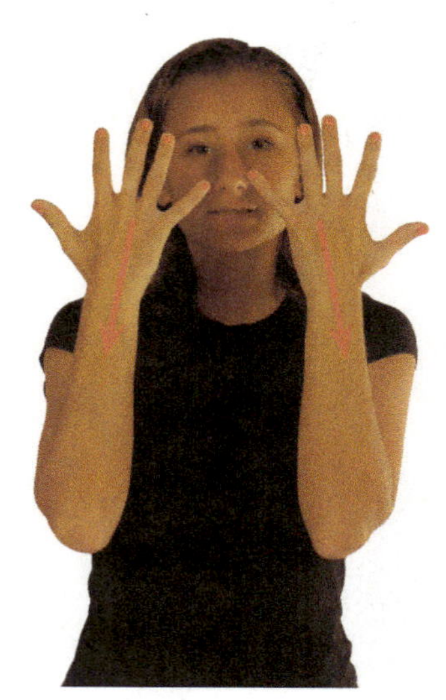

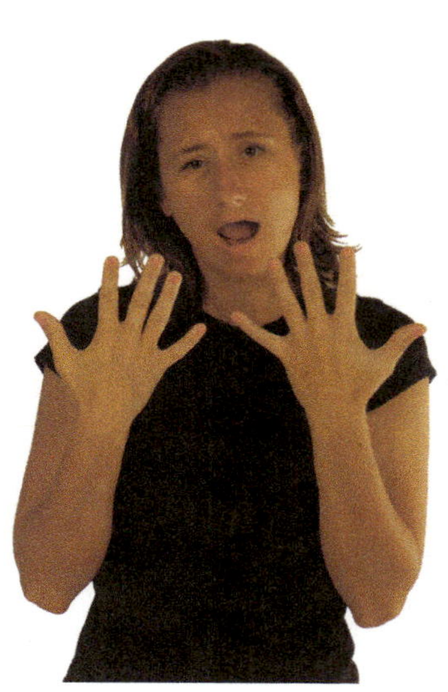

21. HARD

1st "V" bended handshape facing sideways in front of yourself stays still while the 2nd "V" bended handshape on top of the 1st "V" bended handshape once.

22. EASY

Sign "easy" as above.

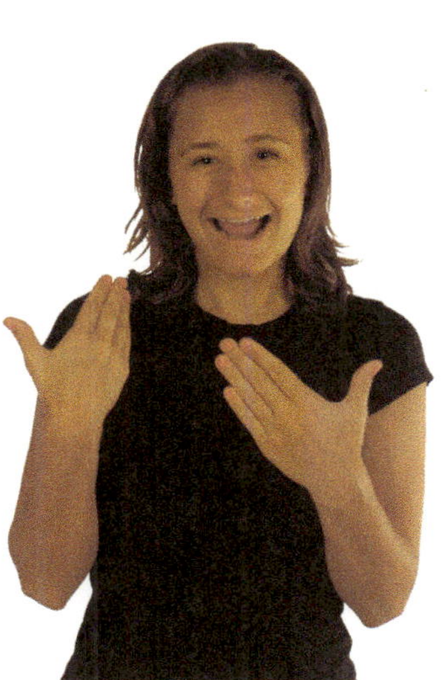

23. HEAVY

Both "5" open handshapes facing up at your stomach height move down once while using facial expression.

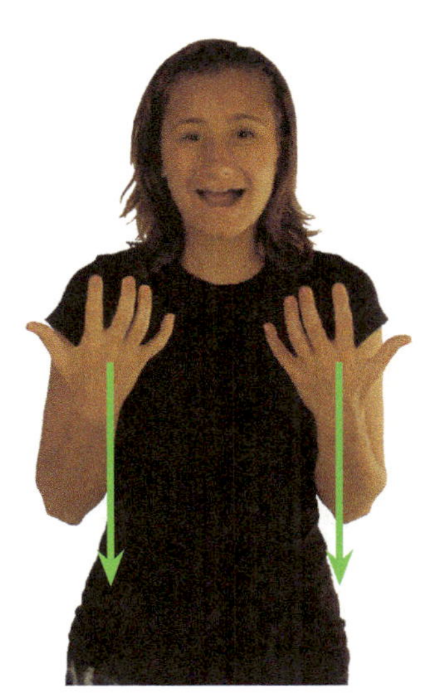

24. LIGHT

Both "middle finger" handshapes touch on your chest and move upward once.

25. HERE

1. Both "1" handshapes point down once.

2. Both "5" closed handshapes facing up move in an opposite circular motion at the same time continually.

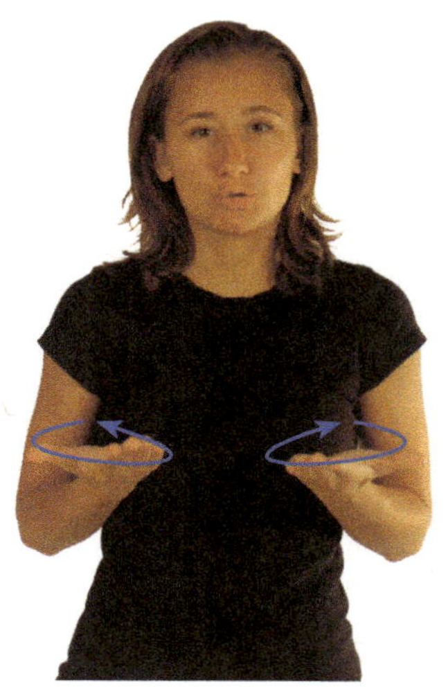

26. THERE

"1" handshape points over there at a certain thing.

27. HIGH

"H" handshape away from your body moves upward once.

28. LOW

"L" handshape away from your body moves downward once.

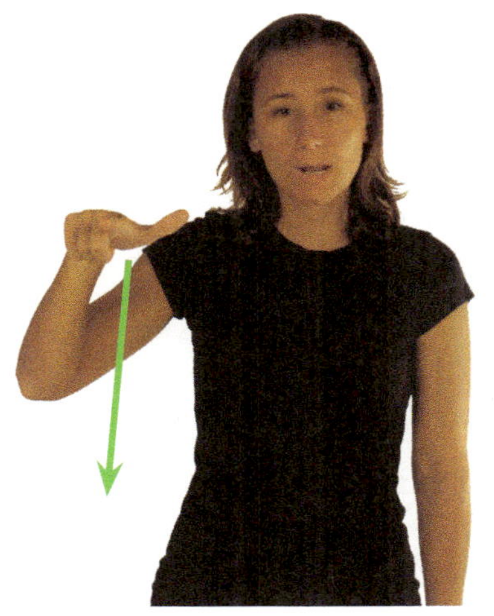

29. HOT

"5" handshape facing down in front of your chin moves and turns downward once.

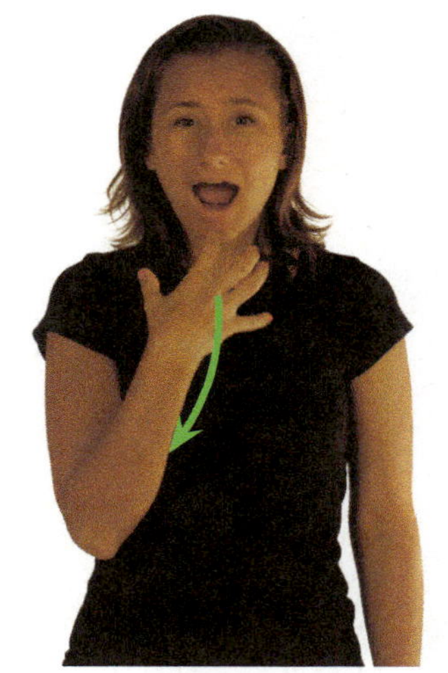

30. COLD

Both "S" handshapes facing sideways away from your body move in and out in an opposite direction repeatedly.

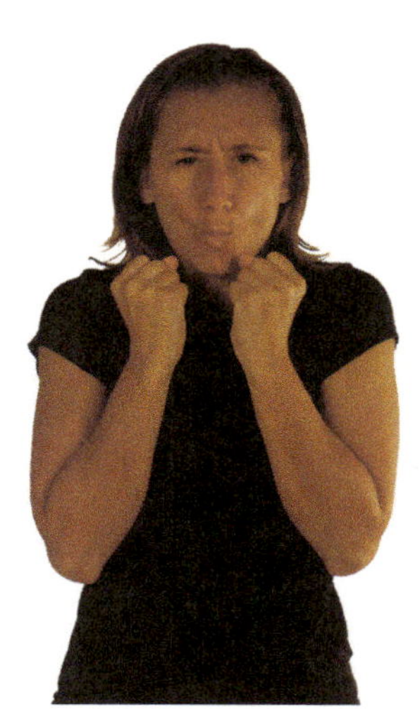

31. IN

1st "O" handshape facing down stays still while the 2nd "O" closed handshape's fingers move into the first "O" handshape once.

32. OUT

1st "O" handshape facing down stays still while the 2nd "O" closed handshape's fingers move out of the first "O" handshape once.

33. INSIDE

Sign "in" as above repeatedly.

34. OUTSIDE

1. Sign "out" as above repeatedly.

2. "5" bended handshape facing down taps on your shoulder repeatedly.

35. BRIGHT

Both "O" closed handshapes sideways touch each other in front of yourself move upward while changing to both "5" open handshapes once.

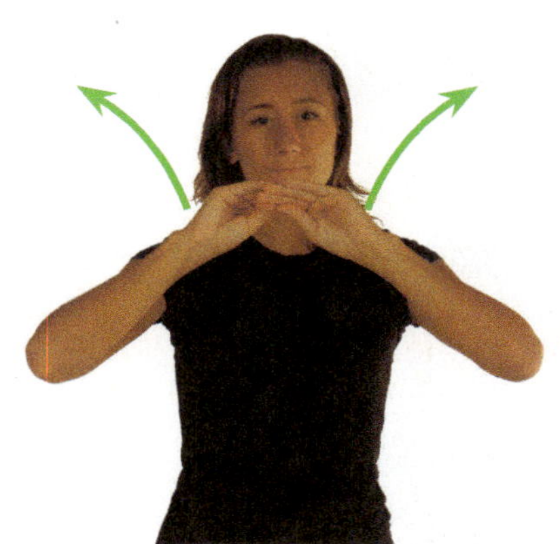

36. DARK

Both "5" closed handshapes in front of your face move toward each other and downward once.

37. LONG

1st "5" closed handshape facing down stays still while the 2nd "1" handshape's finger touches the 1st "5" closed handshape's hand then slides backwards once.

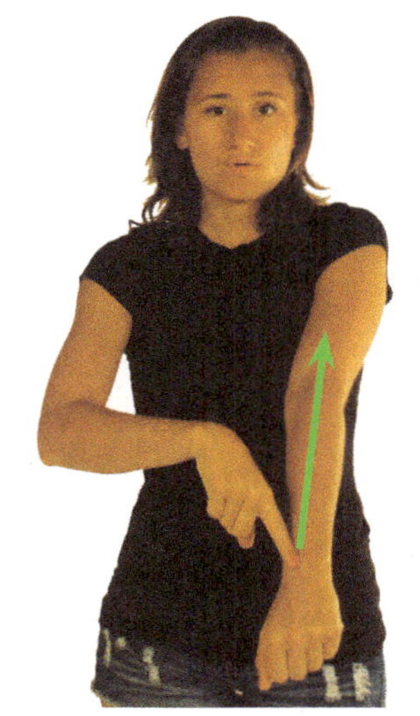

38. SHORT, BRIEF

1st "H" handshape facing sideways stays still while the 2nd "H" handshape facing sideways on the top of the 1st "H" handshape moves forward and backward repeatedly.

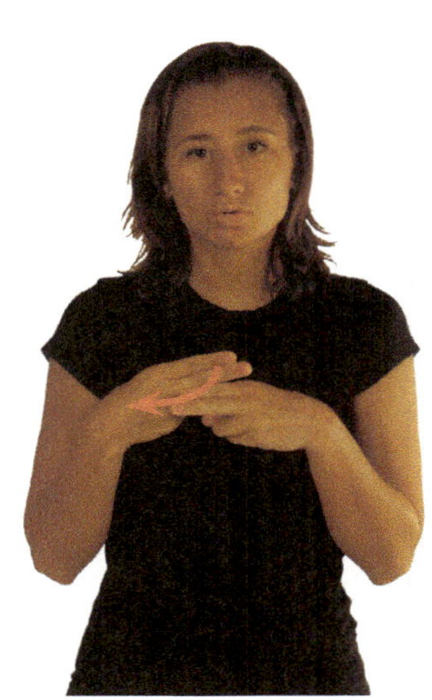

39. MANY

Both "S" handshapes facing yourself move from your body outward and change to "5" open handshapes once or repeatedly.

40. FEW

"S" handshape facing up moves sideways while the fingers change to "5" open handshape once.

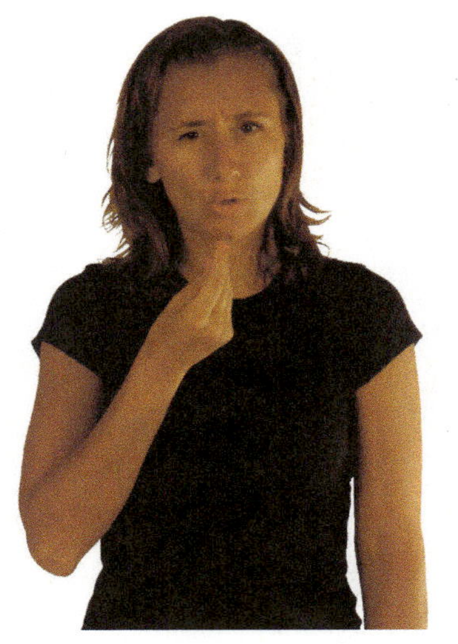

41. OLD

"S" handshape facing sideways on the bottom of your chin moves downward once.

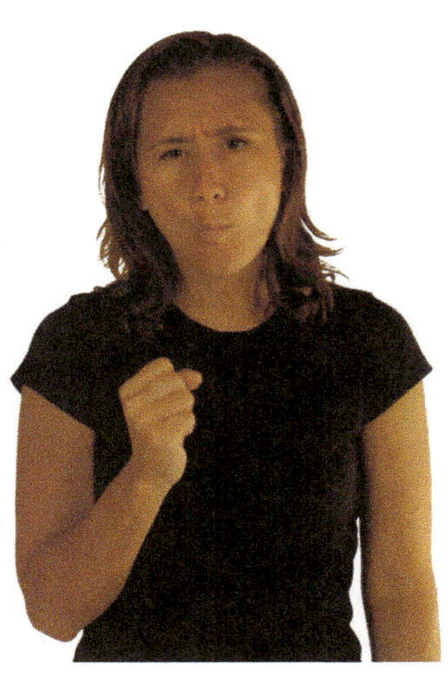

42. NEW

1st "5" closed handshape facing sideways in front of yourself stays still while the back of the 2nd "5" closed handshape slides upward against the palm of the 1st "5" closed handshape once.

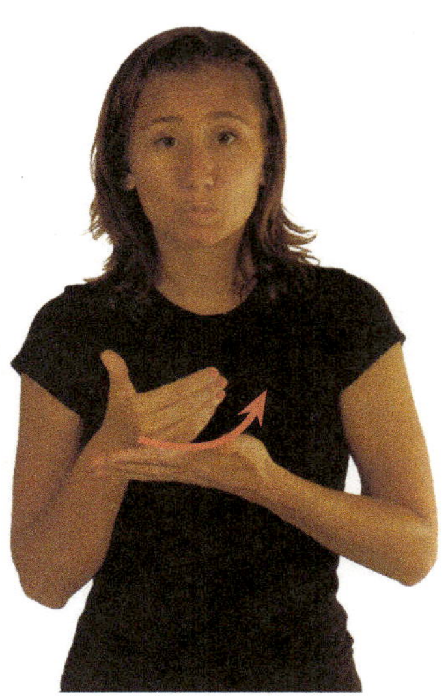

43. RICH

1. 1st "5" open and bended handshape facing up stays still while the 2nd "5" open and bended handshape facing down touches the palm of the 1st "5" open and bended handshape then moves upward once.

2. 1st "5" closed handshape facing up near your stomach stays still while the 2nd "S" handshape on the top of the 1st "5" closed handshape's palm moves upward and changes to "5" open handshape once.

44. POOR

1st "5" closed handshape sideways and halfway down stays still while the 2nd "5" bended and closed handshape, like "G" squeezes your elbow of the 1st "5" handshape moves downward once or repeatedly.

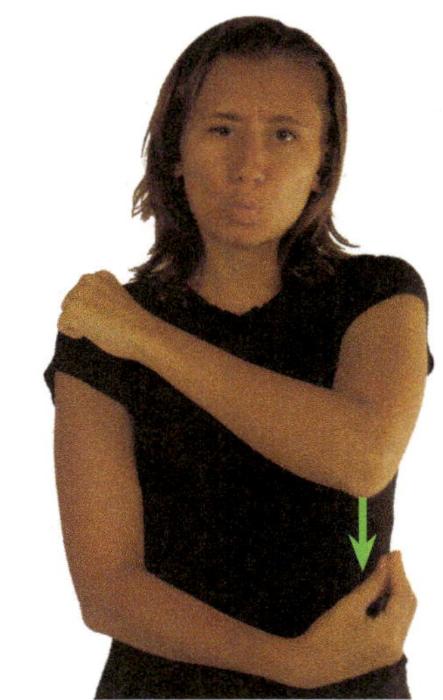

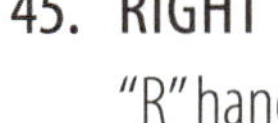

45. RIGHT

"R" handshape facing down moves away from your body to the right (directions).

46. LEFT

"L" handshape moves away from your body to the left (directions).

47. RIGHT (CORRECT)

Both "1" handshapes facing sideways touch on top of each other once.

48. WRONG

"Y" handshape facing yourself moves toward your chin once.

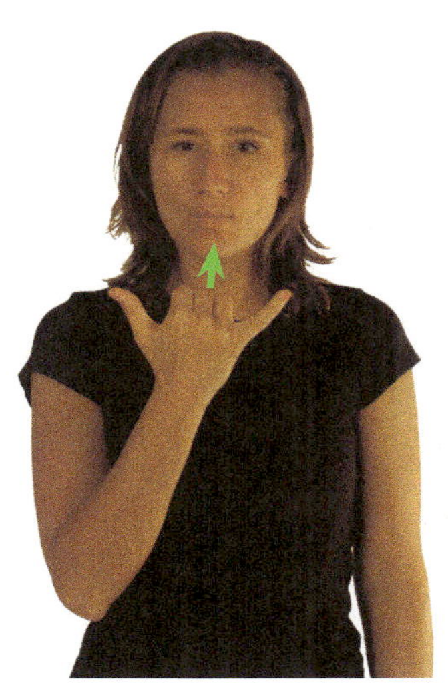

49. SAFE

Both "S" handshapes facing sideways cross each other at the wrists and turn outward once.

50. DANGEROUS

1st "10" handshape facing sideways in front of yourself stays still while the 2nd "10" handshape's thumb brushes up on the back of the 1st "10" handshape repeatedly.

51. SINGLE

"1" handshape facing sideways on the side of your chin moves down and repeats on the other side of your chin once.

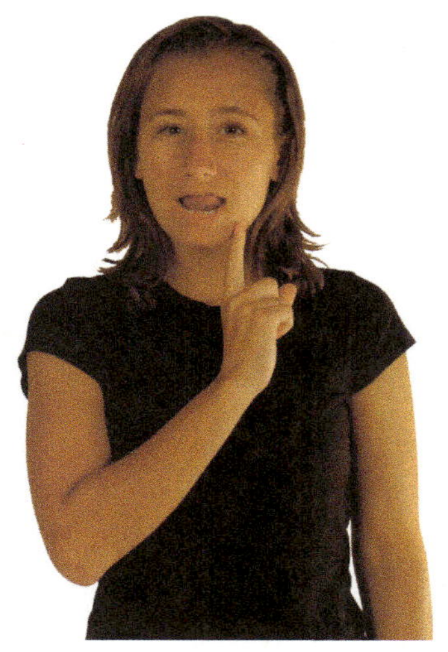

52. MARRIED

1st "5" closed and curved handshape facing up stays still while the 2nd "5" closed and curved handshape facing down clasps together at the same time.

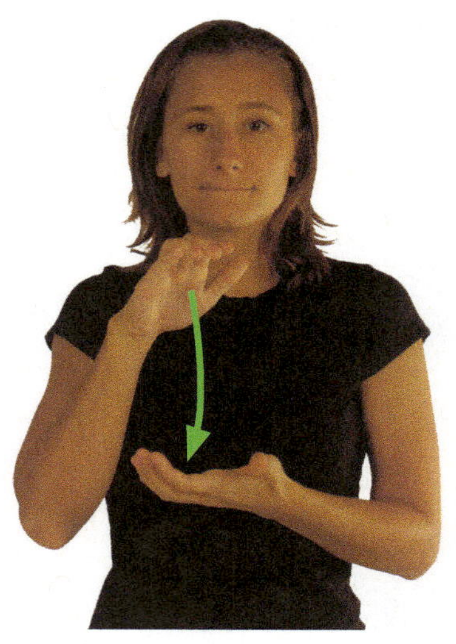

53. SMOOTH

Sign "clean" as above.

54. ROUGH

1st "5" open and bended handshape facing up stays still while the 2nd "5" open and bended handshape brushes from back of palm to fingers once.

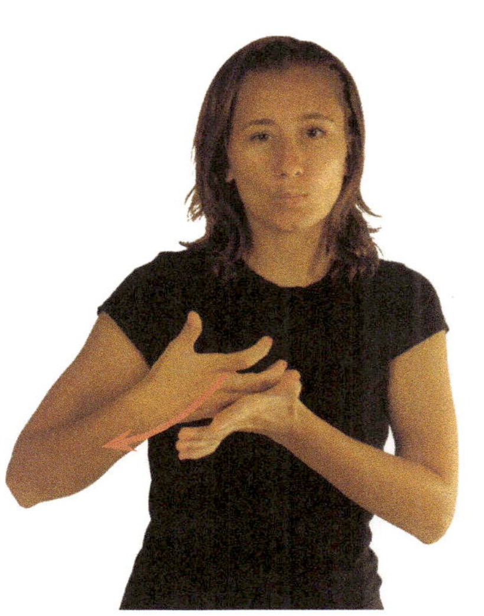

55. SOFT

Both "5" closed and bended handshapes facing up away from your body move downward and change to "O" closed handshapes once.

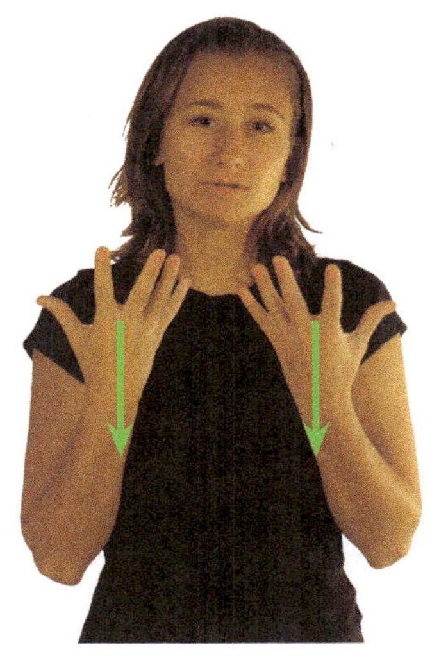

56. HARD

Sign "hard" as above.

57. STRONG

Both "S" handshapes facing sideways, move from one side to the other side of your body once.

58. WEAK

1st "5" bended handshape facing up stays still while the 2nd "5" bended handshape facing down touches the palm of the 1st "5" bended handshape bends repeatedly.

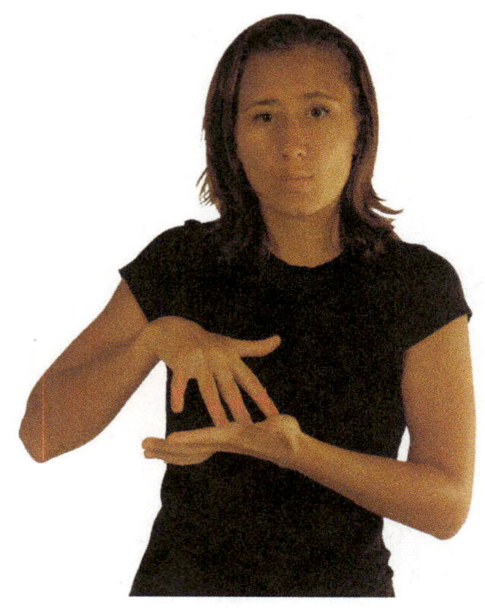

59. TALL

"5" closed and bended handshape moves upward (to show height).

60. VERY TALL

"5" closed and bended handshape moves upward higher (to show height).

61 MEDIUM HEIGHT

"5" closed and bended handshape away from your head stays still.

62. SHORT

"5" closed and bended handshape moves downward (to show height).

63. VERY SHORT

"5" closed handshape moves downward much lower (to show height).

64. WARM

"O" closed handshape's fingers on your chin move upward and change to "5" open handshape once.

65. COOL

Both "5" closed handshapes in front of yourself move back and forth repeatedly.

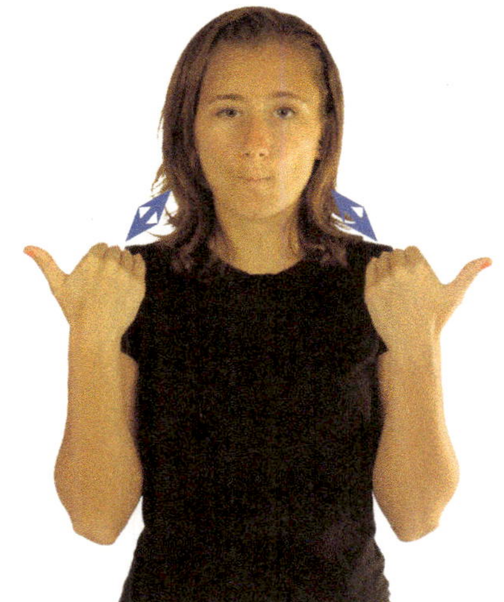

66. WET

1. Both "5" open handshapes in front of yourself move downward and change to "O" closed handshapes once.

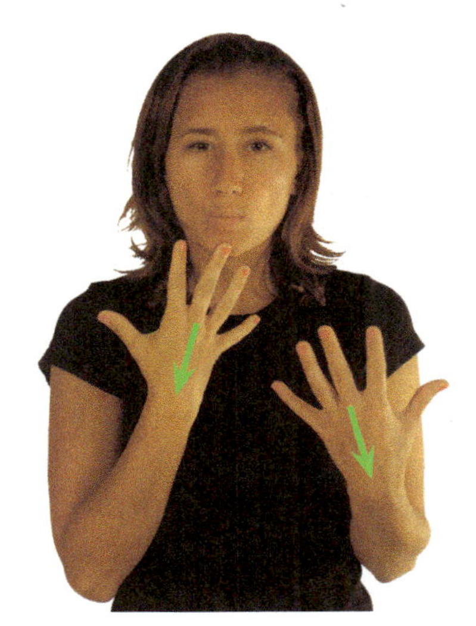

67. VERY WET

Both "5" open handshapes in front of yourself move downward and change to "O" closed handshapes once with your facial expression.

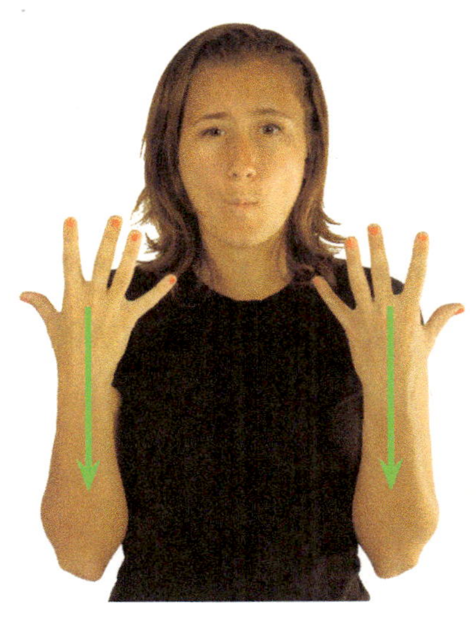

68. DRY

"X" handshape on your chin slides from one side to the other side once.

69. WIDE

Both "5" closed handshapes facing sideways move opposite at the same time.

70. NARROW

Both "5" closed handshapes facing sideways move toward each other once.

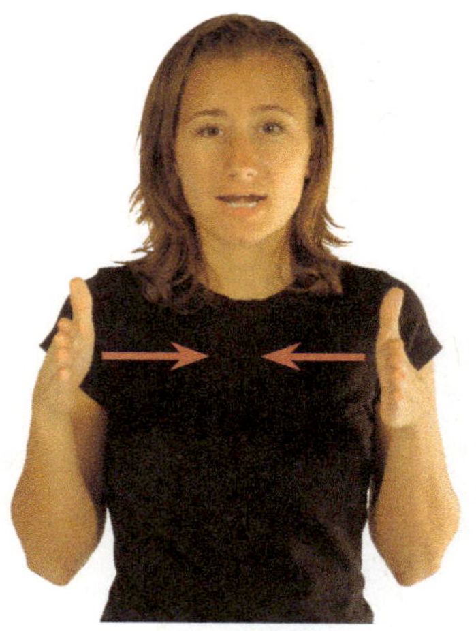

71. YOUNG

Both "5" closed and bended handshape's fingertips on your chest move upward once.

72. OLD

Sign "old" as above.

73. UP

"1" handshape points upward once.

74. DOWN

"1" handshape points downward once.

CHAPTER

14 Education

1. EDUCATION

    1. Both "E" handshapes facing sideways on both sides of your temple move back and forth repeatedly.

    2. Fingerspell "E" on both sides of your temple move forward and change and fingerspell "D" once.

2. SCHOOL

1st "5" closed handshape facing up stays still while the 2nd "5" closed handshape facing down clap each other repeatedly.

3. SCHOOL FOR THE DEAF

1. 1st "I" handshape facing down away from your body stays still while the 2nd "I" handshape taps on the top of the 1st "I" handshape's fist move up and down repeatedly.

4. MAINSTREAMED PROGRAM

Both "5" open handshapes outward at your shoulders move forward away from your body and both "5" open handshapes end by touching on top of the other once.

5. ORAL SCHOOL
   "V" bended handshape facing yourself in front of your mouth moves in a circular motion continually and sign "school" as above.

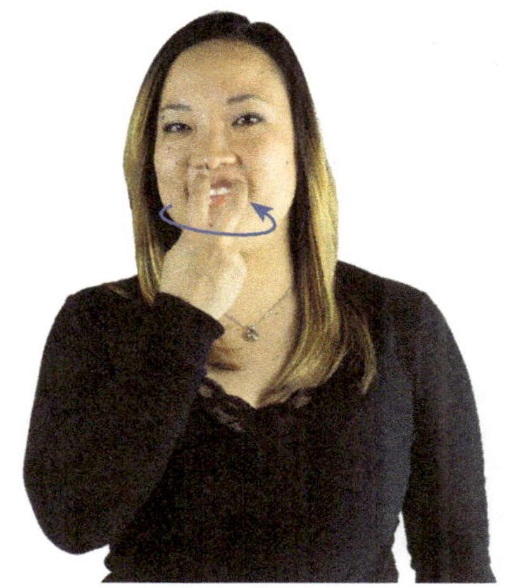

6. PRIVATE SCHOOL
   "A" handshape on your chin moves back and forth slightly and repeatedly then sign "school" as above.

7. **CHARTER SCHOOL**
   Fingerspell C-H-A-R-T-E-R and sign "school" as above.

8. **PRESCHOOL**

   1st "5" closed handshape facing yourself to your stomach stays still while the 2nd "P" handshape touches the 1st "5" closed handshape's palm and moves toward your stomach once and sign "school" as above.

9. **KINDERGARTEN**

   1st "5" closed handshape facing down stays still while the 2nd "K" handshape facing sideways under the 1st "5" closed handshape moves sideway repeatedly.

10. ELEMENTARY SCHOOL
"E" handshape on the side of your body moves sideways repeatedly then sign "school" as above.

11. MIDDLE SCHOOL
1st "5" closed handshape facing up stays still while the "middle finger" handshape facing down moves around halfway and touches on the top of the 1st "5" closed handshape's palm once and sign "school" as above.

12. **HIGH SCHOOL**
    Fingerspell "H" facing yourself changes to "S" handshape sideways once.

13. **PUBLIC SCHOOL**
    "1" handshape touches on your chin and moves up and down like a circular motion.

14. COLLEGE

1st "5" closed handshape facing up stays still while the 2nd "5" closed handshape on the top of the 1st "5" closed handshape's palm moves upward half circle once.

15. UNIVERSITY

1st "5" closed handshape facing up stays still while the 2nd "U" handshape facing down on the top of the 1st "5" closed handshape's palm moves upward half circle once.

16. CERTIFICATE
Both "C" handshape's thumbs touch each other in front of your body while both "C" handshapes bounce off each other repeatedly.

17. LICENSE
Both "L" handshapes. Both thumbs touch each other in front of your body bounce off each other repeatedly.

18. LANGUAGE
1. Both "L" handshapes facing down away from your body while two thumbs touch each other and wiggle outward in opposite direction.

2. LANGUAGE/SENTENCE: (no picture) Both "F" handshapes facing down away from your body while two fingers and thumbs touch each other and wiggle outward in opposite direction,

19. GRAMMER

Both "G" handshapes facing down touch each other and wiggle outward in opposite direction.

20. WRITING

1st "5" closed handshape facing up stays still while the 2nd "L" closed handshape touches on the palm of the 1st "5" handshape and moves like the way you write.

21. **LESSON**

1st "5" closed handshape facing yourself away from your body while the 2nd "5" curved handshape touches on the top of the 1st "5" closed handshape's fingers move downward once.

22. **LECTURE, PRESENTATION**

"5" closed handshape facing sideways on the side of your head moves back and forth repeatedly.

23. **PHYSICAL EDUCATION**

Both "P" handshapes move from your chest to your stomach once and fingerspell "E-D" as above.

24. TUTOR
Both "T" handshapes facing sideways on both sides of temple move back and forth repeatedly.

25. ATTENDANCE
Both "1" handshapes facing forward away from your body move up and down repeatedly.

CHAPTER 15 Business and Technology

1. BUSINESS
   1st "B" handshape facing down in front of yourself stays still while the 2nd "B" handshape's wrist on the top of the 1st "B" handshape's finger moves sideways repeatedly.

2. TECHNOLOGY
   1st "A" handshape facing yourself sideways while the 2nd "middle finger" handshape facing up touches the bottom palm of the 1st "A" handshape taps up and down repeatedly.

3. COMPUTER

1. "C" handshape facing sideways on your upper arm moves up and down repeatedly.

2. 1st "5" closed handshape facing down stays still while the 2nd "C" handshape facing sideways on the top of the 1st "5" closed handshape moves sideways repeatedly.

3. Both "middle finger" handshapes away from your body move in a circular motion continually.

4. CELL PHONE

"E" handshape taps on your cheek once.

5. PAGER

Both "A" handshape facing sideways touching each other while both thumbs move up and down repeatedly.

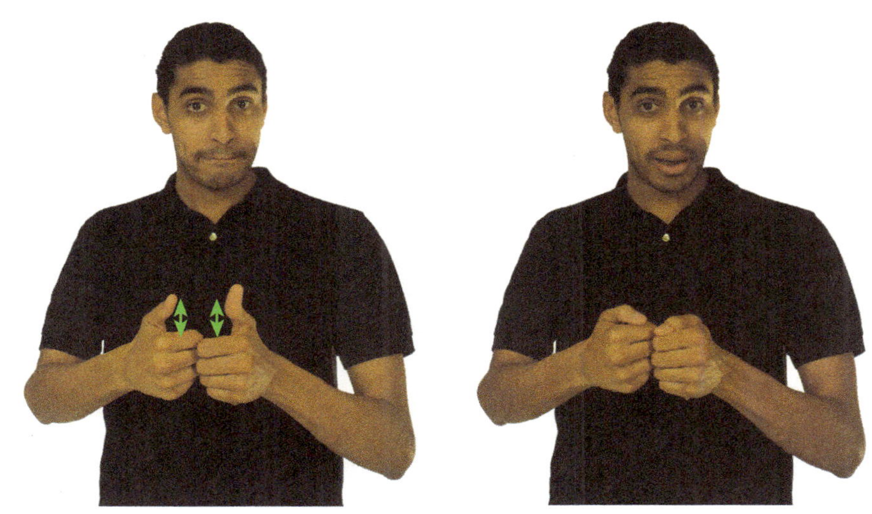

6. EMAIL

1st "5" closed handshape facing sideways (the shape of "G") facing yourself stays still while the 2nd "B" handshape facing down in-between the 1st "5" handshape moves back and forth repeatedly.

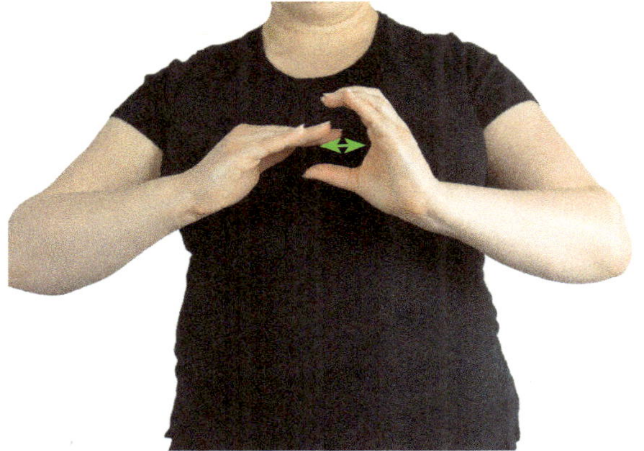

7. ACCOUNTANT

1. 1st "5" closed handshape facing sideways in front of yourself stays still while the 2nd "F" handshape on the palm of the 1st "5" closed handshape moves sideways repeatedly then sign both "5" closed handshapes on both sides of your ribs move downward once.

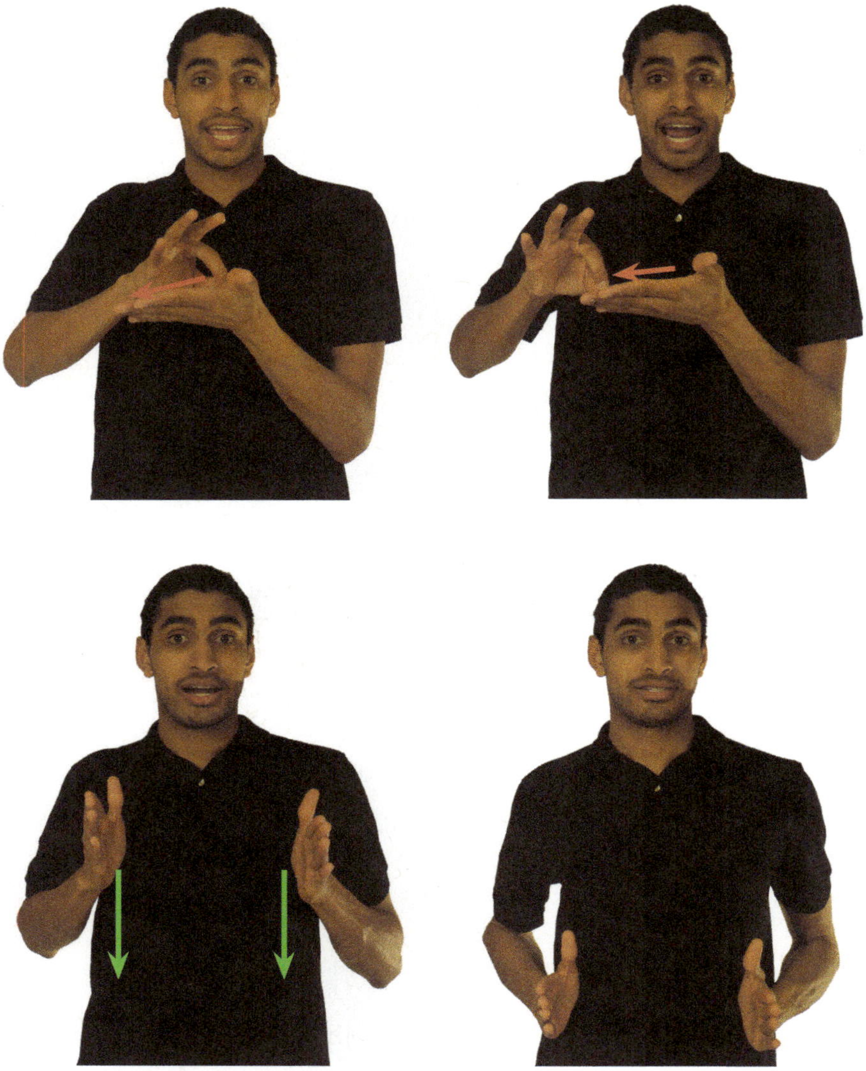

2. 1st "5" closed handshape facing sideways in front of yourself stays still while the 2nd "A" handshape facing sideways on the palm of the 1st "5" handshape slides down once then sign both "5" closed handshapes on both sides of your ribs move downward once.

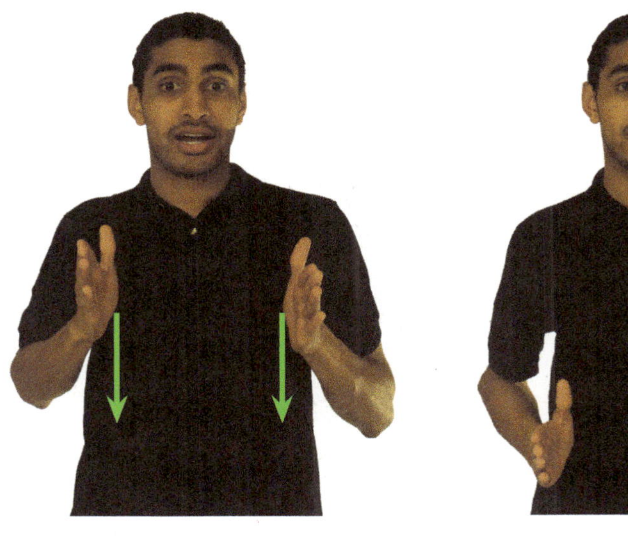

8. CONSULTANT

1st "5" closed handshape facing down in front of yourself stays still while the 2nd "O" closed handshape on the top of the 1st "5" closed handshape moves outward once and changes to "5" open handshape then sign both "5" closed handshapes on both sides of your ribs move downward once.

9. COORDINATOR
Both "9" handshapes touching each other move in a circular motion then sign both "5" closed handshapes on both sides of your ribs move downward once.

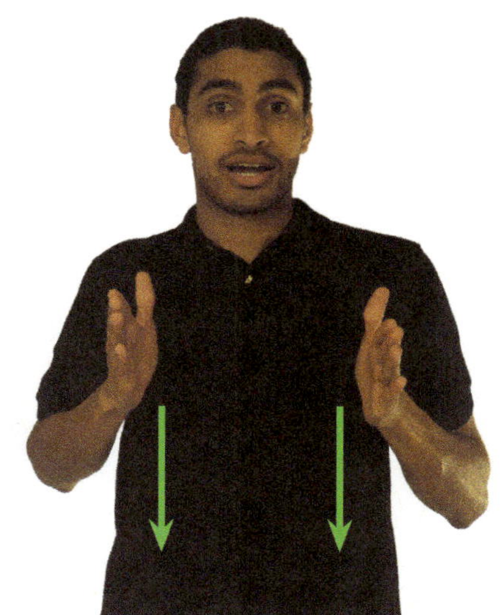

10. CUSTOMER
Both "C" handshapes facing down on both sides of your body moves from your chest to your stomach once.

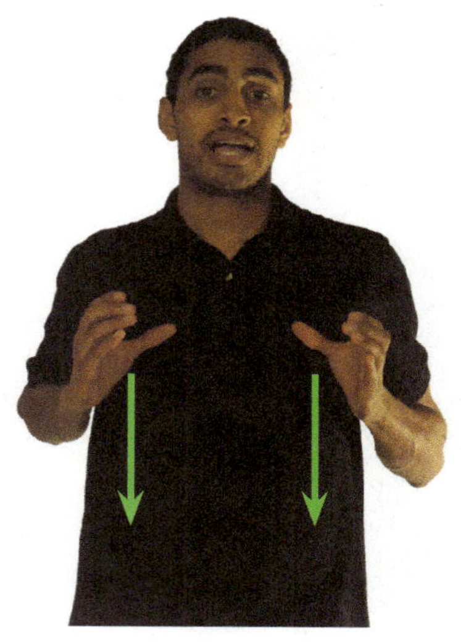

11. DESIGNER

1st "5" closed handshape facing sideways stays still while the 2nd "D" handshape on the top of the 1st "5" closed handshape's palm moves downward like the shape of "Z" once then sign both "5" closed handshapes on both sides of your ribs move downward once.

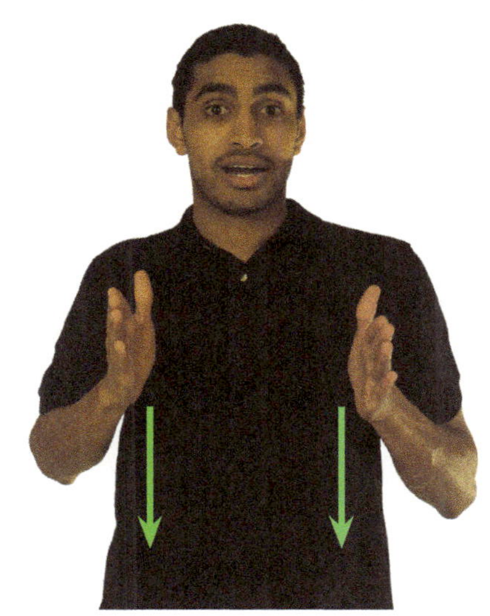

12. SCIENTIST

Both "10" handshapes facing down away from your body move alternating continually then sign both "5" closed handshapes on both sides of your ribs move downward once.

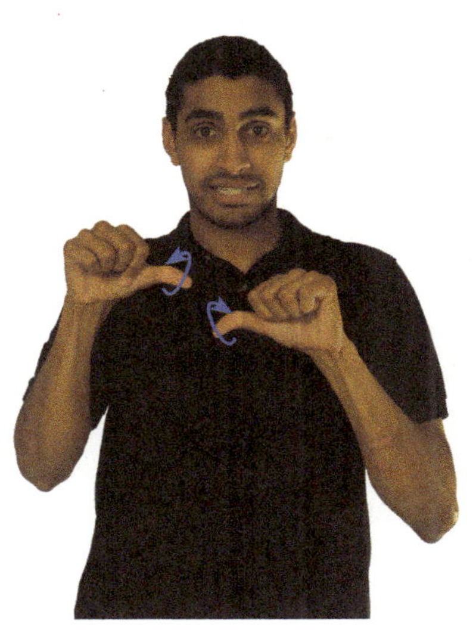

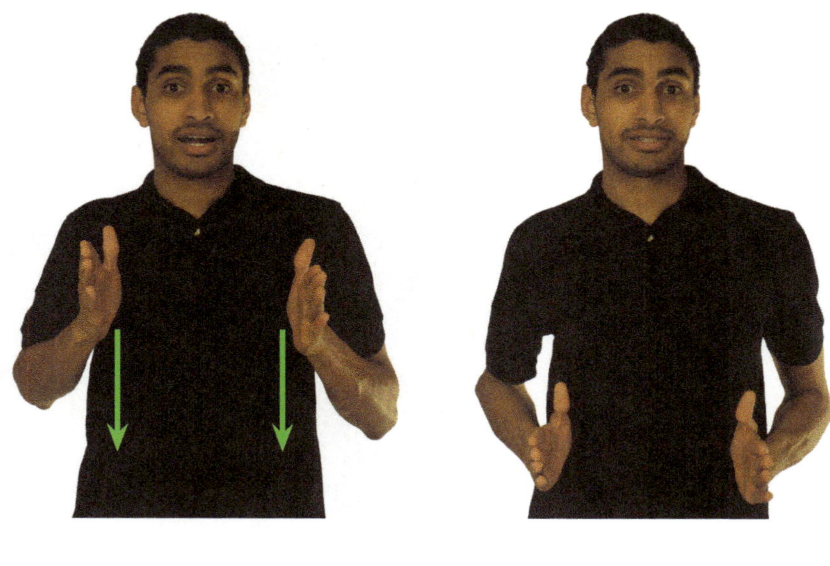

13. **FACULTY**
"F" handshape facing down and sideways on the side of your shoulder moves to the other side of your shoulder once.

14. **SPECIALIST**
1st "B" handshape facing sideways away from your body stays still while the 2nd "1" handshape touches on the top of the "B" handshape and slides outward once.

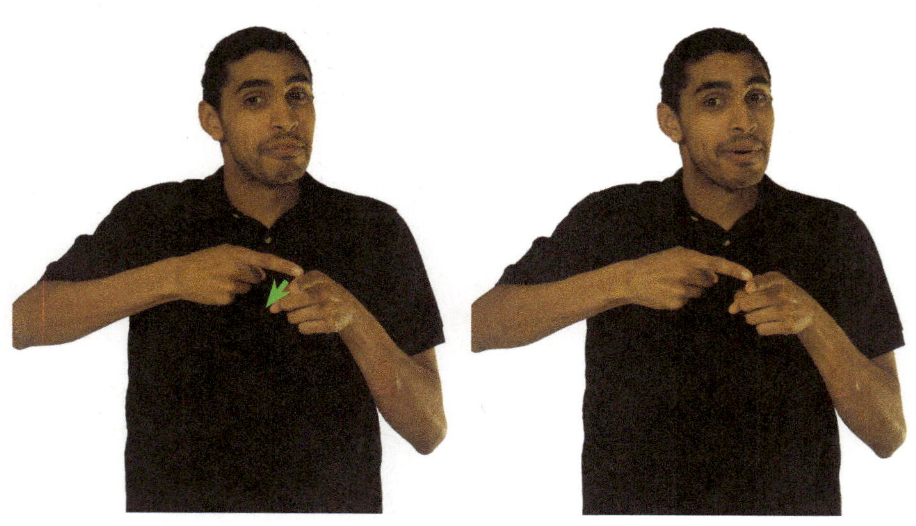

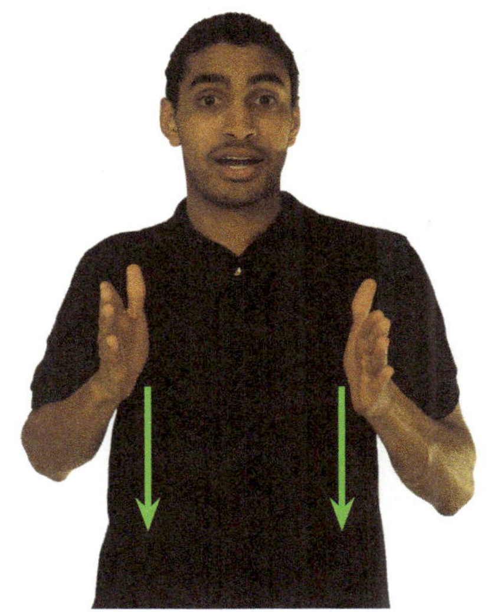

15. ADVERTISEMENT
    1st "S" handshape facing sideways stays still while the 2nd "S" handshape touches the bottom of the 1st "S" handshape and moves downward and changes to "5" open handshape repeatedly.

16. BORROW
    1st "K" handshape facing sideways stays still while the 2nd "K" handshape on the top of the 1st "K" handshape move together toward yourself once.

17. LOAN

    1st "K" handshape facing sideways stays still while the 2nd "K" handshape on the top of the 1st "K" handshape move together outward once.

18. CALCULATE

    1st "5" closed handshape stays still while the 2nd "5" open handshape's fingers wiggle and move up and down on the top of the 1st "5" handshape repeatedly.

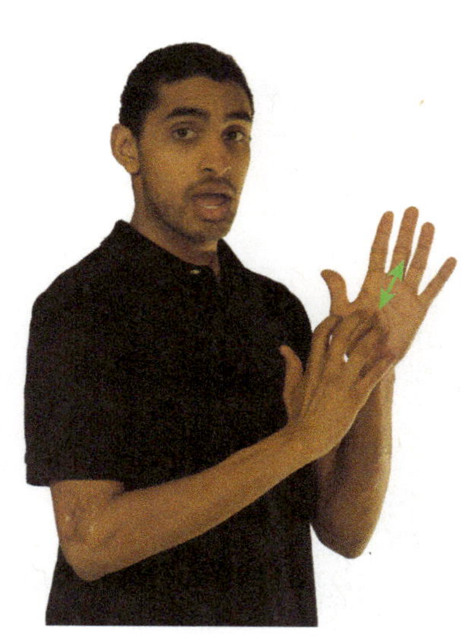

19. BUY

1st "5" closed handshape facing up stays still while the 2nd "O" closed handshape on the top of the 1st "5" handshape's palm moves outward once.

20. CHARGE, TAX

1st "5" closed handshape facing sideways stays still while the 2nd "X" handshape touches on the palm of the 1st "5" closed handshape moves downward once.

21. CREDIT CARD

1st "5" closed handshape facing up stays still while the 2nd "S" handshape facing sideways moves back and forth repeatedly.

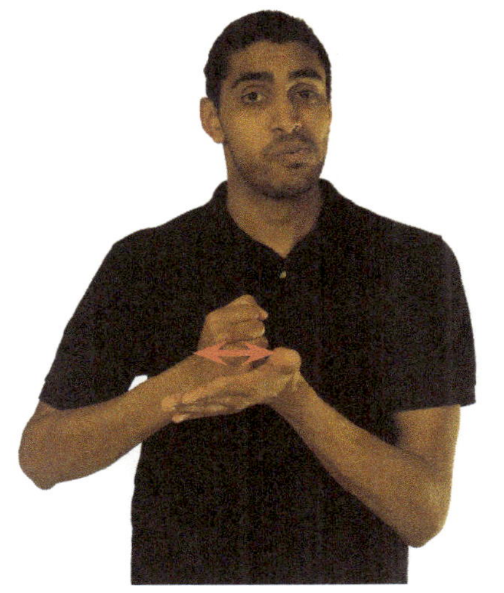

22. CHECK

Both "L" bended handshapes touching each move sideways and both fingers and thumbs move downward and touch each other once.

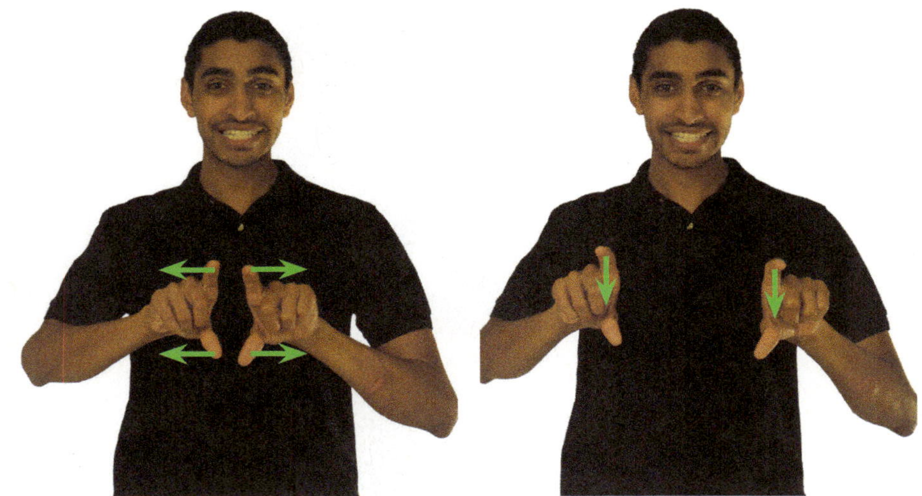

23. DEPOSIT

Both "10" handshape's thumbs touching each other move downward once.

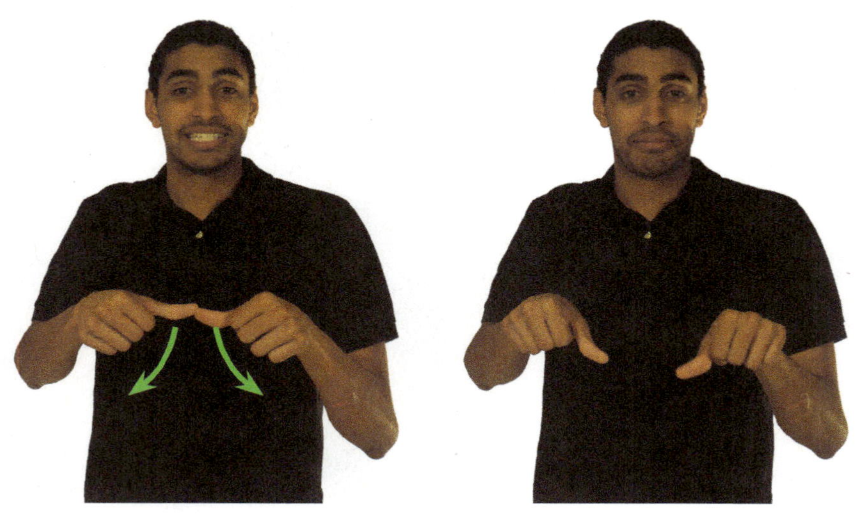

24. INVESTMENT

Both "3" bended handshapes facing forward away from your body alternate upward and downward in a circular motion repeatedly.

25. DOWN PAYMENT

1st "5" closed handshape facing up stays still while the 2nd "C" handshape on the palm of the 1st "5" closed handshape moves outward and then downward once.

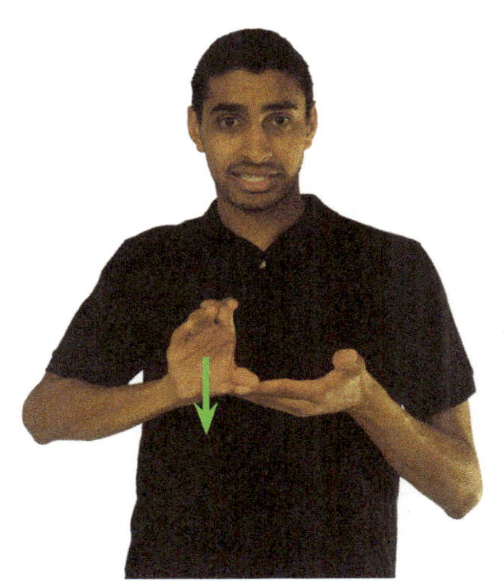

26. SAVINGS

1. 1st "S" handshape facing yourself while the 2nd "V" handshape facing yourself taps on the top of the 1st "S" handshape repeatedly.

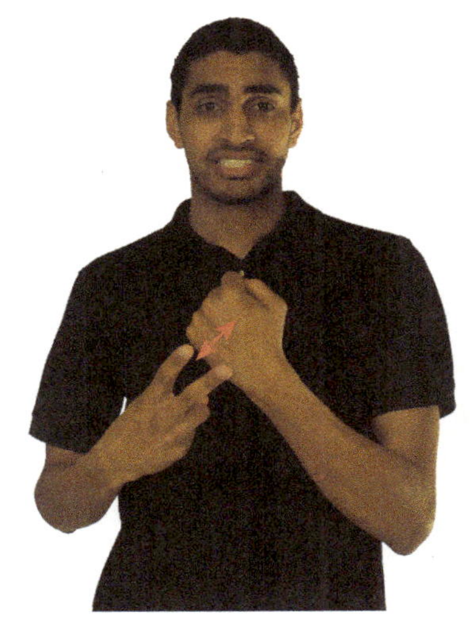

2. 1st "O" closed handshape in front of yourself stays still while the 2nd "O" closed handshape's fingers move in and out of the 1st "O" closed handshape repeatedly.

27. **COUNT**

1st "5" closed handshape facing sideways in front of yourself stays still while the 2nd "F" handshape on the palm of the 1st "5" closed handshape moves sideways once or repeatedly.

28. **EMPLOYEE**

1st "S" handshape facing down away from your body stays still while the 2nd "S" handshape on the top of the 1st "S" handshape moves up and down then changes to both "5" closed handshapes on both sides of your ribs move downward once.

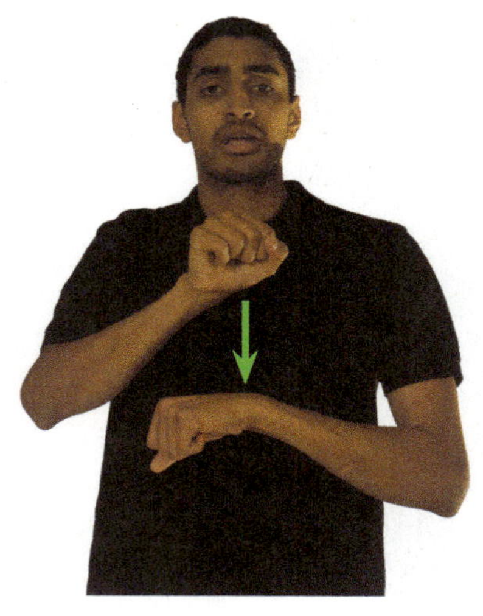
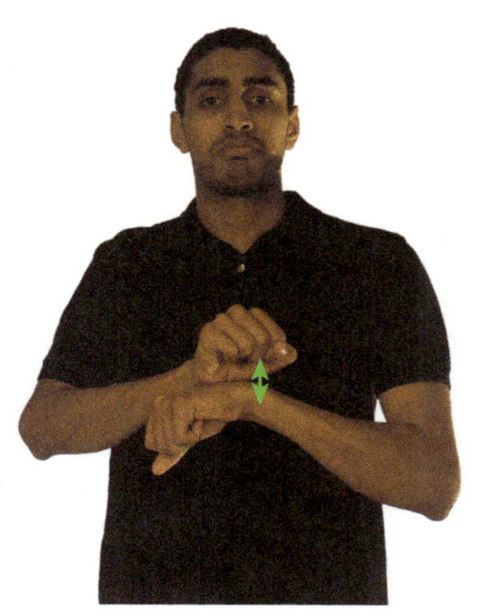

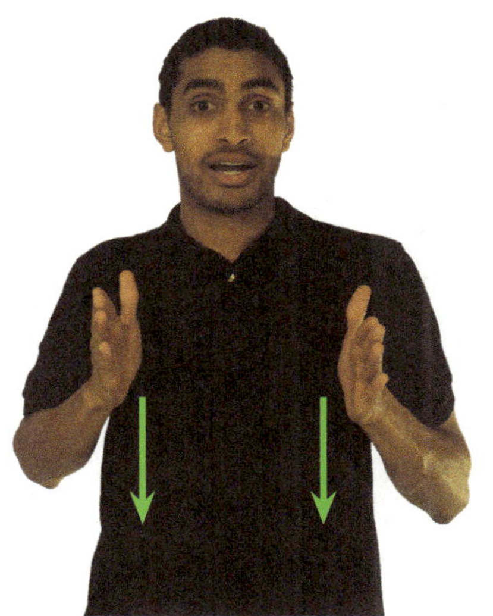

29. ESTIMATE

"5" open handshape facing forward away from your body moves in a circular motion continually.

30. EXCHANGE

Both "A" handshapes facing sideways away from your body move alternating once.

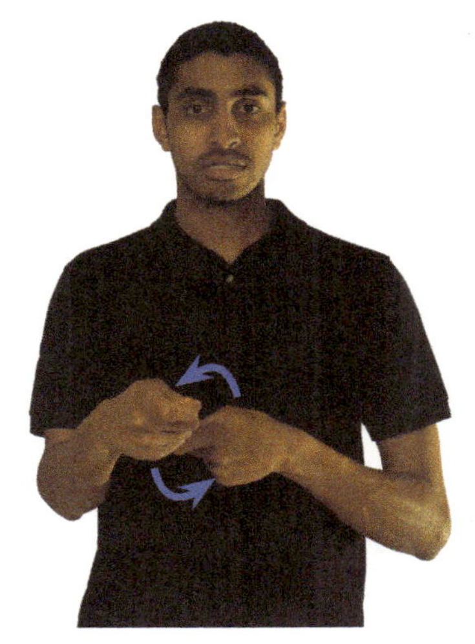

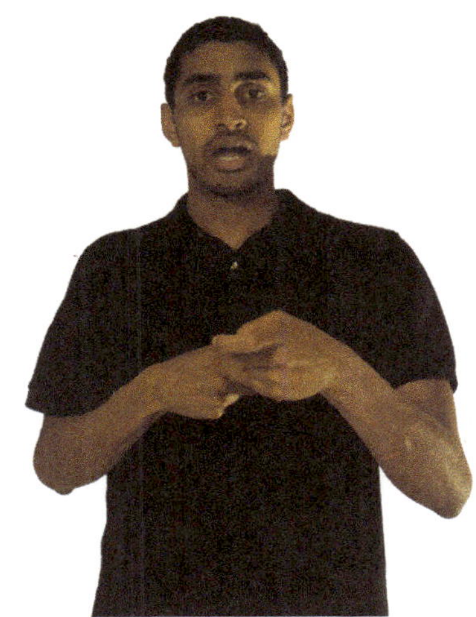

31. MANAGER

Both "A" handshapes facing sideways away from your body move back and forth alternating once then changes to both "5" closed handshapes on both sides of your ribs move downward once.

32. ORGANIZE, PLAN

Both "5" closed handshapes facing sideways away from your body move to the side at the same time repeatedly.

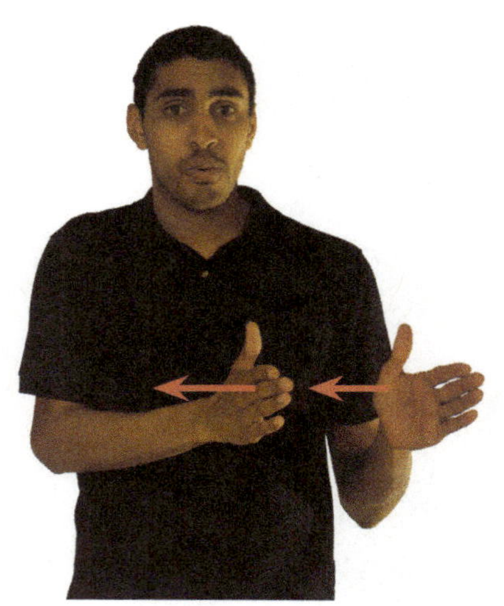

33. OWE, DEBT

1st "5" closed handshape facing sideways stays still while the 2nd "1" handshape points on the palm of the 1st "5" closed handshape repeatedly.

34. PAY

1st "5" closed handshape facing up away from your body stays still while the 2nd "1" handshape points on the palm of the 1st "5" handshape moves outward once or repeatedly.

35. INTEREST

1st "5" closed handshape facing down stays still while the 2nd "little finger" handshape on the top of the 1st "5" closed handshape moves in a circular motion.

36. PERCENT

"O" closed handshape moves the shape of the percent sign once.

37. ANALYSTS

Both "V" bended handshapes facing down touching each other move outward once or repeatedly then changes to both "5" closed handshapes on both sides of your ribs move downward once.

38. APPLICANT

"9" handshape facing down and sideways touches on the top of your shoulder moves up and down repeatedly then changes to both "5" closed handshapes on both sides of your ribs move downward once.

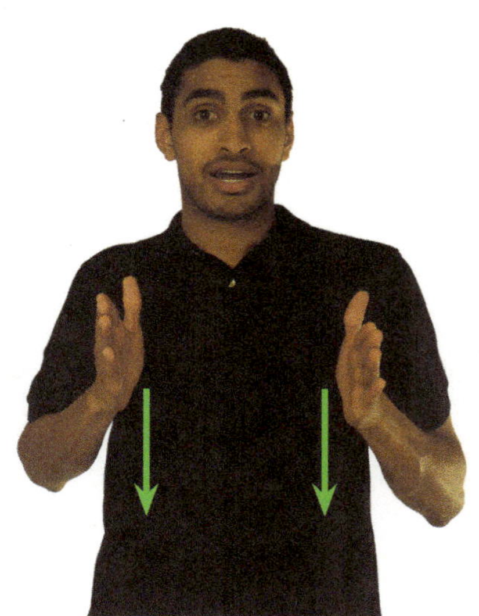

39. CERTIFICATE
Both "C" handshapes thumbs touching each other and bounce back and forth slightly and repeatedly.

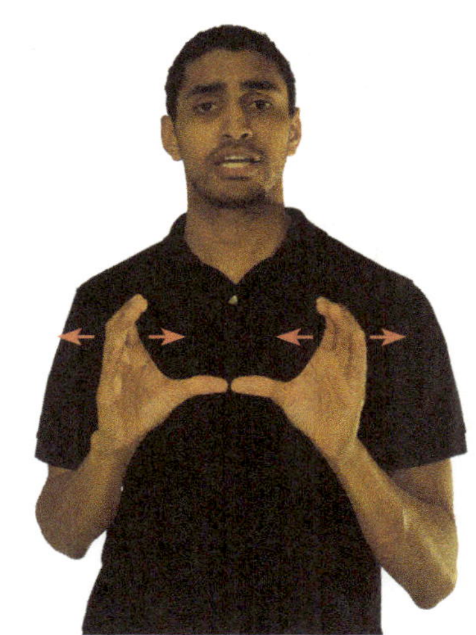

40. CERTIFY
Both "C" handshapes thumbs touching each other bounce back once.

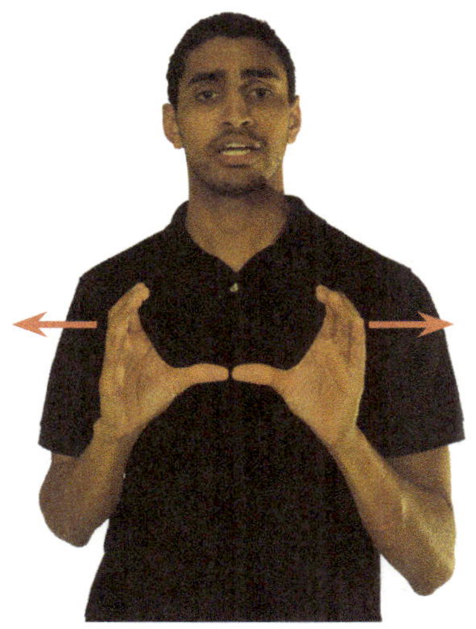

41. LICENSE
Both "L" handshapes thumbs toughing each other and bounce back and forth slightly and repeatedly.

42. PROMOTION
Both "5" closed and bended handshapes facing sideways above your shoulders move up once or repeatedly.

43. PUBLISHING, PRINT
1st "5" closed handshape facing up stays still while the 2nd "G" handshape facing outward on top of the 1st "5" closed handshape thumb and finger moves up and down repeatedly.

44. RESEARCH

1st "5" closed handshape facing up away from your body stays still while the 2nd "R" handshape's fingertips on the top of the 1st "5" closed handshape's palm slides outward repeatedly.

45. RESOURCES

1st "5" closed handshape facing up away from your body stays still while the 2nd "R" handshape facing up on the top of the 1st "5" closed handshape's palm moves outward.

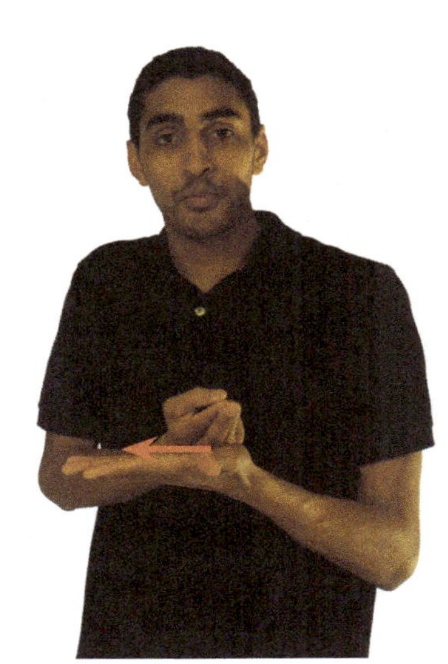

46. TRANSFER

"V" bended handshape facing down toward your body moves sideways in front of your body and twists to the other side of your body once.

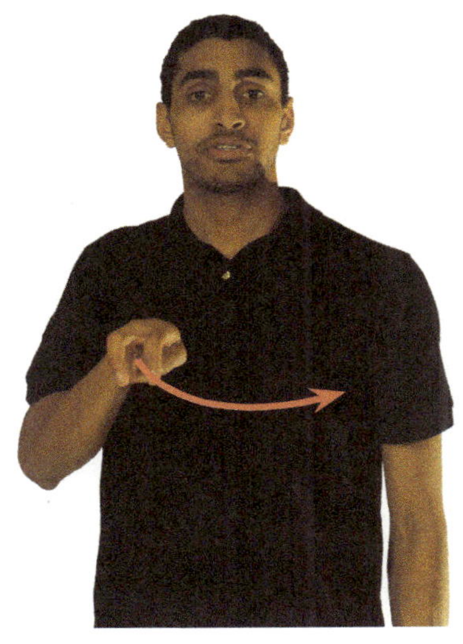

47. EQUIPMENT

    1st "5" closed handshape facing up away from your body stays still while the 2nd "E" handshape facing up on the top of the 1st "5" closed handshape moves outward once or repeatedly.

48. FINANCIAL

    1st "5" closed handshape facing up in front of yourself stays still while the 2nd "F" handshape facing up on the palm of the 1st "5" closed handshape moves up and down repeatedly.

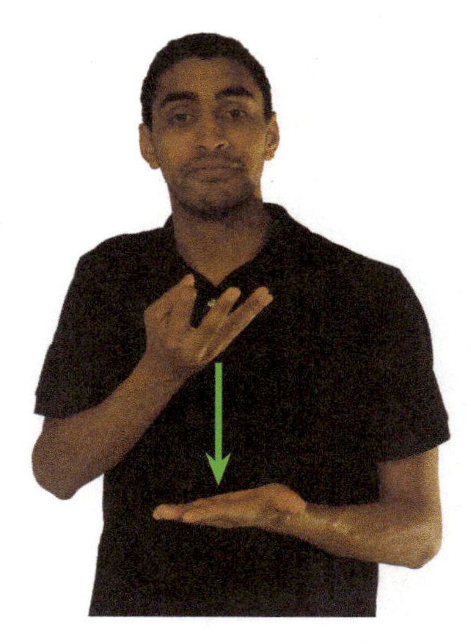

49. LABORATORY

    Fingerspell L-A-B.

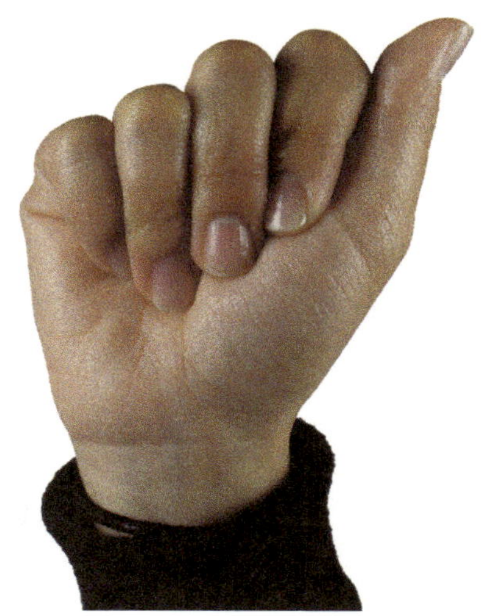

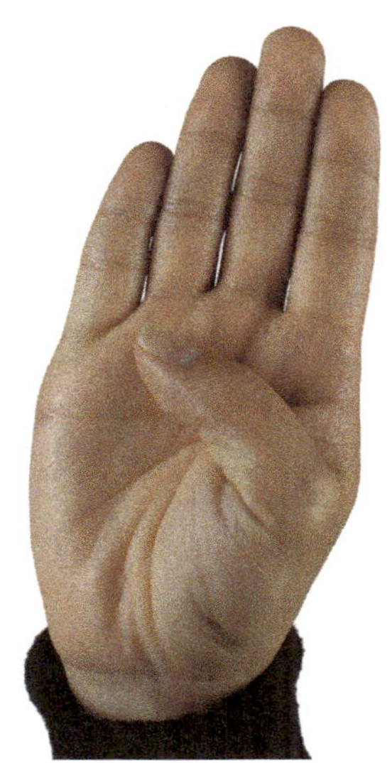

50. OFFICE

Both "O" handshapes facing down away from your body move like the shape of a box once.

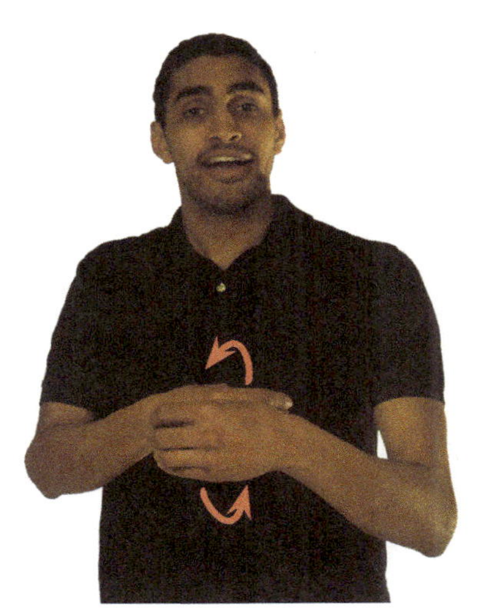

51. PROGRAM

1st "5" closed handshape away from your body stays still while the 2nd "P" handshape touches on the palm of the 1st "5" closed handshape moves upward and turn over and touches the other side of the 1st "5" closed handshape once.

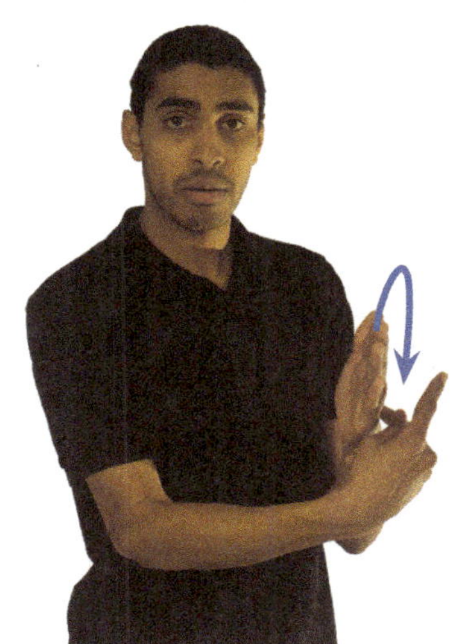

52. **PROJECT**

1st "5" closed handshape away from your body stays still while the 2nd "P" handshape on the palm of the 1st "5" closed handshape moves upward and turn over and change to "J" handshape on the other side of the 1st "5" handshape once.

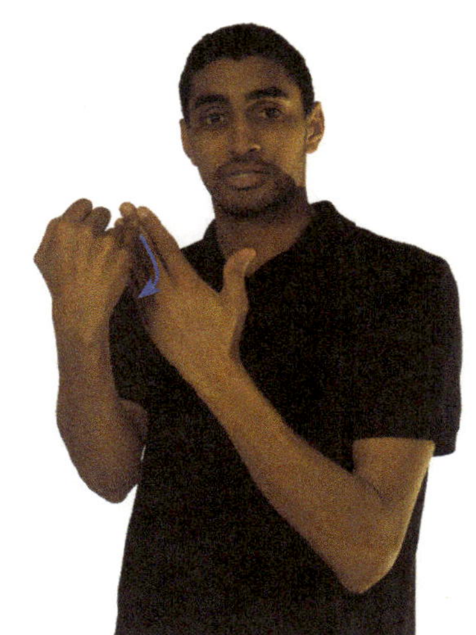

53. **TRAINING**

1st "1" handshape facing sideways in front of yourself stays still while the 2nd "T" handshape on the top of the 1st "1" handshape's finger moves back and forth repeatedly.

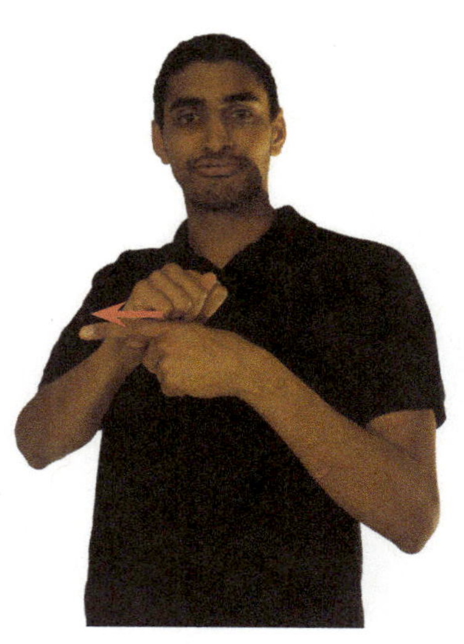

54. WORKSHOP

both "W" handshapes facing outward touching each other turn to "S" handshapes facing yourself once.

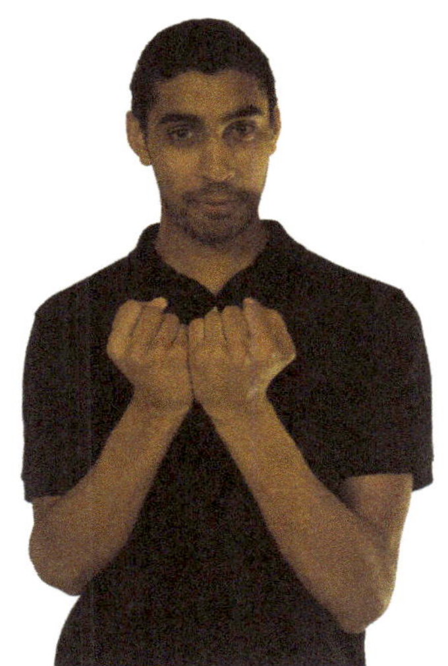

CHAPTER

16 Occupations

1. ACTOR, ACTRESS
   Both "A" handshapes facing sideways on your chest move upward and downward alternating continually then sign both "5" closed handshapes on both sides of your ribs move downward once.

2. DIRECTOR
Both "D" handshapes facing down away from your body move back and forth alternating repeatedly then sign both "5" closed handshapes on both sides of your ribs move downward once.

3. MANAGER
Both "A" handshapes facing up sideways away from your body move back and forth alternating repeatedly then sign both "5" closed handshapes on both sides of your ribs move downward once.

4. **TECHNICIAN**
   Sign "technology" as in Chapter 15 then sign both "5" closed handshapes on both sides of your ribs move downward once.

5. **ARCHITECT**
   Same sign as in Chapter 15.

6. PHOTOGRAPHER

Both "1" bended handshapes near your eyes. The 1st "1" bended handshape stays still while the 2nd "1" bended handshape's pointer finger clicks once then sign both "5" closed handshapes on both sides of your ribs move downward once.

7. ACCOUNTANT

Same sign as in Chapter 15.

8. CHEMIST

Both "C" handshapes away from your body move upward and downward alternating then sign both "5" closed handshapes on both sides of your ribs move downward once.

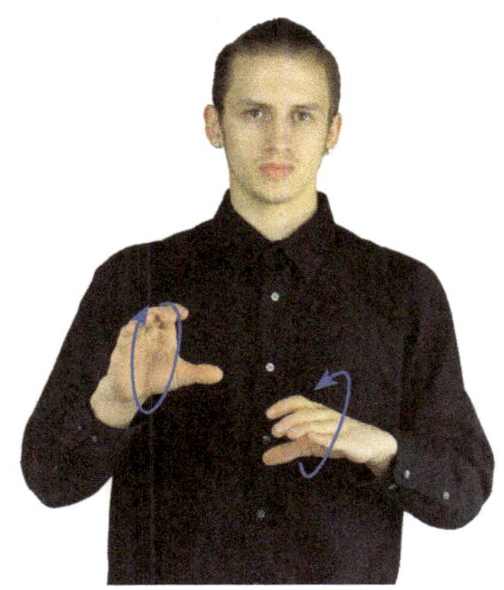

9. SCIENTIST
   Same sign as in Chapter 15.

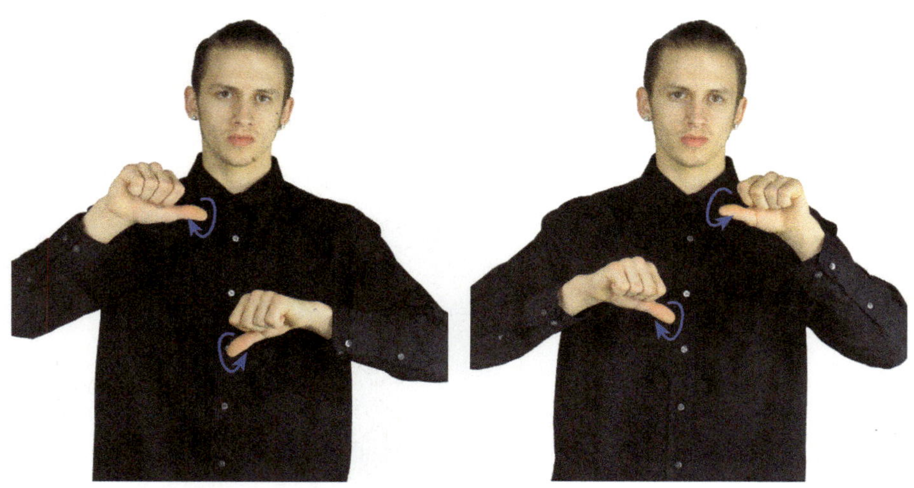

10. **HAIRSTYLIST, HAIRDRESSER**

Both "V" handshapes facing sideways on both sides of your temple move sideways back and forth repeatedly (to show cutting your hair).

11. **BARTENDER**

"10" handshape's thumb on your chin moves back and forth repeatedly then sign both "5" closed handshapes on both sides of your ribs move downward once.

12. ELECTRICIAN

Both "X" handshapes facing down bounce against each other repeatedly then sign both "5" closed handshapes on both sides of your ribs move downward once.

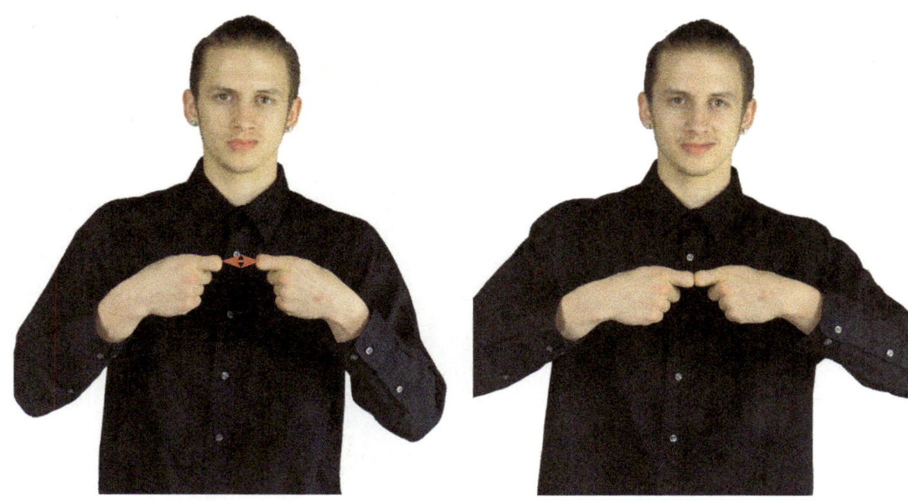

13. INSPECTOR

1st "5" closed handshape facing up stays still while the 2nd "1" handshape brushes against the palm of the 1st "5" closed handshape once then sign both "5" closed handshapes on both sides of your ribs move downward once.

14. CARPENTER

1st "A" handshape facing sideways away from your body stays still while the 2nd "A" handshape away from the 1st "A" handshape moves up and down once (to show using a hammer) then sign both "5" closed handshapes on both sides of your ribs move downward once.

15. DOCTOR

1. 1st "5" closed handshape facing up away from your body stays still while the 2nd "W or 4" closed handshape touches on your wrist of the 1st "5" closed handshape move up and down repeatedly.

2. 1st "5"closed handshape facing up away from your body stays still while the 2nd "D" handshape's fingers touch on your wrist of the 1st "5" closed handshape move up and down repeatedly.

16. NURSE

1st "5" closed handshape facing up in front of yourself stays still while the 2nd "U" handshape facing down touches on the top of the 1st "5" closed handshape's wrist repeatedly.

17. DENTIST

1. "10" handshape facing sideways little finger touching your cheek and bounces on your cheek repeatedly.

2. "10" handshape facing yourself on your mouth moves from one side to the other side once.

3. "X" handshape facing sideways taps on your teeth repeatedly.

18. PILOT

"I-L-Y" handshape facing down away from your head moves outward then sign both "5" closed handshapes on both sides of your ribs move downward once.

19. DANCER

1st "5" closed handshape facing up away from your body stays still while the 2nd "V" handshape facing down (without touching) above the 1st "5" closed handshape's palm moves sideways repeatedly then sign both "5" closed handshapes on both sides of your ribs move downward once.

20. ENGINEER

Both thumbs of "Y" handshapes away from your body touch each other and stay still while the 2nd "Y" handshape's thumb stays with the 1st "Y" handshape's thumb while the 2nd "Y" handshape moves downward and upward repeatedly.

21. FARMER

"5" open handshape's thumb under your chin moves from the side of your chin to the other side of your chin once then sign both "5" closed handshapes on both sides of your ribs move downward once.

22. POLICE

1. "L" bended handshape taps on your upper shoulder once.

2. "5" open and bended handshape facing sideways taps on your upper shoulder once or repeatedly.

3. "C" handshape taps on your upper shoulder once.

23. PAINTER

1. "5" closed handshape facing sideways in front of yourself, stays still while the 2nd "U" handshape touches on the palm of the 1st "5" closed handshape and brushes up and down repeatedly.

2. "5" closed handshape facing sideways in front of yourself stays still while the 2nd "5" closed handshape touches on the palm of the 1st "5" closed handshape and brushes up and down repeatedly.

24. SECRETARY

1. "5" closed handshape facing sideways in front of yourself stays still while the 2nd "V or K" handshape taps on your lower cheek and moves downward and touches on the palm of the 1st "5" closed handshape and slides out once.

2. "5" closed handshape facing sideways in front of yourself stays still while the 2nd "U" handshape taps on your lower cheek and moves downward and touches on the palm of the 1st "5" closed handshape and slides out once.

25. JUDGE

1st "F" handshape facing sideways away from your body while the 2nd "1" handshape taps on the corner of your forehead and changes to "F" handshape downward. Both "F" handshapes move down once at the same time.

26. JUDGE, COURT

Both "F" handshapes move up and down alternating and repeatedly.

27. LAWYER

1st "5" closed handshape facing sideways stays still while the 1st 2nd "L" handshape facing sideways taps on the 1st "5" closed handshape's fingers and slides down slightly then sign both "5' closed handshapes on both sides of your ribs move downward once.

28. MECHANIC

"1" handshape facing sideways in front of yourself stays still while the 2nd "V" handshape facing sideways places the "1" handshape between the pointer and middle fingers then moves up and down repeatedly.

29. MUSICIAN, SINGER

1st "5" closed handshape facing sideways in front of yourself stays still while the 2nd "5" closed handshape above the 1st "5" handshape's palm and arm swings back and forth repeatedly.

30. PRINCIPAL
1st "5" closed handshape facing down in front of yourself stays still while the 2nd "P" handshape moves in a half-circle then touches on the top of the 1st "5" handshape once.

31. PRESIDENT
Same sign as in Chapter 18.

32. VICE PRESIDENT
Same sign as in Chapter 18.

33. PRINTER

1st "5" closed handshape facing up stays still while the 2nd "G" handshape facing outward on top of the 1st "5" closed handshape thumb and finger moves up and down repeatedly then sign both "5" closed handshapes on both sides of your ribs move downward once.

34. TEACHER

Both "O" closed handshapes on both sides of your head move forward then sign both "5" closed handshapes on both sides of your ribs move downward once.

35. DESIGNER

Same sign as in Chapter 15.

36. ARTIST

1st "5" closed handshape facing sideways in front of yourself stays still while the 2nd "I" handshape touches on the palm of the 1st "5" closed handshape and moves downward like a "Z" then sign both "5" closed handshapes on both sides of your ribs move downward once.

37. DRIVER

Both "S or A" handshapes facing sideways away from your body move up and down alternating repeatedly then sign both "5" closed handshapes on both sides of your ribs move downward once.

38. EYE DOCTOR

"1" handshape points to your eye then change to 1st "5" closed handshape facing up away from your body stays still while the 2nd "W" closed handshape touches on your wrist of the 1st "5" closed handshape move up and down repeatedly.

39. COOKER, CHEF

1st "5" closed handshape facing up in front of yourself stays still while the 2nd "5" closed handshape moves back and forth on the palm of the 1st "5" closed handshape repeatedly then sign both "5" closed handshapes on both sides of your ribs move downward once.

40. SALESPERSON

Both "O" closed handshapes facing down away from your body move outward then sign both "5" closed handshapes on both sides of your ribs move downward once.

41. **BAKER**

1st "5" handshape facing down away from your body stays still while the 2nd "5" handshape facing up moves under the 1st "5" handshape's palm once.

42. EMPLOYEE

Same sign as in Chapter 15.

43. VOLUNTEER

"9" handshape facing down and sideways touches on the top of your shoulder moves up and down repeatedly.

CHAPTER 17 Healthcare and Medicine

1. MEDICINE
   1st "5" closed handshape facing up in front of yourself stays still while the 2nd "middle finger" handshape touches on the top of the 1st "5" closed handshape's palm and moves back and forth continually.

2. PILL
   "L" closed handshape facing sideways flicks toward your mouth repeatedly.

3. X-RAY

1. "S" handshape facing yourself moves toward your stomach and changes to "5" open handshape once or repeatedly. (To show where you take an x-ray, i.e., arm, leg, etc.)

2. Fingerspell X-R-A-Y

4. PATIENT

"P" handshape taps on your upper arm and turns over to "K" handshape facing up once.

5. DOCTOR

Same sign as in Chapter 16.

6. NURSE

Same sign as in Chapter 16.

7. BLOOD PRESSURE

"C" handshape grasps your upper arm and squeezes repeatedly.

8. PAIN, ACHE

1. Both "1" handshapes facing sideways in front of yourself move back and forth at the same time repeatedly (to show you have a stomach ache or point at a certain area like headache, ear ache, etc.)

2. Variation of "Pain", headache

9. HEARTH

"Middle finger" handshape taps on your chest near your heart repeatedly.

10. HEART ATTACK

1st "5" closed handshape facing sideways in front of yourself stays still while the "middle finger" handshape taps on your chest near your heart once and change to "S" handshape facing sideways hits on the palm of the 1st "5" closed handshape once.

11. BODY

Both "5" closed handshapes on your upper chest moves down and touch on sides of your stomach once.

12. HEAD

"5" bended handshape facing down taps on your temple and moves down shortly and taps on your cheek once.

13. EYES

"1" handshape facing down taps on your upper cheek near your eye once and moves to the other side of your cheek and taps near your eye once.

14. NOSE

"1" handshape facing down points at your nose once.

15. MOUTH

"1" handshape facing down moves in a circular motion in front of your mouth continually.

16. ARM

"5" closed handshape points at your arm and slides down shortly once.

17. LEG

1. "5"closed handshape facing sideways taps on your thigh repeatedly.

18. FACE

"1" handshape facing down moves in a circular motion in front of your face once.

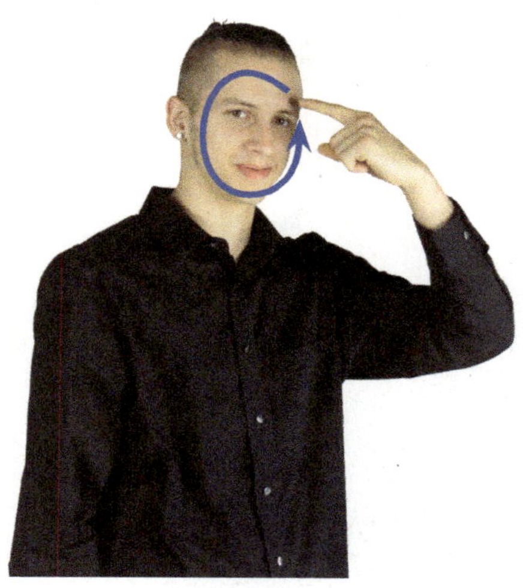

19. EAR

"1" handshape facing down points at your ear once.

20. TEETH

"1" handshape facing down points at your teeth once.

21. TONGUE

"1" handshape facing down points at your tongue once.

22. FEET

"1" handshape facing down points at your both feet.

23. HANDS

1st "B" handshape facing sideways in front of yourself stays still while the 2nd "B" handshape facing sideways on the top of 1st "B" handshape's finger move alternating repeatedly.

24. DEAF

1. "1" handshape facing down points at your ear and moves down and taps on your lower cheek once.

2. "1" handshape facing down points at your lower cheek and moves upward and taps on your ear once.

25. HARD OF HEARING

"H" handshape facing sideways moves sideways shortly once.

26. HEARING

"1" handshape facing sideways taps on your chin and moves in a circular motion continually.

27. SEE, VISION

"2" handshape's second finger taps on your upper cheek near your eye and moves outward once.

28. BLIND

"V" bended handshape facing yourself taps on your cheeks on both sides of your nose.

29. TASTE

"Middle fingers" handshape taps on your lower lip repeatedly.

30. SMELL

"5" closed handshape facing sideways brushes on your nose in a circular motion continually.

31. DIE

1st "5" closed handshape facing up away from your body stays still while the 2nd "5" closed handshape facing down away from your body and both "5" closed handshape turn over once.

32. BREATHE

"5" open handshapes facing sideways in front of yourself moves forward and backward repeatedly.

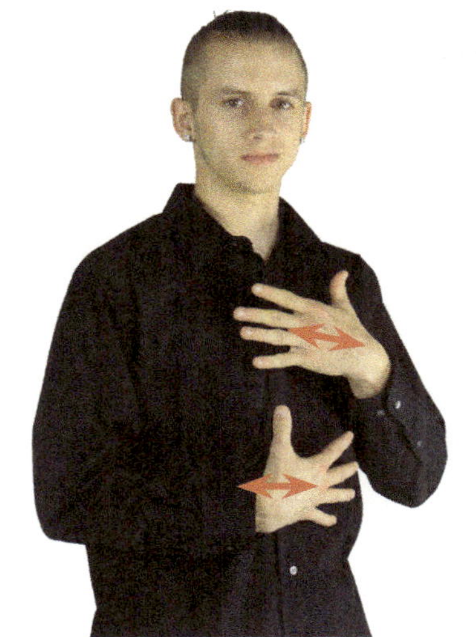

33. SLEEP

"5" open handshape in front of your face moves downward slightly and changes to "O" closed handshape once or repeatedly.

34. SORE

"A" handshape's thumb on your chin stays still and twists back and forth repeatedly.

35. SWEAT

Both "S" handshapes on both sides of your face move downward slightly and change to "5" open handshape facing down once or repeatedly.

36. DIZZY

"5" open and bended handshape in front of your face moves in a circular motion continually.

37. UPSET

1. "K" handshape facing sideways in front of yourself taps on your stomach and turns over once.

2. "5" closed handshape facing sideways in front of yourself taps on your stomach and turns over once.

38. VOMIT

1st "5" open handshape facing sideways in front of your stomach stays still while the 2nd "5" open handshape facing sideways in front of your chest above but not touching each other. Both handshapes move outward once (to show how you throw up).

39. NERVOUS

Both "5" open handshapes facing down in front of yourself shakes a little bit continually.

40. SHOT, INJECTION

1. "3" bended handshape taps on your arm (or hip , etc.) once.

2. Variation of "Shot, Injection"

41. BLOOD TEST

1st "5" closed handshape facing sideways in front of yourself stays still while the 2nd "1" handshape on your chin moves down once and changes to "X" handshape then changes to "5" open handshape's fingers wiggle on the top of your 1st "5" closed handshape

once then sign both "1" handshapes facing forward then move downward and change to "X" handshapes once.

42. TEMPERATURE

1st "1" handshape forward in front of yourself while the 2nd "1" handshape facing down taps on your forehead and moves downward and touches the knuckle of the 1st "1" handshape and moves up and down slightly and repeatedly.

43. HOSPITAL

"H" handshape taps on your upper arm and turns over once.

44. DENTIST

1. Same sign as in Chapter 16.

2. Variation of "Dentist"

3. Variation of "Dentist"

45. EYE DOCTOR

Same sign as in Chapter 16.

46. SURGERY, OPERATION

1st "5" closed handshape facing up in front of yourself stays still while the "10" handshape's thumb taps on the palm of the 1st "5" closed handshape and moves downward slightly (to show how you cut). *Variation: you show where you have a surgery like stomach surgery, leg surgery, etc.

47. BLOOD

1st "5" closed handshape facing sideways in front of yourself stays still while the 2nd "1" handshape on your chin moves down once and changes to "X" handshape then changes to "5" open handshape's fingers wiggle on the top of your 1st "5" closed handshape once.

48. HEARTBEAT

1st "5" bended handshape facing sideways in front of yourself stays still while the 2nd "S" handshape facing yourself taps the palm of your 1st " 5" bended handshape repeatedly.

49. PNEUMONIA

Both "P" handshapes on your upper chest on both sides of your chest move in a circular motion continually.

50. BRONCHITIS

Both "B" handshapes facing down on your upper chest on both sides of your chest move up and down continually.

51. SORE THROAT

"L" closed handshape facing yourself touches on your neck and moves up and down repeatedly.

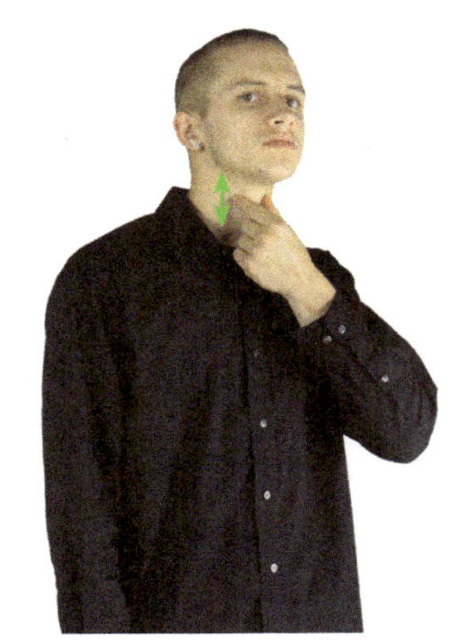

52. EAR INFECTION

Sign "ear" as above then sign "I" handshape away from your body moves sideways back and forth repeatedly.

53. EYE INFECTION

Sign "eye" as above then sign "I" handshape away from your body moves sideways back and forth repeatedly.

54. CHICKEN POX

Sign "bird" in Chapter 7 then sign measles as below.

55. MEASLES
Both "5" open and bended handshapes on both upper cheeks tap downward repeatedly.

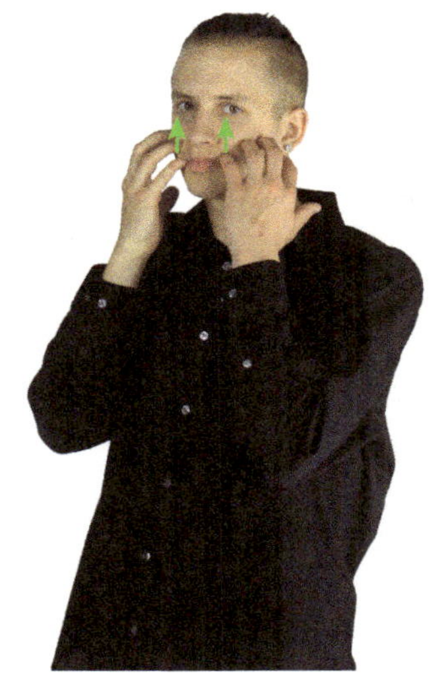

56. MUMPS
Both "5" open and bended handshapes touch both sides of your neck once.

57. MENSTRUATION
"A" handshape facing sideways taps on your lower cheek repeatedly.

58. BREAST
"5" closed and bended handshape taps on your upper chest and moves to the other side of upper chest once.

59. ABORTION
1st "5" closed handshape facing sideways stays still while the 2nd "A" handshape taps on the palm of your 1st "5" closed handshape moves downward and change to "5" open handshape once.

60. BAND AID
1st "5" closed handshape facing down stays still while the 2nd "U" handshape facing down touches on the top of the 1st "5" closed handshape and moves down toward your thumb once.

61. HANDICAPPED
Fingerspell H-C.

CHAPTER

18 Government

1. PRESIDENT
   Both "5" open handshapes facing outward on both sides of your head move upward and change to "S" handshapes facing outward once.

2. VICE PRESIDENT
   "V" handshape facing outward touches on your temple and moves downward and change to "P" handshape once.

3. **DEMOCRATIC**
"D" away from your chest shakes back and forth repeatedly.

4. **REPUBLICAN**
"R" away from your chest shakes back and forth repeatedly.

5. **INDEPENDENT**
Both "I" handshape's little fingers touching each other in front of your body move outward once.

6. LEGISLATURE

"L" taps on your upper shoulder and moves to other upper shoulder once.

7. ELECTION/VOTE

"S" handshape facing sideways stays still while the 2nd "F" handshape facing down touches on the top of the fist "S" handshape and moves up and down repeatedly.

8. FEDERAL

"F" handshape away from your temple turns over and taps on your temple once.

9. GOVERNMENT

1. "G" handshape facing down away from your temple turns over and taps on your temple once.

2. "1" handshape facing outward away from your temple turns over and taps on your temple once.

10. REPRESENTATIVES

1. "R" handshape facing down taps on your upper shoulder and moves to other upper shoulder once.
2. (no picture) "5" closed handshape facing sideways in front of your body stays still while the 2nd "R" handshape touches the palm of the 1st "5" closed handshape and move forward once .

11. SENATE
"S" handshape facing down taps on your upper shoulder and moves to other side of shoulder once.

12. SENATOR
Same sign "senate" as above and changes to "person". Both closed "5" handshapes on each side of your body move from your chest to your waist once.

13. GOVERNOR

1. "1" handshape pointing to your temple turns over and taps on your temple once. Both closed "5" handshapes on each side of your body move from your chest to your waist once.

2. "G" handshape pointing to your temple turns over and taps on your temple once. Both closed "5" handshapes on each side of your body move from your chest to your waist once.

14. JUDGE, COURT

Both "F" handshapes facing down, move up and down, alternating repeatedly.

15. CONGRESS

"C" handshape facing down taps on your upper shoulder and moves to the other side of your shoulder once.

16. LAW

1st "5" closed handshape facing sideways stays still while the 2nd "L" handshape facing sideways taps on the 1st "5" closed handshape's fingers and slides down slightly once.

17. REGULATIONS, RULE

1st "5" closed handshape facing sideways upward stays still while the 2nd "R" handshape facing sideways fingertips tap on the 1st "5" closed handshape's fingers and slides down slightly once.

18. POLICY

1st "5" closed handshape facing sideways stays still while the 2nd "P" handshape facing down taps on the 1st "5" closed handshape's fingers and slides down slightly once.

19. BOARD

"B" handshape facing sideways taps on your upper shoulder and moves to the other side of your upper shoulder once.

20. ADMINISTRATION

Fingerspell A-D-M.

21. POLITICAL

"K" handshape from your temple turns over and taps on your temple once.

22. CONSTITUTION

1st "5" handshape facing sideways outward stays still while the 2nd "C" handshape facing sideway taps on the 1st "5" closed handshape's fingers and slides down slightly once.

CHAPTER

19 Ethnicities

1. ETHNICITY
    1. Fingerspell E-T-H-N-I-C-I-T-Y.

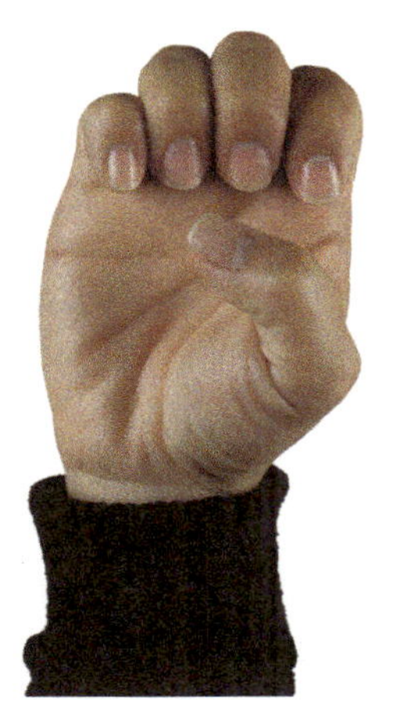

2. ARAB

Fingerspell A-R-A-B.

3. ASIAN

"A" handshape in front of yourself moves upward in a half-circle motion and change to "5" open handshape once to complete the circle.

4. BLACK/AFRICAN AMERICAN

   1. "1" handshape sideways on your forehead moves from side to side once.

   2. Sign "Africa" then sign "USA" as in Chapter 19 then sign both "5" closed handshapes on both sides of your ribs move downward once.

5. SPANISH
   1. 1st "X" handshape facing down stays still while the 2nd "X" handshape taps on your upper shoulder and touches on top of the 1st "X" handshape once.

   2. Sign "Spain" as in Chapter 19.

6. INDIAN, INDIA
   "10" handshape's thumb facing yourself taps on your forehead and twists back and forth repeatedly.

7. INDIAN, AMERICAN

"F" handshape facing sideways, taps on your lower cheek and moves upward and taps on the top of your head once.

8. WHITE

1. "5" open handshape facing sideways taps on your chest and moves outward and changed to "O" closed handshape facing sideways then moves upward and changes to "5" open handshape toward your face once.

CHAPTER

20 Countries and Continents

1. AFRICA
   "5" open handshape facing outward away from your body moves downward like curve and changes to "O" closed handshape once (to show a shape of Africa's continent).

2. AFGHANISTAN
   1st "3" bended handshape's thumb facing sideways touches on your forehead moves across once.

3. ARGENTINA

   1st "5" bended handshape facing up away from your body stays still while the 2nd "5" curved handshape facing yourself away from your body moves up and down repeatedly (to show you play a guitar).

4. ASIA

   "A" handshape facing outward turns around like a half-circle and changes to "5" open handshape once.

5. AUSTRALIA

   Both "8" handshapes facing down near your body move outward and flick once.

6. AUSTRIA

1. 1st "V" bended handshape facing sideways in front of your body stays still while the 2nd "V" bended handshape touches on the top of the 1st "V" bended handshape. Both "V" bended handshapes' fingers move up and down twice.

2. 1st "X" handshape in front of your body stays still while the 2nd "X" handshape touches on the top of the 1st "X" handshape. Both "X" handshapes move up and down twice.

7. BELGIUM

"B" handshape facing sideways in front of your mouth moves outward once.

8. BELIZE
   "B" handshape facing sideways in front of your body moves like the shape of "Z" once.

9. BRAZIL
   "B" handshape facing sideways away from your body moves downward in a swirling motion once.

10. BOLIVIA
    "1 finger & little finger" handshape facing outward away from your body twists back and forth repeatedly.

11. CAMBODIA

"C" handshape facing down touches your hip moves to the other side of your hip and changes to "S" handshape once.

12. CANADA

1. "A" handshape facing yourself knocks on your upper shoulder moves back and forth repeatedly.

2. "5" handshape taps on your chest repeatedly.

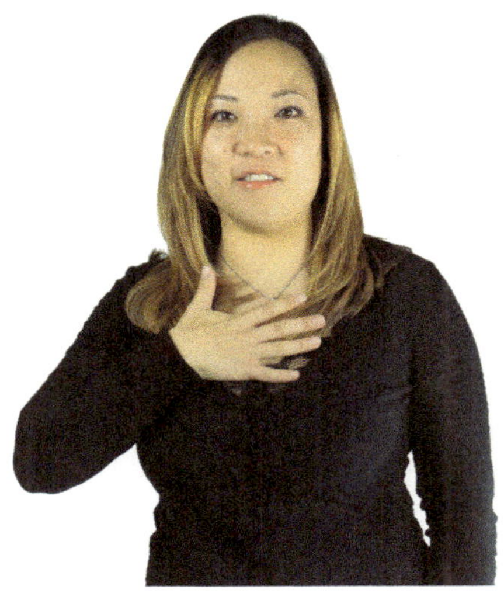

13. CENTRAL AMERICA
1st "5" open handshape facing sideways away from your body while the 2nd "5" open handshape facing forward thumbs touching each other once.

14. CHILE
"8" handshape on your upper shoulder flicks repeatedly.

15. CHINA
"L" handshape facing yourself taps on your upper chest and moves to other side of chest then moves downward once.

16. COLOMBIA
"C" handshape facing yourself away from your face moves back and forth repeatedly

17. COSTA RICA
Fingerspell C-R

18. CUBA

"C" handshape's wrist facing outward touches on your forehead.

19. CZECH REPUBLIC

"5" bended handshape's wrist facing up touches under your chin.

20. DENMARK

"3" handshape sideways facing yourself in front of your stomach moves up, down, and backward from one side of your stomach to the other side of your stomach.

21. DOMINICAN REPUBLIC

1. "R" handshape facing yourself taps on your forehead moves downward and changes to "D" handshape on your chin once.

2. "D" handshape facing yourself taps on your forehead moves downward and changes to "R" handshape on your chin once.

22. ECUADOR

1st "5" handshape facing down away from your body stays still while the 2nd "E" handshape touches on the top of the 1st "5" handshape moves up and down repeatedly.

23. EGYPT

1. "X" handshape facing outward taps on your forehead once.

2. 1st "5" closed handshape facing sideways in front of your body while the 2nd "5" closed handshape touches on the tip of the 1st "5" closed handshape's fingers move downward like the shape of pyramid then turn hands sideways and repeat movement once.

24. EL SALVADOR

"E" handshape sideways facing yourself on your upper shoulder moves downward to the other side of hip and changes to "S" handshape once (to show sash).

25. ENGLAND

1. "5" bended handshape facing down away from your body stays still while the 2nd "5" bended handshape facing down touches on the top of the 1st "5" bended handshape once.

2. "L" bended handshape sideways facing yourself touches on your chin once.

26. EUROPE

"E" handshape facing yourself near your forehead moves in a circular motion continually.

27. FINLAND

"X" handshape facing yourself taps on your chin repeatedly.

28. FRANCE

"F" handshape sideways away from your body twists once.

29. GERMANY

1. "1" handshape's wrist sideways taps on the top of your head repeatedly.

2. 1st "5" open handshape facing sideways halfway in front of your body stays still while the 2nd "5" open handshape facing sideways touches on top of the 1st "5" open handshape while all fingers wiggle repeatedly.

30. GREECE

1. "G" handshape facing up slides down your nose repeatedly.

2. 1st "1" handshape facing outward stays still while the 2nd "1" handshape facing sideways yourself taps on the 1st "1" handshape repeatedly.

31. GUATEMALA

1st "5" open handshape facing down away from your body stays still while the 2nd "3" handshape on the top of the 1st "5" open handshape moves sideways in a circular motion continually.

32. HAITI

"H" handshape facing yourself on your cheek near your mouth taps and moves sideway and changes to "I" handshape facing outward once.

33. HOLLAND

Both "5" closed handshapes' fingers touch on each side of your head move downward and change to "O" closed handshapes at the same time once.

34. HONDURAS

"H" handshape facing sideways taps on your chin repeatedly.

35. HONG KONG

"O" closed handshape facing yourself in front of your nose changes to "5" open handshape repeatedly.

36. HUNGARY

"L" handshape's finger facing yourself sideways touches on your upper lip and moves outward sideways and snap once.

37. ICELAND

"A" handshape facing sideways on your chin moves down once.

38. INDIA

1. "10" handshape's thumb facing yourself taps on your forehead and twists back and forth repeatedly.

2. "Middle finger" handshape facing yourself taps on your forehead and brushes up repeatedly.

39. IRAN

1st "5" closed handshape facing up away from your body stays still while the 2nd "10" handshape's thumb taps on the top of the 1st "5" closed handshape's palm and moves up and down repeatedly.

40. IRAQ

1st "5" closed handshape facing up away from your body stays still while the 2nd "Q" handshape taps on the top of the 1st "5" closed handshape's palm and moves up and down repeatedly.

41. IRELAND

1. "B" handshape facing sideways on your temple moves back and forth repeatedly.

2. 1st "S" handshape facing down away from your body stays still while the 2nd "V" bended handshape moves in a half-circle and touches on top of the 1st "S" handshape once

42. ISRAEL

"L" handshape facing yourself touches on the side of your chin and moves to the other side of your chin once.

43. ITALY

1. "L" bended handshape away from your body moves downward quickly and changes to "L" closed handshape once in a swirling motion.

2. "I" handshape facing yourself taps on your forehead and moves down slightly then moves to straight line to the end of your forehead once.

44. JAMAICA

"B" handshape facing down away from your body stays still while the 2nd "5" closed and curved handshape touches the tip of the 1st "B" handshape's fingers from one side to the other side once.

45. JAPAN

Both "L" open handshapes touching each other away from your body move sideways and change to "L" closed handshapes once.

46. KOREA

"5" closed and bended handshape's fingers facing sideways touches on your temple moves outward slightly and downward and touches your cheek once.

47. LEBANON

Both "3" closed handshapes facing sideways on each side of your head and move downward 3 or 4 times once.

48. LIBYA

"5" closed handshape facing sideways taps on your temple and slides downward to your cheek.

49. MALAYSIA

Both "5" closed handshapes facing sideways moves up and down alternating repeatedly.

50. MEXICO

"V" handshape facing down taps on your forehead and moves back and forth repeatedly.

51. NEW ZEALAND

1st "5" closed handshape facing sideways away from your body stays still while the 2nd "U" handshape facing down touches the tip of the 1st "5" closed handshape's fingers slides down slightly once and changes to "5" closed handshape and moves outward and touches back to the 1st "5" closed handshape's palm once.

52. NICARAGUA

Both "5" closed handshape's fingers facing sideways away from your body touch each other and move outward and change to both "O" closed handshapes at the same time once.

53. NORTH KOREA

54. NORWAY

"3" closed handshape facing sideways near your stomach moves like the shape of "mountain" from the side of your stomach to the other side of your stomach once.

55. PAKISTAN

1st "1" handshape facing sideways away from your body stays still while the 2nd "F" handshape's two closed fingers tap on the tip of the 1st "1" handshape repeatedly.

56. PANAMA

Both "5" closed handshape's fingers touching each other in front of yourself and bend toward your body repeatedly.

57. PERU

"R" handshape facing outward taps on your forehead repeatedly.

58. PHILLIPPINES

1st "5" closed handshape facing down away from your body stays still while the "P" handshape moves in a circular motion and touches on the top of the 1st "5" closed handshape.

59. POLAND

"5" closed and bended handshape's fingertips on the upper side of your chest moves to the other side of your chest once.

60. PORTUGAL

"1" bended handshape taps on your forehead then taps on your nose then taps on your chin once.

61. PUERTO RICO

Fingerspell P-R.

62. ROMANIA

Both "5" closed handshapes touching each other in front of your body (like a shape of triangle) and changes to "5" closed handshapes sideways twice.

63. RUSSIA

1. "1" handshape facing sideways slides across on your chin and changes to "X" handshape then turn to "1" handshape downward once.

2. Both "5" closed handshapes facing down touch on each side of your hips moves sideways repeatedly.

64. SAUDI ARABIA

"S" handshape facing up away from your waist moves up and changes "H" handshape facing yourself and taps on your forehead then go back to your waist and changes to "S" handshape facing up once.

65. SCOTLAND

"4" open handshape facing yourself slides across your upper arm then turns over and slides down once.

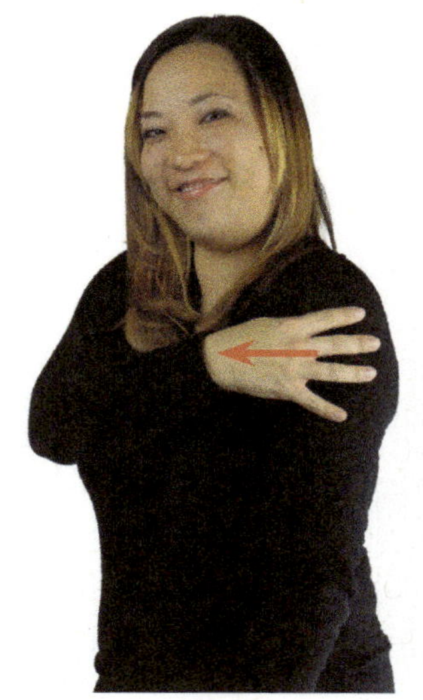

66. SINGAPORE

"5" open handshape facing sideways stays still while the 2nd "L" closed handshape on the 1st "5" open handshape's elbow flicks repeatedly.

67. SOUTH KOREA

"S" handshape away from your body moves downward once then sign "Korea" as above.

68. SPAIN

1. "X" handshape facing yourself on your upper shoulder turns over "X" handshape facing outward once.

2. 1st "X" handshape facing down away from your body stays still while the 2nd "X" touches on your shoulder and moves towards the 1st "X" handshape once.

69. SUDAN

"A" handshape's thumb taps on your temple and slides down to your lower cheek once.

70. SWEDEN

1st "5" closed handshape facing down away from your stomach stays still while the 2nd "5" closed handshape on the top of the 1st "5" closed handshape moves up and down repeatedly.

71. SWITZERLAND

"C" handshape facing down taps on your upper middle chest and moves down then changes to face sideways and moves from one side of your chest to your other chest once.

72. SYRIA

"5" closed handshape facing sideways stays still while the 2nd "H" handshape facing down taps on the 1st "5" closed handshape repeatedly.

73. TAIWAN

"S" handshape facing down and facing yourself in front of your chin and moves up and down to the other side of your chin once.

74. THAILAND

"1" handshape facing yourself sideways touches on the tip of your nose and moves outward repeatedly (to show elephant's trunk).

75. TRINIDAD

Both "A" handshapes facing up away from your body moves up and down alternating repeatedly (to show beating on a drum).

76. TURKEY

"L" bended handshape facing yourself taps on your forehead twice.

77. UGANDA

1st "5" closed handshape facing sideways stays still while the 2nd "G" handshape taps on the palm of the 1st "5" closed handshape repeatedly.

78. UNITED KINGDOM

Fingerspell U-K.

79. USA (AMERICA)

Both "5" open handshapes fingers clasp together and move around in front of your body continually.

80. VENEZUELA

"V" handshape away from your body moves downward in a swirling motion.

81. VIETNAM

1. "V" handshape taps on your temple and moves down shortly and changes to "N" handshape facing outward on the bottom of your cheek once.

2. "L" closed handshape facing yourself taps on your chin moves downward once.

CHAPTER

21 States in the USA

1. ALABAMA
   Fingerspell A-L-A.

2. ALASKA

"A" handshape facing down on your ear moves upward and over your head and changes to "5" open handshape on the other once.

3. ARIZONA

"A" handshape facing sideways slides down on the corner of your chin and moves to the other corner of your chin once.

4. ARKANSAS

Fingerspell A-R-K.

5. CALIFORNIA

1. "1" handshape facing yourself taps on your ear and changes to "Y" handshape facing downward once.

2. "I-L-Y" handshape's pointer finger taps on your chin and changes to "Y" downward once.

3. "Middle finger" handshape touches on your chin and brushes down repeatedly.

6. COLORADO

1. "5" open handshape facing yourself taps on your chin while wiggling then fingerspell A-D-O.

2. 1st "5" closed handshape facing down away from your body stays still while the 2nd "C" handshape on the top of the 1st "5" closed handshape's elbow moves sideways (to show a shape of mountain).

7. CONNECTICUT

Fingerspell C-O-N-N.

8. DELAWARE
   1. "D" handshape taps on your temple repeatedly.

   2. Fingerspell D-E-L.

9. FLORIDA

Fingerspell F-L-A.

10. GEORGIA

Fingerspell G-A.

11. HAWAII

"H" handshape in front of your face and moves in a circular motion continually.

12. IDAHO

1. 1st "S" handshape facing down stays still while the 2nd "V" bended handshape facing down taps on the top of the first "S" handshape repeatedly.

2. Fingerspell I-D-A-H-O.

13. ILLINOIS

1. Fingerspell I-L.

2. Fingerspell I-L slides once.

3. "L" handshape facing sideways away from your body turns to "L" downward once.

14. INDIANA

Fingerspell I-N-D.

15. IOWA

Fingerspell I-O-W-A.

16. KANSAS

Fingerspell K-A-N.

17. KENTUCKY
Fingerspell K-Y.

18. LOUISIANA
Fingerspell L-A.

19. MAINE

1. "F" handshape facing down taps on your upper shoulder and moves down and outward once.

2. Fingerspell M-A-I-N-E.

20. MARYLAND

Fingerspell M-D.

21. MASSACHUSETTS

Fingerspell M-A-S-S.

22. MICHIGAN

Fingerspell M-I-C-H.

23. MINNESOTA

Fingerspell M-I-N-N.

24. MISSISSIPPI

Fingerspell M-I-S-S.

25. MISSOURI
"M" handshape facing yourself moves outward and changes to "O" once.

26. MONTANA
Both "M" handshapes touching each other and move sideways then go downward once.

27. NEBRASKA

Fingerspell N-E-B.

28. NEVADA

1. Fingerspell N-E-V.

2. Fingerspell N-V.

29. NEW HAMPSHIRE

Fingerspell N-H.

30. NEW JERSEY

Fingerspell N-J.

31. NEW MEXICO

Fingerspell N-M.

32. NEW YORK
1st "5" closed handshape facing up away from your body stays still while the 2nd "Y" handshape on the top of the first "5" closed handshape and moves back and forth repeatedly.

33. NORTH CAROLINA
Fingerspell N-C.

34. NORTH DAKOTA
Fingerspell N-D.

35. OHIO

Fingerspell O-H-I-O.

36. OKLAHOMA

Fingerspell O-K-L-A.

37. OREGON

1. "O" handshape facing yourself taps on the top of your shoulder moves outward like a swirl once.

2. "O" handshape facing yourself away from your body moves back and forth repeatedly.

38. PENNSYLVANIA

Fingerspell P-A.

39. RHODE ISLAND

Fingerspell R-I.

40. SOUTH CAROLINA

Fingerspell S-C.

41. SOUTH DAKOTA

Fingerspell S-D.

42. TENNESSEE

Fingerspell T-E-N-N.

43. TEXAS

"X" handshape facing outward away from your body moves sideway then go downward once.

44. UTAH

1. "U" handshape facing sideway taps on your upper cheek and slides down to the bottom of your cheek slightly.

2. Fingerspell U-T-A-H.

45. **VERMONT**
Fingerspell V-T.

46. **VIRGINIA**
Fingerspell V-A.

47. WASHINGTON

"W" handshape's fingers facing yourself touch on the top of your shoulder and moves outward like a swirl once.

48. WASHINGTON, D.C.

Same sign "Washington" as above then fingerspell D-C.

49. WEST VIRGINIA

1. "W" handshape away from your body moves sideways then fingerspell V-A.

2. Fingerspell W-V-A.

50. WISCONSIN

1. Fingerspell W-I-S.

2. Fingerspell W-I-S-C.

51. WYOMING

1. Both "W" handshapes touching each other move sideways then change to "Y" handshapes downward once.

2. "W" handshape moves downward and changes to "Y" handshape then moves upward and changes to "O" handshape once.

CHAPTER

22 Holidays

1. HOLIDAY
   Both "5" open handshapes facing sideways thumbs tap on your upper chest repeatedly.

2. NEW YEAR
   Sign "new" as in Chapter 13 then sign "year" as in Chapter 5.

3. MARTIN L. KING
Fingerspell M-L-K.

4. PRESIDENT'S DAY
Sign "president" as in Chapter 18 then sign "day" as in Chapter 5.

5. VALENTINE'S DAY
   Both "middle fingers" handshapes on your chest draw a heart and sign "day" as in Chapter 5.

6. ST. PATRICK'S DAY

"1" and "thumb" handshape on your upper arm and twist over one time and sign "day" as in Chapter 5 (to show pinching your arm).

7. MEMORIAL DAY

"2" handshape on the corner of your eye and move backward one time and sign "day" as in Chapter 5.

8. **4TH OF JULY**
   "4" handshape facing away from yourself twists and sweeping movement then fingerspell J-U-L-Y.

9. LABOR DAY

1. 1st "S" handshape facing down in front of yourself stays still while the other "S" handshape taps on the top of 1st "S" handshape's wrist moves up and down repeatedly then sign "day" as in Chapter 5.

2. (no picture) Finger spell L-A-B-O-R and sign "day" as above.

10. COLUMBUS DAY

"C" handshape upright and twists back and forth repeatedly then sign "day" as in Chapter 5.

11. HALLOWEEN

1. 2 "H" handshapes facing up in front of your eyes move together and apart repeatedly.

2. "1 finger and little finger" handshapes in front of your eyes moves back and forth sideways repeatedly.

12. VETERAN'S DAY

1st "S" handshape facing yourself near your stomach stays still while the 2nd "S" handshape facing yourself on your upper shoulder like holding a rifle move forward and backward repeatedly and sign "day" as in Chapter 5.

13. THANKSGIVING

1. "G" handshape facing yourself taps on your chin and moves downward and taps on your lower neck once.

2. Both "5" closed handshapes touch on the sides of your chin moves upward twice in a swirl.

14. HANUKKAH

Both "4" handshapes away from your body with pointer fingers touching each other move away from each other once.

15. CHRISTMAS

1st "5" closed handshape facing down in front of yourself stays still while the 2nd "C" handshape's elbow touches the fingertips of the 1st "5" closed handshape. "C" handshape turns facing yourself once.

16. NEW YEAR'S EVE

Sign "new" as in Chapter 13 and sign "year" as in Chapter 5 then fingerspell E-V-E.

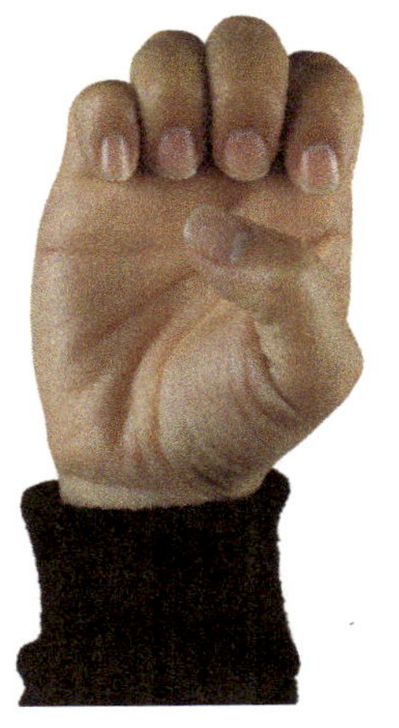

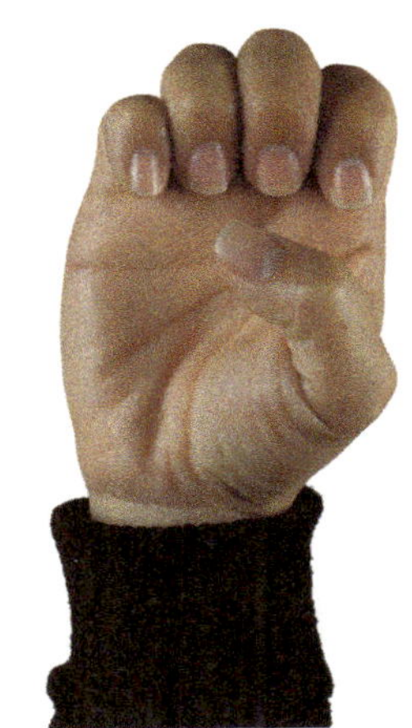

17. CHRISTMAS EVE

Sign "Christmas" as above and fingerspell E-V-E.

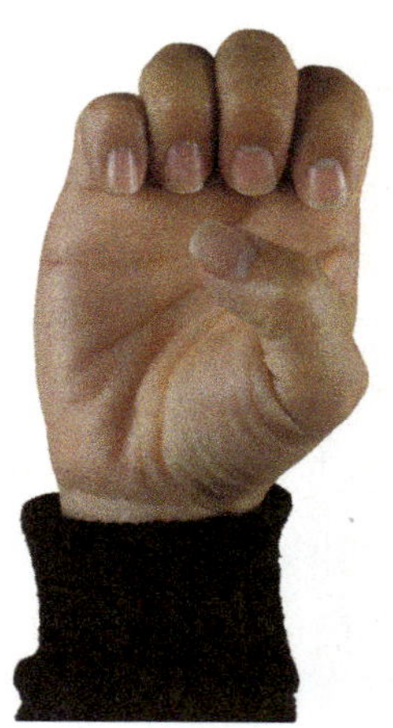

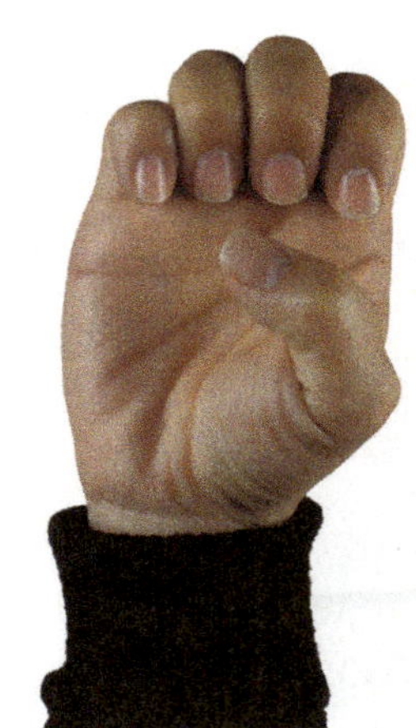

18. EASTER

1. Both "E" handshapes away from your body move shake back and forth repeatedly.

2. 1st "5" closed handshape facing up in front of yourself stays still while the 2nd "V" handshape facing down touches on the top of the 1st "5" closed handshape and moves upward like shape of a small "Z" repeatedly.

19. KWANZAA

1st Both "1" handshapes facing of yourself away from your body touch each other then change to "3" handshapes facing outward and move away from each other once.

20. BIRTHDAY

1. 1st "5" closed handshape in front of yourself stays still while the 2nd "5" closed handshape touches on the palm of 1st "5" closed handshape then moves under the 1st "5" closed handshape once.

Same sign "day" as in chapter 5

2. "Middle finger" handshape touches on your chin and moves down to your chest repeatedly

3. "5" closed handshape taps on your shoulder moves in a circular motion continually.

4. 1st "S" handshape near your stomach stays still while the 2nd 1st "1" handshape facing sideways taps on your chin and moves down then change to "5" open handshape and touches on the top of the 1st "S" handshape once.

5. 1st "5" closed handshape near your stomach stays still while the 2nd "5" closed handshape on your chest moves downward and touches the palm of the 1st "5" handshape once.

Biographies

STEFANI BRINKMAN

Stefanie Brinkman, a Hard of Hearing Minnesotan and a Mother of two lovely hearing children.

MELISSA "ELLI" HALVERSON

Melissa "Elli" Halverson, A Deaf Minnesotan, is a student at Gallaudet University. Her major is Biology. Her dream is to become a Dentist and help children all over the world by providing necessary dental services and to encourage them to explore life and learn about love.

TRAVIS LAUDERBAUGH

Travis Lauderbaugh, a Deaf Minnesotan, is employed and he is actively involved in activities in the Deaf Community. He has a Deaf family.

MIKELL SANDBERG

Mikell Sandberg, a Deaf Minnesotan, is a mechanic and participates in various activities in the Deaf Community and The Bread of Life Lutheran Church for the Deaf.

DAVID PENNEY, PHOTOGRAPHER

David Penney, a Hearing New Jerseyan, is an artist and graphic designer. He is currently working towards his BFA in Fine Art at the University of Minnesota. His work has been seen at Art shows in New Jersey and Minnesota. Some of the formats that he has shown include photography, painting, 3-D design, graphic design, and ceramics.

DIANE MCDONAGH, AUTHOR

Diane McDonagh has been deaf since birth. She received her B.A. and M.A. from California State University at Northridge, California. She has been teaching ASL for 34 years at North Hennepin Community College and 18 years at Augsburg College in Minnesota. This book is the result of her long-time dream to establish a book that is practical for everyone (Deaf, Hard of Hearing and Hearing) to use and meet everyone's needs. Throughout her life and travels, she has met with many Deaf and Hard of Hearing people who use different regional signs. As understanding those differences are so important to communication, she has incorporated some of those differences into this book. Thanks to my two wonderful and faithful friends, Lori Kruger and Dini Sullivan who proofread my explanations and assisted with arrow design and placements. They have been so helpful through the whole process.

Again thank you very much!